AGENTS OF CHANGE

agents *of* change

POLITICAL PHILOSOPHY IN PRACTICE

BEN LAURENCE

Harvard University Press   *Cambridge, Massachusetts | London, England*

2021

First printing

Library of Congress Cataloging-in-Publication Data

Names: Laurence, Ben, author.
Title: Agents of change : political philosophy in practice / Ben Laurence.
Description: Cambridge, Massachusetts : Harvard University Press, 2021. |
    Includes bibliographical references and index.
Identifiers: LCCN 2021012225 | ISBN 9780674258419 (cloth)
Subjects: LCSH: Political science—Philosophy. | Pragmatism. | Change.
Classification: LCC JA71 .L38 2021 | DDC 320.101—dc23
LC record available at https://lccn.loc.gov/2021012225

*For my father, Martin Washburn, who helped make me
an intellectual and taught me, when necessary,
to swim against the currents of contemporary fashion*

CONTENTS

AGENTS OF CHANGE

Introduction

*P*olitical philosophy promises to shed light on the considerable problems of our shared social world. One naturally hopes it will help us understand the injustices and political pathologies confronting us in our political life. And having helped us to say what is wrong with our social world, one hopes that it will help us say what might make it right, orienting us toward a better possible future for the sake of political action. The naive appeal of political philosophy is that it is practical.

This is not easy to understand. One question concerns the relation of theory and practice. Political philosophy is surely theory. And isn't theory opposed to practice? Practice concerns the doing of things in particular circumstances, whereas theory concerns the articulations of general truths, strung together in structures of evidentiary and inferential dependence. Granted, we might think, theory can inform action—it can serve as information in light of which one acts. But beyond this, what can it possibly mean to say that political philosophy is itself practical? One wonders whether there is something on the order of a category mistake implicit in the promise and naive appeal of political philosophy. Surely action is one thing and philosophy another. Philosophy happens in the ivory tower, not the halls of government, much less the streets.

This general puzzlement can be developed further when we reflect on the normativity of political philosophy. For if political philosophy articulates truths about normative matters, about what
justice requires—our duties, right and wrong—reasoning about
what to do appeals to a broader set of considerations. Intelligent
political action requires a realistic sense of the obstacles confronting
us in the form of general human foibles as well as the organized
forces of political opposition. It also requires us to think realistically about opportunities—weak spots in the armor of unjust status
quos, the agents who might exploit these weaknesses, and the possibilities for transformative action. But such realistic thoughts, so
crucial for intelligent action, seem alien constraints on our normative theorizing. To introduce them into the very stuff of normative
reflection is to lower the horizons of our normative reflection. The
theory of normativity is something higher and better than this. We
must not allow it to be compromised by pragmatic considerations
but rather carefully parse the hard-won insights of philosophy from
the actionable intelligence required for political action. The theory
of justice is a purely normative inquiry.

When confronted with this seemingly elevated and austere conception of the theory of justice, it is natural to recoil. Even if one
feels its pull, it is hard to be satisfied with it. By distancing political
philosophy from practice for the sake of maintaining the purity of
philosophical reflection about justice, it seems to abandon, or at
least hopelessly qualify, the practical aspiration that animates the
whole enterprise. If we think that the point of political philosophy
is the light it casts on the confrontation with injustice, then this
method of purification seems headed for heartbreak. This disap-
pointment naturally receives theoretical expression in different pictures of political philosophy that abandon, or seriously qualify, the
idea of political philosophy as theory. For example, one might
think of political philosophy as reactive to the pathological situations that confront us, looking for normatively attractive partial

fixes to our current afflictions taken seriatim. The task of political philosophy is to produce a set of jerry-rigged fixes in an experimental spirit without orientation to a guiding ideal. One might think of political philosophy as enabling comparative judgments among currently feasible alternatives, a grown-up version of the children's game "Would you rather?"

The problem is that while apparently pragmatic, and motivated by an admirably steady sense of the importance of the confrontation with injustice, it is also hard to be satisfied by these proposals. In their antitheoretical zeal, they seem to abandon too lightly the systematic aspirations of political philosophy, aspirations to bring reason and self-consciousness to our political judgments. They also seem to sever political philosophy from a long engagement with the utopian aspiration for a just political world. But isn't the utopian aspiration for a just society actually important to practice? Aren't these views saddled with the unappetizing project of convincing us to abandon our hope for a just future? One wants a more satisfying approach that grants central place to the confrontation with injustice while not sacrificing system and aspiration—if only one could have it.

The message of this book is that we can. This book interprets and defends the idea that political philosophy is practical. It aims to vindicate the naive picture, preserving its full allure, while defusing the worries to which it gives rise. By explaining how theory can be practical, I aim to dispel the allure of the austere picture, simultaneously removing the impetus for the understandable but unsatisfying antitheoretical reaction to this picture. My goal is to resolve this dialectic through a positive account of the practical nature of political philosophy.

I develop the claim that political philosophy is practical by following a tradition that distinguishes practical from theoretical reason. To say that political philosophy is practical is to say that it is an exercise of practical rather than theoretical reason. Political philosophy begins by reflecting on the engaged exercise of our sense of justice in our ordinary political life, as we make piecemeal and fragmentary judgments for the sake of action, issuing and responding to claims on one another to reorder our shared institutions in light of the injustices that afflict us. This practical context is largely one of contestation around salient alleged injustices and often raises the question of which side the thinker is on in an ongoing struggle. Political philosophy raises this engaged practical thought to self-consciousness by articulating principles of justice that gather together and explain low-level judgments about justice and injustice, and reveal their dependence on high-level judgments. Together the principles of justice constitute a unitary end for our political hope and action. Working from this end, political philosophy reasons back to the conditions of action in the injustice that confronts us. As an exercise of practical reason, it does not stop short of action. When carried to completion, such reasoning comes all the way back to an agent of political change and the question of what is to be done.

The themes with which this book engages are at the center of contemporary conversations in political philosophy, which is in a state of productive ferment.[1] The death of John Rawls is one cause of this upheaval. Canonical in the discipline, his work set the agenda in the United States and beyond for more than three decades. His lexicon provided a handy lingua franca, a set of familiar terms and concepts that could be presupposed as a common basis for discussion. Since his death, book upon book has questioned his method and made the case for a radical reorientation of the discipline.[2] This onslaught of methodological critique has coincided with a demographic and political crisis in academic philosophy in the United States. Growing concern about the underrepresentation of women and minorities in the profession has gone hand in hand with a mainstreaming of political topics that were previously marginalized in Rawlsian political philosophy—for example, the philosophy of race and feminist approaches to a variety of subjects. An older generation of scholars who have been working for a long time in these areas are receiving overdue recognition.

One place where these different currents come together, making for turbulent waters, is the literature sometimes called "the ideal theory debates." Rawls thought the main concern of political philosophy was the theory of justice. He divided the theory of justice into two parts. The first was ideal theory discussing the nature and aims of a just society. The second was nonideal theory discussing the pressing and urgent injustices that confront us in our actual politics. Rawls argued that ideal theory was prior to, and provided the basis for, nonideal theory. He discussed ideal theory at great length in the famous defense of his two principles of justice and in his sketch of institutions that might satisfy them, especially the regime he called "property-owning democracy." But he said much less about nonideal theory than one would have anticipated given its prominence in his two-part conception of the project of political philosophy.

The ideal theory debates concern the best understanding, and evaluation of the merits, of this approach. Variations of the dialectical themes I have traced play out here. On one line of thought, Rawlsian orthodoxy defends the purity of normative theorizing in a way that is objectionably disconnected from political practice and the confrontation with injustice.[3] Philosophers with this perspective view Rawls's conception of the theory of justice as the root of the problem. Either it is utopian, and so insufficiently realistic for practice, or it (inadvertently) serves the role of ideological distraction or distortion that deflects critique of pressing injustice. In any case, the complex of methodological ideas is not well suited to play the practical role that political philosophy should. Some critics writing in this vein locate the problem in the alleged priority of ideal theory over nonideal theory. They argue that we ought to view nonideal theory as prior to ideal theory: the solution is to conceive nonideal theory as the queen rather than the handmaiden of political philosophy. Others go further back, objecting to the very division of the theory of justice into two parts and urging us to replace it with alternative unitary accounts on comparative or reactive models. Others go further still, arguing that political philosophy should not be mainly concerned with justice, which is only one political value among many. They add that focus on justice, rather than power, efficiency, legitimacy, or freedom, leads to an overly moralized political philosophy.

But in this debate, one finds another line of criticism of this Rawlsian complex, coming from the other direction.[4] On this view, Rawls is too concessive to considerations of realism and so insufficiently utopian. By allowing considerations about feasibility and stability, and various motivational foibles and limitations, into his account of the principles of justice, he sullies the purity of justice with the muck of human failure. His theory is practical all right, but in the wrong place and the wrong way. To treat the pragmatic questions that arise from the need to cope with human failings as matters of first (political) philosophy is to give up on the fundamental question of the nature of justice. Rawls's theory compromises at crucial moments, failing to maintain the austere picture of normative theorizing. It is, in a sense, too practical.

As one can see from even this stratospheric summary of the ideal theory debates, big questions lie an inch beneath the surface of these troubled waters. Here are some of the most obvious: What is it for political philosophy to be practical? Practical as opposed to what? Supposing political philosophy is theory, what relationship does theory have to practice? Being practical seems to have something to do with being realistic, but what are the requirements of realism? How are they to be distinguished from the objectionable cynicism into which talk about realism so readily veers? Or to grasp the stick from the other end, presumably (idle) utopianism is in some way a failure to be practical. In what way is it a failure? Is there a place for the utopian impulse in political philosophy? Is there a good kind of utopianism?

Notwithstanding the profundity of the lurking questions, it would be hard to blame someone if they walked away from the ideal theory debates with the impression that it was, at the end of the day, largely a debate about the legacy of Rawls and his system. If one reads his critics and defenders, it would be natural to conclude that Rawls introduced the division between ideal theory and nonideal theory as either a brilliant or a hopelessly idiosyncratic conceptual innovation, on a par with his reworking of Harsanyi's veil of ignorance, or the Difference Principle, or the two moral powers of citizens. This suggests that the fate of the division between ideal theory and nonideal theory might be tightly linked with the fortunes of Rawls's substantive theory, "justice as fairness." (Or, if not with Rawls's theory alone, perhaps with the conjunction of late twentieth-century theories influenced by Rawls's approach, including, for example, those of Ronald Dworkin and Robert Nozick.)

The problem with this impression is that the connected suite of big questions about the practicality of political philosophy is as old as political philosophy.[5] Something corresponding to the Rawlsian complex of ideas shows up as attempted answers in a dizzying number of forms throughout the history of political philosophy. Take three illustrious historical figures displaying diverse political commitments and falling over more than two millennia: Aristotle, Kant, and the young Marx.

In *Nicomachean Ethics*, Aristotle famously makes a division between practical and theoretical intellect.[6] He tells us that *politike* is one deployment of practical wisdom, the perfection of the power of the practical intellect, exercised by citizens in their deliberations about their common life together.[7] When orienting the reader to his project, he says that the subject matter of the *Nicomachean Ethics* is itself "some kind of *politike*," implying that the philosophical work is itself an exercise of the practical rather than theoretical intellect, indeed a use of the very same power that ordinary citizens use when reasoning practically about justice and the common good.[8] Famously, he approaches this task by articulating the *prakton agathon*, a practical good that guides the practical intellect in general, both in politics and in private life. And in *Politics*, where Aristotle turns to more narrowly political uses of this idea, what method does he employ? He distinguishes between the (ideal) theory of the best of the practically possible political communities and the (nonideal) theory of various suboptimal regimes, including those found in the Greece of his day. Furthermore, he maintains that ideal theory is (in some sense) prior to nonideal theory.[9]

Immanuel Kant, too, operates with a division between practical reason and theoretical reason. He treats political philosophy, which he calls "the doctrine of Right," systematically in the *Metaphysics of Morals*. The doctrine of right, like the other part of morality (the doctrine of virtue), consists in a series of a priori principles issuing from practical reason.[10] When it comes to public right, the aspect of right that concerns the political community, he treats the relevant principles as comprising the idea of a republic.[11] This is an idea of reason that can be approached ever closer but that can never be realized in experience. It serves to orient us in practice, guiding the course of social reform and functioning as a practical good for politics.[12] Furthermore, when Kant embeds public right in the broader context of international and cosmopolitan right in his essay "Towards Perpetual Peace," he introduces precisely a distinction between ideal theory and nonideal theory in the form of the distinction between "preliminary" and "definitive" articles for perpetual peace.[13] Indeed, it's this essay that Rawls himself follows in *The Law of Peoples* when drawing the division between the ideal and nonideal theories of international justice.[14]

Or, to take a rather different sort of theorist, consider the young Marx. The young Marx is obsessed with the practicality of political philosophy. His eleventh thesis on Feuerbach famously reads, "The philosophers have only interpreted the world, in various ways; the point is to *change* it."[15] The central preoccupation of his early writings is an analysis of the alienation, exploitation, and domination of the worker under the capitalistic mode of production. This analysis was, in keeping with the eleventh thesis, produced with a view to changing the world. He thought that to do so, it was necessary not only to critique the present but to limn the possible future with which the present order was pregnant. In this possible future, humanity could finally free itself from alienation, exploitation, and domination and, for the first time, realize its species being in an association of free producers.[16] To be sure, he did not frame the critique of capitalism or the alternative of revolutionary socialism in terms of *Recht*, which he saw as a pinched framework bound up with capitalist economic forms.[17] But it is no accident that the body of socialist political philosophy following him contains some of the richest reflections on utopianism, realism, political change, theory, and practice found in the tradition.

As should be obvious from my list, including, as it does, a defender of ancient slavery, bourgeois republicanism, and revolutionary socialism, my point is not that these philosophers agree with one another in some unbroken tradition of political philosophy. Nor is my point that Rawls is somehow reproducing an unchanging classical doctrine. The point is rather that Rawls is presenting, under particular historical circumstances, and in relation to his own theory of justice, a constellation of concepts that have been developed in a variety of historical, philosophical, and political milieus. In their most profound articulations, they have also been related in determinate ways to systematic divisions between theoretical and practical deployments of reason, so as to answer versions of the big questions that I have said lurk just beneath the surface in the ideal theory debates.[18]

Once one sees this point, the role of Rawls in the ideal theory debates becomes more complicated. The big questions are entangled with fundamental distinctions within philosophy—for example, between practical reason and theoretical reason. They also raise questions about the distance between ordinary and philosophical ways of thinking and about the relationship between philosophical theory and political praxis. The solutions Rawls presents to them, considered at a certain level of abstraction, are not especially Rawlsian, although he develops them in determinate ways in connection with his own project and system. I would forgive someone for thinking that if Rawls looms too large in these debates, perhaps it would be best simply to leave him to one side and focus directly on the big questions.

But at the present juncture, this approach would be naive. Rawls is a profound philosopher who made a systematic attempt to arrive at a set of views on these questions in a late twentieth-century context. Surely there is valuable material here to work with, even if imperfect and problematic. Also, Rawls is a central figure in the ideal theory debates. A theme of the chapters to come is that you cannot understand Rawls's critics without understanding the Rawlsian source of the ideas to which they are reacting. For all their insights, these critics are indebted to Rawls in the unfortunate sense that they inherit confusions that run through his views and are, in a certain sense they do not recognize, laboring in his shadow even as they turn against him. I will be arguing at length that Rawls is the source of many of our troubles: that he ran together (at least) two different conceptions of ideal theory and nonideal theory in a way that obscured the practical rationale for his division of the theory of justice; that he never managed to clearly state the sort of priority that, on his best view, ideal theory must have over nonideal theory; and that in his failure to attend at length to nonideal theory, he did not explore its distinctive conceptual terrain and, for this reason, was never able to pose and answer in a satisfying way the question of the relationship of political philosophy to political action under conditions of injustice. Indeed, the most significant error I will attribute to him concerns his views about the role of political philosophy in an unjust society.

Many are happy to continue in dialogue with Rawls, relating their own work in one or another way to his signal contributions to political philosophy. This book obviously speaks to them, insofar as Rawls is one of my conversation partners. However, increasingly, many feel that it is time to come out of the shadow of his legacy. Part of the message of this book is that there are no shortcuts here. In order to move past Rawls's legacy, a core set of ideas must be separated from the idiosyncrasies of his substantive project. I will argue that some of these ideas, once freed from these trappings and once their practical conceptual logic is made clear, are defensible and compelling. Whether or not the reader agrees, my hope is that by engaging with Rawls sufficiently to explain the sometimes unhelpful ways his views are taken up even by critics, I make a contribution to moving out of the shadow of his legacy.

Here is a road map of the course we will follow. In Chapter 1, "Two Conceptions of the Theory of Justice," I work to identify two different conceptions of the theory of justice in Rawls. Each divides the theory of justice using the distinction between ideal theory and nonideal theory, but each construes this dyad differently. I call the first "the compliance conception" and the second "the teleological conception." The core insight of the compliance conception is that justice involves right relations between members of society vis-à-vis their shared institutions. Ideal theory idealizes to capture such right relations: institutions and individuals are assumed to comply flawlessly with what justice requires. Nonideal theory relaxes this idealization to consider the messy question of how justice requires us to respond when relations go wrong and individuals and institutions deviate from what justice requires. The teleological conception, by contrast, is motivated by the insight that the theory of justice is practical. It employs the idea of a just society as a practical good to be pursued in our political action. Nonideal theory on this second characterization involves reasoning toward this end in conditions where the end is not yet in reach. Distinguishing these two conceptions of the theory of justice raises the question of whether they can be coherently combined in some way, or whether one of them is preferable to the other, or whether both should be rejected. Making further progress requires further explorations of the motivating insights of each.

In Chapter 2, "From Practice to Theory," I take up this work, probing more deeply the motivation of the teleological conception. Here I introduce the antipracticalist and practicalist critics of the teleological conception. The antipracticalists object to the teleological conception on the grounds that it projects our practical interests onto the theory of justice, which, they allege, is theoretical rather than practical. They maintain the austere normative picture by rejecting the needs of practice as alien intrusions. The practicalists, by contrast, object to the teleological conception from the opposite direction, on the grounds that it fails to take seriously the practicality of political philosophy, since it downplays the centrality of the struggle against injustice for practice.

Taking a cue from Aristotle, I argue that the theory of justice begins with piecemeal judgments of our engaged political intellect, which are initially better known to us than the deliverances of theory. This material is practical per se, since it arises from the claims of others understood as reasons for political action, and revolves around salient injustice and its contestation. Political philosophy ascends from these practical judgments to the principles of justice. These principles together constitute a conception of a just society that serves as a necessary end for political action. That justice serves as such an end is not, I argue, a projection of our purposes onto the theory of justice, but rather a structure internal to justice, flowing from the fact that the valid claims of others place us under stringent necessity to reform or replace unjust institutions and practices. Orientation to this end belongs to the political philosopher qua political philosopher and, contra the antipracticalists, is no imposition on theory.

In Chapter 3, "From Theory to Practice," I continue my exploration of the teleological conception, focusing now on the response to the practicalists. Although they are right about the starting points of inquiry and the salience of injustice, I argue that they are wrong that ideal theory is unhelpful in the confrontation with injustice. I distinguish two broad ways in which the end of a just society informs our engagement with injustice. First, it guides practice dynamically by allowing us to specify paths of transformation toward justice as an end, including the specification of an agent of change, and the determination of obstacles, hazards, and opportunities that populate the practical terrain. Second, it guides practice immanently by illuminating ways in which the struggle against injustice is both intrinsically significant and principled. I argue these immanent and dynamic dimensions together reveal the practical-explanatory sense in which ideal theory is prior to nonideal theory.

In Chapter 4, "Agents of Change," I extend the analysis by considering the distinct conceptual issues raised by nonideal theory in an attempt to shed light on the relationship of theory to practice. If, on the teleological conception, ideal theory articulates a just society as an end for practice, nonideal theory brings the course of reasoning about justice back to action in our present circumstances of injustice. Here, I criticize the widespread tendency to appeal to the citizen in general, or a universal "we," as the addressee of political philosophy. Since entrenched injustices are stably reproduced over time, in part through the operation of ordinary politics, it is often the case that political change comes from agents that are neither coextensive with the political community nor identified with the organized elements of representative government. I argue that the

practical proposals of nonideal theory stand in a special relationship to the agent so specified and that the relationship of theory to
agents of change is a central and unavoidable topic for theory.

In Chapter 5, "Against Strict Compliance," I turn finally to consider the compliance conception of the theory of justice. I argue
that we have reason to be suspicious of the role this conception
grants strict compliance in ideal theory. I draw on some Kantian
ideas about the centrality of the response to injustice and of rights
of resistance to the characterization of relations of justice between
equals. One of the essential aspects of justice that sets it apart from
other domains of morality is the fact that violations of the duties of
justice license responses intended to prevent, counteract, or rectify
these failures. This authorization to resist injustice is part of the
normative force of the original duties of justice, which limn a space
of deontic enforcement. Being a free equal is, in large part, having
the standing to hold one another to fulfillment of our mutual obligations. My conclusion is that the justice we are after is one that is
compatible with and responds to various dimensions of human
imperfection.

In Chapter 6, "Against the Antipracticalists," I respond further
to the antipractical critics who see concessions to imperfection as
alien intrusions on our thought about the fundamental requirements of justice. I do so by staging a dialogue with David Estlund's
critique of "utopophobia." I find much that is true in Estlund, especially a certain interpretation of his view that justice must not bend
to our unwillingness to do right. However, I criticize Estlund's defense of what he calls "hopeless nonconcessive theory," saying why
and how a hopeless theory would fail as a theory of justice. I also
explain how the theory I have presented responds to the challenge
of a cynic about the possibility of realizing justice. This chapter
ends by connecting the teleological conception with the claim that
practical hope is a justified presupposition of our thinking about
justice.

In my concluding Chapter 7, "Political Philosophy as Practical Reasoning," I present an overview of the teleological conception defended in the first six chapters. I next consider the senses in which political philosophy is an exercise of practical reason on this conception, before turning to some objections this conception is likely to attract. In my closing pages I meditate on what it means to present a conception of political philosophy, asking in what sense this book is itself practical and how the arguments within it fit into the conception of political philosophy defended here.

For those who want to focus narrowly on the positive conception of political philosophy I present, Chapters 2–4 and the analytic overview of the teleological conception presented in §§1–3 of Chapter 7 should provide an accurate sense of this book's position.

Before we embark on this journey, I would like to say a word about the historical sources of inspiration for different portions of my argument. My book focuses on contemporary debates and does not directly take up historical figures, aside from a brief discussion of some leitmotifs from Aristotle's practical philosophy in Chapter 2 that draws selectively on secondary scholarship. Nevertheless, these historical figures loom large in the background. The entirety of Chapters 2 and 3, which defend a conception of political philosophy as oriented toward a practical good and divide political philosophy into ideal and nonideal parts on this basis, might be thought of as the Aristotelian moment of my argument. My argument that political philosophy is itself an exercise of the same sense of justice deployed by citizens in their common deliberations is intended to echo directly Aristotle's cryptic but exhilarating claim that his philosophical investigation is an exercise of politike. And my discussion of different kinds of ends, and the sense in which justice is an end, is heavily indebted to Aristotle's distinction between praxis and poesis.

The argument of Chapter 4 about political action in opposition to injustice draws inspiration from the tradition of Marxist political philosophy. This tradition consisted of practically oriented political thinkers who sought maximally ambitious social and political change in the face of what they viewed to be the production and reproduction of staggering injustice. They were thus forced to confront in especially stark ways the conceptual difficulties of both identifying an agent of change and articulating the relationship of the theorist to the political practice of such an agent. Since my argument is intended to apply to views across the political spectrum, it depends neither on their political convictions about the evils of capitalism and the emancipatory power of socialism nor on their solutions (different in different thinkers) to the difficult question of the role of the theorist. But the lines of influence will be unmistakable for those familiar with this tradition, as I seek to present a sort of generalized form of some common and recurring themes in the tradition of socialist political theory.

Chapter 5 brings some of the peculiar features of justice into view as a way of arguing against the compliance conception. This might be viewed as the Kantian moment of my argument. The thought that to articulate duties of justice one must discuss the forms of opposition to injustice that they license is intended to echo Kant's claim that right (justice) is internally connected with the authorization to hinder a hindrance to freedom. This has been a centerpiece of Arthur Ripstein's recent work on Kant's political philosophy, and I am indebted both to Kant's text itself and to the broad sweep of the current resurgence of scholarship on *The Metaphysics of Morals*.[19] The general conception of justice as involving necessitation from another that figures heavily in this chapter is unmistakably Kantian in origin.

My hope is that these historical sources of inspiration have helped me to free some of the issues in the ideal theory debates from their entanglement with Rawls and his critics. I am convinced that this tradition can help us understand the role, character, and method of political philosophy as an exercise of practical reason. We can draw on the resources of this tradition in our contemporary moment to contribute to the renewal of political philosophy in the changing circumstances of action that confront us. Whether I have succeeded in making such a contribution is for the reader to judge.

Two Conceptions of the Theory of Justice

§1.1: THE THEORY OF JUSTICE

Our central question is how we are to understand the relation of successful political philosophy to practice. The primary concern of political philosophy is justice. As a reflective enterprise, the work of political philosophy is theory—the theory of justice. But how does the theory of justice relate to practice when done right? What are the consequences of this orientation toward action for our understanding of theory? What is the role of the political philosopher, as one who engages in this theory, in political action?

These are big and hardly neglected questions, the subject of a vibrant and growing conversation in contemporary political philosophy in what is sometimes called "the ideal theory debate." This debate concerns the viability of a conception of the theory of justice as dividing into two parts, "ideal theory" and "nonideal theory." Anyone who has waded into this conversation knows there is an unusual amount of cross talk, even by the high standards of philosophy, and a tendency for the meanings of key terms to shift. The literature discussing this distinction has reached the point where helpful interventions have produced taxonomies in attempts to dispel the terminological confusion.[1] Without gainsaying the distinctions introduced by these subtle taxonomies, I believe we can identify two main conceptions of the ideal theory / nonideal theory dyad animating the contemporary discussion. Although they are often not clearly distinguished, each is motivated by a different philosophical insight, and each carves up the theory of justice— and so the enterprise of political philosophy—in different ways. This contributes to the unstable conceptual atmosphere of these discussions.

The story begins with John Rawls, who reintroduced the distinction between ideal theory and nonideal theory into recent political philosophy, and with it the conflation. The shifting meanings of the terms in contemporary discussion are not surprising, given that most critiques of received orthodoxy begin with a criticism of Rawls. This chapter tells the story of how we came to be so productively confused by tracing the problem to its source in his work. For, as we will see as we progress, the critics slide with Rawls between these two conceptions. But the point is not the genealogy of error, for each of the distinctions arises from important insights that we will explore in their own terms in later chapters. The question of how these insights are related to one another and to the idea of justice leads straight to the heart of our topic and promises to shed significant light on the big questions about the relation of theory and practice explored in later chapters.

§1.2: WHAT IS JUSTICE?

According to Rawls, the primary concern of political philosophy is justice. Since philosophy is a reflective enterprise, he thinks this concern naturally takes the form of the construction of a theory of justice. Before we consider his views about the division of the theory of justice into ideal theory and nonideal theory, we need to understand the basic concept of justice that Rawls thinks such a theory determines. What, then, is justice such that political philosophy is the theory of it? I answer this question by highlighting what I take to be a core of insights that structure and motivate his approach.[2] To be clear, I affirm these views about the primitive concept of justice, which serve as the basis for the argument of later chapters (including arguments in criticism of Rawls).

I wish to emphasize three features of the concept of justice in particular: (1) its second-personal form, (2) its stringency, and (3) its role in evaluating the institutions that structure an ongoing system of social cooperation.[3] Although I intentionally leave these marks general and unspecified so they could be accepted by many who would understand them in different ways, they are nonetheless a starting point that some will perhaps find controversial. Later, I will defend them against a few specific challenges, but I will also try throughout to indicate where in my argument I am relying on these marks so that one who disagrees can see clearly what is at stake.

Let us begin with the thought that justice is distinct from other aspects of morality in that it is an essentially relational, or "second-personal," phenomenon in an especially thick sense.[4] When it comes to justice, the duties we are under are "directed duties" that are owed to others.[5] Duties of justice are correlative with the claims on our conduct of those whom we would wrong by failing to fulfill those duties.[6] Given this relational form, to do injustice is not only to act wrongly but to wrong another. Wherever there is injustice, some have a legitimate grievance against others. If no one is wronged, no one has a claim on others that has been unfulfilled, and so no one has a grievance. In that case, there is no injustice.

Justice thus contrasts with other aspects of morality, such as private virtues like temperance, self-discipline, and integrity, where we may be under duties or moral requirements that are, in the first instance, not owed to others. But it also contrasts with other related domains of morality such as beneficence, charity, and generosity. To act ungenerously, for example, is not necessarily to fail to fulfill a legitimate claim that others are entitled to press. For generosity characteristically concerns bestowing kindnesses or favors on others, where a favor in the relevant sense is something the beneficiary is not in a position to claim from us, and so the withholding of which would not wrong them.[7] And yet we should be generous, and so have a duty to act generously, both in general and, perhaps, here and now.[8] Unlike these other moral duties, duties of justice can always be represented as legitimate claims of those to whom the duty is owed. Relatedly, injustice always involves someone being wronged—someone whose legitimate claims are not being upheld and who, as a result, has a determinate grievance.

This relational view of justice receives expression in various contemporary sources. It can be found in the work of philosophers like Joel Feinberg, Michael Thompson, and Stephen Darwall, who emphasize the directedness of duties and the "bipolar" character of justice. It can also be found in the "relational egalitarianism" of authors such as Elizabeth Anderson and Samuel Scheffler. The relational egalitarians argue that a defensible egalitarianism must ground distributive considerations in an account of relations of equality.[9] Anderson writes illuminatingly about the concept of justice underlying relational egalitarian views as "a set of interpersonally justifiable claims . . . expressible as a *demand* that a person makes *on* an agent whom the speaker holds accountable."[10] Such relational views of justice are also familiar from the work of republican theorists, including Anderson, who treat injustice in the political sphere as involving relations of domination and subordination, and so represent duties of political justice as correlative with the claims of those who would be wronged (dominated or subordinated) where these duties are not fulfilled.[11]

Both Anderson and Scheffler have argued persuasively that John Rawls was a relational egalitarian, holding a second-personal conception of justice.[12] I believe they are correct in their interpretation. First, and perhaps most obviously, the relational conception of justice is what underlies Rawls's insistence that the principles of justice specify relations of a certain sort. For he often says that the principles of justice specify what features the basic structure of society must realize in order for them to embody relations of reciprocity between free equals in an ongoing system of social cooperation. Relations of reciprocity hold when the benefits that the social order bestows on each do not disadvantage the others—none gain at the expense of others, and the social arrangements work to the advantage of all. Reciprocity is a feature of the relationship between citizens that has to hold, according to Rawls, in order for their legitimate claims on one another to be satisfied by the social order they share.

We can see this relational view expressed as well in Rawls's favorite adjudicatory metaphor for the role of the principles of justice. For Rawls says that the principles of justice are the final arbiters adjudicating our conflicting claims on one another to order the institutions and structures of society.[13] The picture is that the principles of justice are the ultimate authority we rightly appeal to when making the case to our fellow citizens that the shared structures of our society fail to fulfill our legitimate claims and so wrong us. The relational character of justice is present here in the thought that principles serve as the ultimate authority specifying the legitimate claims that citizens can make on one another to order their shared institutions. When the principles of justice are realized, the valid claims of citizens on one another to order their shared institutions are met. When the principles of justice are not realized, the same valid claims go unfulfilled.

Perhaps most strikingly, Rawls dramatizes the relational character of justice in what we might think of as the primal scene of Rawlsian theory. This is a scene where a person occupying one representative position in society calls on another occupying a different representative position to justify the inequality between them in light of their relationship as free equals in a shared system of social cooperation. The relational character of this scene figures most directly in Rawls's informal discussions, where he makes explicit in discursive form the underlying logic of his arguments.[14] These informal discussions tend to take the form of dialogues where agents occupying different positions in society press claims on one another or argue that institutions would satisfy all legitimate claims if structured thus and so. When he discusses the principles of justice, Rawls thus presents the arguments about justice in dialogic form, as the rendering of reasons from one to another in light of the potential claims that arise between representative persons occupying contrasting positions within a shared social order. The whole of Rawls's theory is thus pervaded by a relational, second-personal, conception of justice, centered on the specification of the valid claims we can press against one another.

In addition to the strongly second-personal or relational form of duties of justice, I take their second mark to be their stringency, or practical primacy over a range of other considerations. This urgent practical character of claims of justice is manifested in the special place we grant judgments about justice in our political thought. When someone points out that institutions are unjust and wrong in some significant way, the appropriate response is to change the institution. As Rawls famously said,

> Justice is the first virtue of social institutions, as truth is of systems of thought. A theory however elegant and economical must be rejected or revised if it is untrue; likewise, laws and institutions no matter how efficient and well-arranged must be reformed or abolished if they are unjust . . . Being first virtues of human activities, truth and justice are uncompromising.[15]

Rawls adds that while the injustice of an institution may not settle it straightaway that it must be reformed, it allows only special kinds of temporary exemptions—for example, the fact that introducing a reform now would create new and greater injustices or obstruct later and farther-reaching reforms. If the institutions of our society are unjust, then absent special exemptions, we must reform them to meet the legitimate claims of those whom they wrong.

G. A. Cohen has raised objections to the stringency of justice, arguing that justice is one value that must be balanced against others and that it might be right to favor injustice in light of these balancing considerations.[16] In maintaining this, he has sought to rescue justice from the limitations that arise from endowing claims of justice with this stringency. Gerald Gaus fairly remarks that Cohen thereby "rescues" justice only by diminishing its significance.[17] But we can note here also that the stringency of justice hangs together with its relational character. Justice is itself not one value to be balanced against another, but rather a view about the proper ordering of different values to meet our claims on one another. If there is no valid claim that anyone has to our adopting a different balancing, then there is no injustice, since no one is wronged and there is nothing to rebalance.[18]

Let us turn to the third mark. It is the combination of their second-personal form with their stringency that explains why those to whom the duties of justice are owed typically have standing to hold us to their fulfillment.[19] If we fail in these duties, then in virtue of being wronged they are entitled to insist or demand that those who are responsible fulfill the duties that are owed to them. Indeed, when it comes to justice, it is a common theme that the wronged need not patiently await the dawning of scruples in their wrongdoers, but are authorized to take an active stance of opposition to the failure to fulfill the obligations. This authorization presumably explains the special relation that many have rightly thought holds between duties of justice and the possibility of justified coercion, a relation that other moral duties typically lack. It also underlies the widely held thought that many duties of justice are ones that individuals can rightly be compelled to fulfill, and that this sets them apart, for example, from duties of charity or piety or friendship.[20] Finally, it grounds the internal connection many thinkers have asserted between rights and enforcement. While I do not mean to identify all claims of justice with rights, nevertheless the fact that rights are claims of justice is a necessary precondition for understanding why, on many accounts that otherwise differ, rights are enforceable moral claims we have on one another, the enforceability of which comes in a variety of modes.[21] Again, a theory of justice will develop concrete views about the relation between justice and enforcement, and here I leave the mark unspecified to make room for a variety of views.

Finally, justice, while by no means exclusively pertaining to institutional questions, since it also touches on practices and individual behavior, nonetheless has an institutional focus. Justice requires institutional realization, and the most significant injustices involve the wrongful ordering and structure of shared institutions. In political philosophy, we are centrally concerned with the evaluations of the basic institutions that structure the shared social life of an ongoing political community. Questions of political justice centrally involve the legitimate claims individuals have on one another to order their shared institutions in ways that fulfill the obligations of justice that are owed to them.

A final note on the concept of justice. I will generally follow Rawls in speaking of a "society" or "political community" as the primary locus of justice, and I will sometimes even speak of the relation between "citizens" when operating in a Rawlsian conceptual atmosphere. I allow myself this dispensation in part out of a conviction that the political community is a crucial unit of analysis for our thought about justice. But it is also clear that relations of justice hold within a single political community between citizens and noncitizens, and across borders between political communities, individuals, and a bewildering variety of different kinds of national and transnational agents. Agents have standing to press for reform of both institutions and patterns of practice in all these cases.

I hope not to prejudge in any real way important questions about how to understand the ordering of different "regimes of right" or "levels of justice" to one another.

§1.3: THE COMPLIANCE CONCEPTION

In *A Theory of Justice*, Rawls first introduced the division between ideal theory and nonideal theory in the following fateful passage:

> [F]or the most part I examine the principles of justice that would regulate a well-ordered society. Everyone is presumed to act justly and to do his part in upholding just institutions. Though justice may be, as Hume remarked, the cautious, jealous virtue, we can still ask what a perfectly just society would be like. Thus I consider what I call strict compliance as opposed to partial compliance theory. The latter studies the principles that govern how we are to deal with injustice. It comprises such topics as the theory of punishment, the doctrine of just war, and the justification of the various ways of opposing unjust regimes, ranging from civil disobedience and conscientious objection to militant resistance and revolution. Also included here are questions of compensatory justice and of weighing one form of institutional injustice against another. Obviously, the problems of partial compliance theory are the pressing and urgent matters. These are the things that we are faced with in everyday life. The reason for beginning with ideal theory is that it provides, I believe, the only basis for a systematic grasp of these more pressing problems. . . . At least, I shall assume that a deeper understanding can be gained in no other way, and that the nature and aims of a perfectly just society is the fundamental part of the theory of justice.[22]

Note first that Rawls's original titles for the two parts of the theory of justice are "strict compliance theory" and "partial compliance theory." The language of ideal theory is only introduced at the end of this passage as an afterthought. Rawls thus originally presents "ideal" as a synonym for "strict compliance." The passage begins by asserting that strict compliance theory is the theory of a "well-ordered society." This is a term of art for Rawls. A society is well ordered if there is public knowledge among its citizens that they all accept the same principles of justice, and if these principles effectively regulate society in that individuals and institutions comply with their requirements.[23] So strict compliance theory operates under the assumption that everyone knows that everyone accepts and lives up to the principles of justice that the theory outlines.

By contrast, partial compliance theory relaxes the assumption of strict compliance and asks how we are to respond to injustice when it arises.[24] The list of subjects Rawls initially includes under this rubric is instructive. He mentions the theories of punishment, compensatory justice, just war, and strategies of protest and resistance to domestic injustice. These topics presuppose departures from the principles of justice and ask how we are to justly cope with them. For example, the theory of punishment presupposes wrongdoing on the part of the criminal. Similarly, just war theory asks what military measures can be taken on the assumption that some nation or rogue group is engaging in unjust military aggression. And so on.

Rawls says that in order to get a "clear and uncluttered" view of a question, we both abstract, leaving out some of the messy and complicated features of the social world, and substitute idealizations for other features.[25] Such abstraction and idealization allow us to simplify a question by focusing precisely on the elements that we believe are most significant for developing an answer to our guiding question.[26] In this context, Rawls remarks, "The idea of a well-ordered society is plainly a very considerable idealization."[27] The theoretical operations of abstraction and idealization that Rawls mentions are familiar from the social and natural sciences, and they are the subject of a burgeoning literature in the philosophy of science.[28] Some authors in this literature have helpfully regimented these terms.[29] On their regimentation, abstraction and idealization are employed for the purposes of constructing models. Abstraction simplifies by omitting information. Idealization simplifies in a different way, by attributing features to entities that diverge from those they possess.

Strict compliance is an idealization in this regimented sense.[30] It involves attributing to citizens an ensemble of cognitive and motivational properties that they do not currently possess. For citizens do not all currently affirm the principles of justice, much less strictly comply with them out of a firm allegiance to justice. The same could be said as well for the functioning of institutions, which are currently plagued by injustice. Rawls grants this idealization of citizens and their shared institutions a central place in ordering the theory of justice because he thinks that it allows us to focus on the considerations relevant for justifying principles of justice. But why?

The principles of justice are the norms that govern the relations of free equals who share a basic structure of institutions as members of one society.[31] The principles of justice characterize the features the social world must possess for people to view and treat one another as free equals. They describe how the social world must be structured for the valid claims of all to be satisfied by their shared practices and institutions. Rawls reasons that if this is what principles of justice are, then strict compliance and the other idealizations contained in the concept of a well-ordered society appear to be reasonable assumptions for modeling them. For only when strictly complying with publicly affirmed principles do agents view themselves and one another through the relevant conceptions and live up to them in their interactions. To the extent that they depart from the principles of justice, they fail to deal with one another as free equals, and so their action fails to express the normative point of view articulated by the principles of justice. To the extent that their institutions fail to comply with the principles of justice, they fail to secure and honor the valid claims free equals have on one another.

Thus, strict compliance is an idealization in a special sense. The entities it describes do not merely possess features that diverge in some way or other from their actual counterparts: they possess the features that are proper to their actual counterparts, and so these idealized features are required for their actual counterparts to be as they should be given that they are related as free equals.[32] The idealization is thus normative in a certain sense that sets it apart from the idealizations employed in physical sciences.[33] The principles of justice specify what it is for members of society to meet the valid claims they have on one another, including claims to organize their shared institutions in ways that can be justified to all.[34]

Of course, the most pressing questions of justice with which we are concerned in ordinary political life arise because of failures to comply with the principles of justice. For this reason, we must in a second stage of theory relax the assumption of strict compliance and consider what, in light of the principles of justice, justice requires in response to injustice. We must complicate our reflections and consider how justice requires us to act when relations are not right and the institutions of our society do not fully honor our valid claims on one another. The theory of justice is thus a two-part affair because of the necessity of considering multiple assumptions about compliance. Strict compliance has a special status because it allows us to specify the principles of justice. Partial compliance brings us from the principles of justice to thought about what justice requires in the nonideal circumstances we confront.

Given the role this conception grants compliance in structuring the theory of justice, employing the division between strict and partial compliance to divide the theory of justice into ideal and nonideal components, I call this "the compliance conception" of the theory of justice. It is motivated by the view of the principles of justice as specifying right relations and by the observation that relations are often not right in the real world. This imperfect state of affairs raises distinct questions that require us to extend our theory. For now we must ask what the principles that govern right relations say about situations where legitimate claims are not being honored and the response to such injustice is lamentably required. To pose this question, we must relax our idealization. Thus, the theory of justice is rightly divided into two parts to handle the questions that arise on different assumptions about compliance.

§1.4: THE TELEOLOGICAL CONCEPTION

In Rawls's writings, a second conception of the theory of justice exists uneasily alongside the compliance conception.[35] This is the conception of ideal theory as presenting a practical good and nonideal theory as reasoning toward this end in conditions of injustice. This conception is clearly present from the beginning in *A Theory of Justice*. There, Rawls writes, "Viewing the theory of justice as a whole, the ideal part presents a conception of a just society that we are to achieve if we can."[36] This reference to achievement sounds a practical note: what ideal theory presents is something to be realized in practice. In the same work, he calls a just society "the end of political action by reference to which practical decisions are to be made."[37] Ideal theory thus presents an end or telos that is meant to serve as a reference point for making political decisions. Elsewhere he describes this end as providing the "objective" or "long-range goal" toward which to strive.[38] He tells us that this goal is to guide us in the course of social reforms, through which we may approach it in steps.[39] On the conception that emerges from these remarks, ideal theory serves to articulate an ideal of a just society that can serve as an aim for political practice.

In later works, Rawls expresses this idea with the intentionally paradoxical phrase "realistic utopia."[40] We could represent each word of this apparently oxymoronic coupling as indicating a requirement on ideal theory. On the one hand, ideal theory must be utopian, because it uses moral ideals and principles to specify the concept of a reasonable and just society that can serve as an end for our political hope and action.[41] Since neither our society nor any other with which we are familiar is just, this involves envisioning a better world that does not exist. Ideal theory is the place in political philosophy where the utopian aspiration and the robust exercise of the political imagination have their home. This utopian aspiration has been a central element of political philosophy from its inception, and it is an expression in theory of the reasonable hope decent people have in the possibility of a human future freed from the evils of marginalization, exploitation, oppression, and domination.

On the other hand, this use of the moral imagination aims to articulate a goal for practice and not an idle fantasy or wish. For this reason, it must be realistic. The end it articulates must be possible to achieve, at least under favorable conditions. It must, as Rawls says, "fall under the art of the possible."[42] The end it determines must be compatible with the facts of human psychology and biology, including our characteristic foibles and vulnerabilities.[43] It must also be compatible with the material and historical conditions of our social world. After presenting an ideal, one must thus be willing to address the most plausible and empirically grounded objections to its feasibility.[44]

In endorsing this requirement of realism, Rawls would seem to be in familiar territory, for it is widely agreed that something is wrong with a political philosophy if it rests on an unrealistic conception of the political subject or of our material or historical conditions.[45] A political philosophy describing a community of angels rather than human beings, or situated in the Garden of Eden rather than in current material conditions, strikes many as misguided. In this context, Rawls appropriates Rousseau's methodological dictum in *On the Social Contract* to take "men as they are, and laws as they might be."[46] Rawls puts the point elegantly in *A Theory of Justice*, writing, "Conceptions of justice must be justified by the conditions of our life as we know it or not at all."[47]

Rawls also connects the requirement of realism with two other features of a theory of justice: workability and stability.[48] A theory of justice is workable if individuals can apply the principles of the theory to their ongoing political affairs. These principles are to provide the terms according to which individuals evaluate their institutions, rendering public justification to one another, and hold one another accountable for failures of justice. For principles to play this role, they must be formulated with concepts that make it possible to determine whether they have been satisfied.[49] They must also place on people demands they are able to fulfill, at least under favorable circumstances.

That Rawls includes stability under the rubric of realism is not surprising, since he identifies the stability of a theory of justice at various points with its feasibility.[50] The concept of stability is a complex one, and I can do no more here than touch on some main points.[51] A theory of justice is stable if it specifies a basic structure that can maintain its justice in the face of inevitable countervailing forces. The system must be able to set in motion sufficient forces to counteract these injustices when they arise. In that case, "the inevitable deviations from justice are either corrected or held in tolerable bounds by the system."[52] Of course, stability can come through many routes, including the barrel of a gun, indoctrination, and moral lethargy. But insofar as this is a requirement on a theory of justice, the stability in question must be what Rawls calls "stability for the right reasons."[53] The countervailing forces must consist of the just mechanisms of enforcement through which citizens secure justice for themselves and through their allegiance to these just institutions. For a theory of justice to be stable, its principles must thus be capable of "generating their own support" among the citizen body.[54] Since Rawls assumes that the way in which one acquires allegiance to principles of justice is through growing up with an experience of being benefited by just institutions, stability has an importantly intergenerational form.[55] The justice of a society must be such that it can be maintained and reproduced over time through the just institutions and the dispositions and actions of its citizens that they secure.

While it might initially seem that realism and utopianism are two unrelated requirements, limiting each other externally, Rawls intends a deeper unity. The heart of the utopian project consists in the identification and defense of principles of justice and their use to characterize a just society. The realism constraint is internal to this project, since the theory of justice is intended to describe a practical good for human beings. The principles of justice are principles for us, intended to regulate our political action and the public claims we make on one another in light of our shared institutions. The claim that the theory of justice must take human beings as they are and laws as they might be is not an alien constraint on this project. Rather, it flows from an understanding of what the principles of justice are and how they must be justified in light of this fact. The utopian aspiration is thus bound up with an element of realism.

The requirement of realism is, in turn, informed by a utopian element. If we consider the requirement of workability, we can see that it expresses the moral idea that principles of justice serve as public standards through which members of society hold one another to account. The principles of justice are to serve as the public charter of our social world.[56] They serve as public standards that members can employ in their deliberations with one another as free equals.[57] Justice thus must be something that can be publicly appealed to in an open way in our political reasoning. Similarly, when it comes to stability, we are concerned with stability for the right reasons. This is a stability that arises from just institutions that rightly enforce our claims on one another, thereby holding injustice within "tolerable bounds" and working to produce their own support in our just dispositions without the help of illusion or ideology.[58] So the requirement of realism is bound up with utopian elements as well.

Realism and utopianism thus turn out to be two sides of the same coin, united in the concept of a just society, understood as a practical good. The central task in ideal theory is to combine the cutting edge of utopianism with the hard steel of realism. By realizing this union, political philosophy at its best expands the horizons of our sense of political possibility by showing us a just world that could become a practical reality. This is why Rawls says that ideal theory "probes the limits of practicable political possibility."[59] If it is successful, it sustains our practical hope that a just world is in fact possible, by showing us how this end might be realistically conceived and orients us toward this end for the sake of action. Let us call this the "realistic utopia" conception of ideal theory.

The corresponding conception of nonideal theory asks how we are to work from our current condition of injustice toward this realistically utopian goal.[60] As John Simmons puts it in a perceptive discussion, "Where ideal theory dictates the objective, nonideal theory dictates the route to that objective (from whatever imperfectly just condition a society happens to occupy)."[61] If ideal theory discusses the long-range goal, nonideal theory discusses the means that can effectively and justly be taken in pursuit of it in the short and middle range.[62] Simmons aptly describes nonideal theorizing on this conception as transitional in character, since it concerns the movement from situations of injustice to the end of a just society. I follow Simmons in calling this conception of nonideal theory "transitional theory."[63]

Since transitional theory strategically navigates toward the goal of a just society, it must systematically identify the injustices that confront us and work to diagnose the underlying causes of the political pathologies that serve as obstacles to forward movement. It must use this diagnosis to propose morally permissible and effective remedies that could be effectuated by some agent of change.[64] It thus must identify permissible policies that would be effective in moving us toward justice and resistance in the face of a likely well-defended status quo. It looks for courses of action and policy that are morally permissible and likely to be effective, and it works to identify agents of change who might bring them about through morally permissible and productive transformational strategies of political action.[65]

On this conception of the theory of justice, ideal theory is "realistic utopian theory." It presents a conception of a just society as an end or practical good to be realized through our political action. The paired version of nonideal theory is "transitional theory," consisting of reasoning toward this end in conditions of injustice. Given its use of the relation to an end or telos to structure the theory of justice, I call this conception of the theory of justice the "teleological conception."

§1.5: THE PROBLEM WITH CONFLATING THE CONCEPTIONS

Rawls mingles these two conceptions of ideal theory everywhere; many critics and apologists follow his lead. Here is a representative passage from *A Theory of Justice*:

> It will be recalled that strict compliance is one of the stipulations of the original position; the principles of justice are chosen on the supposition that they will be generally complied with. Any failures are discounted as exceptions. By putting these principles in lexical order, the parties are

choosing a conception of justice suitable for favorable conditions and assuming that a just society can in due course be achieved. Arranged in this order, the principles define then a perfectly just scheme; they belong to ideal theory and set up an aim to guide the course of social reform.[66]

In dizzying fashion, Rawls turns back and forth between the two conceptions. On the one hand, ideal theory is formulated on the supposition of strict compliance; failures are to be idealized away ("discounted as exceptions"). On the other hand, ideal theory assumes that a just society so described can be achieved "in due course"; it sets up an aim guiding the course of social reform. After the quoted passage, Rawls goes on to say social reform is treated by a nonideal theory that asks what justice requires when we relax the assumption of strict compliance. In short, ideal theory presents a strictly complying society as a realistic utopia, and nonideal theory considers how we are to transition from a partially complying society to such a realistic utopia.

But on the face of it, these seem like two distinct conceptions, motivated by different concerns, deploying different criteria of classification, and setting different stakes for locating a phenomenon on either side of the dyad.

On the realistic utopian conception, ideal theory describes the end of a just society. This is a practical good. Nonideal theory discusses how we are to move from conditions of injustice towards this good. This teleological structure of end, and strategic reasoning toward this end, is specific to practical endeavors.[67] Since the good in question is practical, it follows that the just society treated by ideal theory must be practicable, something that could be brought about and sustained through our collective action. For this reason, our description of the just society must be compatible with our nature, including facts about human psychology and development, disability and the susceptibility to illness, and the material conditions of our world.

Furthermore, since the end in question is a practical good, the classification of something as belonging to ideal theory has immediate practical significance. For, on the teleological conception, to locate some phenomenon in ideal theory is to say that it is part of a just society that is the proper aim of our political hope and action; to classify some phenomenon as belonging to ideal theory is to say that, as a matter of practical political conviction, it is a component of a realistic utopia for which we are to strive. By contrast, to locate some phenomenon (only) in nonideal theory is to declare it to be an element of society that we must transform in the name of justice; it is to say that, as a matter of fundamental political conviction, we are to strive against the structure of which it is a part, as it is ultimately incompatible with the just society to which we aspire.

When we put the two features of practicality and goodness together, we see that on the realistic utopian conception, the dividing line between ideal theory and nonideal theory has momentous political implications. To say that some phenomenon belongs to nonideal theory is to say that it can and must be overcome. It is at best a necessary way station and at worst an obstacle on the route to a just society. By contrast, to classify some phenomenon as belonging to ideal theory is to say that it is an element of an end that can and must be achieved. It is a component of the just society toward which our action ought to be directed.

On the compliance conception, by contrast, ideal theory applies the operation of idealization to the case of identifying principles of justice. It does so by working with a model of a well-ordered society that includes strict compliance. The idealizations employed in the model conception of a well-ordered society involve attributing dispositions to the citizen and the functioning of institutions that are in flawless accord with the principles of justice. We are to consider a situation where everyone lives up to their commitments and honors the principles of justice from a flawless righteousness.

Now, some of these assumptions about human motivation are possible for human beings only if certain individuals are excluded from consideration, as when Rawls initially excludes children from ideal theory, on the grounds that, owing to the undeveloped state of their moral powers, they cannot strictly comply.[68] Admittedly, this sounds bad, as though Rawls is saying that society would be better off without these individuals or, even worse, that we should somehow try to bring about a society without them. But in fact, there is no such implication. True, in this case, idealization is being employed to isolate a relationship of free and equal citizens that is related to the idea of justice. But Rawls is not saying that it would be practically good if society lacked individuals who do not possess the features of the citizen, and he is not proposing excluding them as a practical goal.

But even for adult citizens who possess their full range of practical powers, it may not be within the practical power of the political community to bring about or maintain a state of affairs where all are always disposed to treat one another justly.[69] In this sense, even if it is possible for each individual to spontaneously comply with the principles of justice, such a state of affairs might not be a practicable political end.[70] Producing such a condition, or maintaining it, might not be possible. As Rawls himself argues, a practical good that could serve as an end of our collective action would include a stable set of institutions that function to respond to injustices as they arise by holding them in check and counteracting their effects so as to produce and reproduce the just status quo across time. The utopia of a just society must also be realistic. It may thus involve various mechanisms of enforcement that would be unintelligible if we conceived everyone as strictly complying with the principles of justice from their own disposition. Indeed, we have seen that the enforceability of justice is part of what sets it apart from the rest of morality—a feature the strict compliance conception strangely seems to have no way to represent, as I will argue at some length in Chapter 5.

Thus, to say that something belongs to ideal theory on the compliance conception is not to say that it is something to be brought about through our political action; it is to say only that it is what should be considered for the purposes of specifying the principles of justice that would characterize right relations. Similarly, to say that some phenomenon belongs to nonideal theory is not to say that it is something to be overcome through our action; it is to say only that it involves phenomena that depart from right relations and is best treated in a second moment of theoretical reflection, where we must relax our idealizations once clarity on the principles of justice has been achieved. In short, the compliance conception is not motivated by, and does not issue immediately in, the idea of a practical good.

The two conceptions of the theory of justice are heterogeneous. The grounds for treating something as belonging to ideal theory on each conception are distinct, and the decision to so treat something has different consequences in each case. We should not use the teleological and compliance conceptions simultaneously as two ways to make what is thought to be the same division between ideal theory and nonideal theory. In reality, the terms "ideal theory" and "nonideal theory" track a different distinction when understood in one way or the other.

This naturally raises the question of how these heterogeneous distinctions are related to each other. Should we employ one but not the other to structure the theory of justice? Since each is motivated by what seem to be philosophical insights, rejecting either will require philosophical thought. No doubt there are many possible ways of combining aspects of each. Can we find a place for them both without conflation? Should we reject one, or both, and if so, how?

From Practice to Theory

We have inherited multiple ways of carving up the theory of justice, motivated by different philosophical insights. In order to make progress, I propose we explore the rationale and consequences of the view that political philosophy is practical. For if political philosophy is practical, there should be consequences for how the theory of justice is structured and what it is for theory to succeed. Furthermore, those who criticize the division of the theory of justice into ideal and nonideal components typically do so precisely on the grounds that this division is misguided in light of the practical aim of the confrontation with injustice.

Sometimes seeing what is involved in denying a claim helps illuminate what is at stake in affirming it. Luckily for our purposes, G. A. Cohen and Adam Swift have recently denied that political philosophy is practical. Cohen writes strikingly,

> [S]uppose that, like me, you think that political philosophy is a branch of philosophy, whose output is consequential for practice, but not limited in significance to its consequences for practice. Then you may, as I would, protest that the question for political philosophy is not

what we should do but what we should think, even when
what we should think makes no practical difference.[1]

Cohen says a philosophical inquiry into justice answers the question of what we should think about justice rather than what to do
about justice. Political philosophy is an inquiry aiming to produce
knowledge about the nature of justice rather than practical proposals about how we should organize our community or respond
to injustice. Cohen grants, of course, that deciding what to think
about justice has consequences for deciding what to do about justice. But his view is that political philosophy addresses the former
rather than the latter; the influence it has on the latter flows entirely
from its answers to the former.

To support this view, Cohen draws an analogy to arithmetic and
its application to the empirical world. He writes,

> It is not the purpose of fundamental principles [of justice]
> to guide practice, any more than it is the purpose of arith-
> metic to reach by calculation truths about the empirical
> world. Arithmetic indeed serves that purpose, when it is
> yoked to facts about the world, but that purpose is not
> constitutive of what arithmetic is: if the world were to
> become too chaotic for arithmetic to be applied to it,
> arithmetic would remain exactly what it now is. And fun-
> damental principles indeed serve the purpose that (when
> combined with the facts) they tell us what to do, but their
> standing, too, lies upstream from their serving practical
> purposes. So one cannot say "The purpose of funda-
> mental principles is to guide practice," even though they
> of course do so.[2]

On this analogy, arithmetic serves the purpose of allowing us to
know things about the empirical world through calculation. We
"yoke" arithmetic to facts about the world—facts that are not

mathematical facts but rather empirical ones—so that arithmetic might serve our purposes. Were the facts to change in such a way that it was no longer possible to yoke them to arithmetic to serve this purpose of ours, "arithmetic would remain exactly what it now is." Thus, the purpose of arriving at truths about the empirical world through calculation is not a purpose that is constitutive of arithmetic. It is one of our purposes, something we bring to arithmetic from the outside.

Similarly, Cohen suggests, the principles of justice serve the purpose of telling us what to do about justice when yoked to various facts about our social life. But this purpose is not constitutive of our philosophical thinking about justice. Arithmetic lies "upstream" from "serving practical purposes" of arriving at knowledge of empirical matters through calculation, just as philosophical thought about justice lies "upstream" from the purpose of thinking about political practice.

Cohen draws the conclusion that if someone happened not to have this purpose in doing political philosophy, and so wasn't guided by it in any way in their inquiry, they wouldn't be misunderstanding political philosophy. He writes, "One may or may not care about practice, but one may also care about justice, as such, one may be interested in what it is, even if one does not care about practice at all."[3] It would take an unusual psychological constitution to care about what justice is without caring about what to do about justice, Cohen tells us. But he reassures us that he is not unusual in this way, since of course he does "personally happen" to care about political practice.[4] But this concern is not constitutive of philosophical thinking about justice, which is directed to the question of what justice is rather than the question of what to do. So it is not a mistake, at least not one of political philosophy, to pursue its study without being guided by any concern to receive guidance about what to do.[5]

We see here what is involved in denying that political philosophy is practical. Political philosophy aims not at action, but rather at (perhaps practically inert) belief. Remove any engagement with practice from it, and political philosophy "would remain exactly what it now is." So if practical reasoning has characteristics and structures different from those of theoretical reasoning, the differences will not inform the structure or methods of the theory of justice. For we bring our practical purposes to the theory of justice from the outside; understandable and legitimate as they are, they are nonetheless ours, things we "personally happen" to care about.[6] If for some reason claims about justice are not able to serve our practical purposes, this is no criticism of the claims, just as it would be no criticism of arithmetic if some branch of it could not be employed to arrive at knowledge of the empirical world through calculation.

Cohen makes these remarks in the context of criticizing Rawls's constructivism, which treats the theory of justice as an exercise of practical reason. We can also see how Cohen's view leads him to reject in particular a number of concepts associated with the teleological conception. Most obviously, he rejects the idea that the theory of justice (in part) articulates a realistic utopia.[7] For the requirement of realism flows from the thought that the utopia so articulated must be capable of playing a certain role in practice. This constraint would only make sense if playing such a role were constitutive of the theory of justice.

Connectedly, Cohen rejects the idea that the theory of justice is a theory for us, a theory for human beings. He emphatically rejects the thought that it might be justified in light of, or even constrained by, facts about human life or our historical condition.[8] Such facts are, of course, of great practical import when we make our thinking about justice serve our practical purposes, since they must be taken account of to arrive at sensible proposals for action. But they are alien intrusions to the theory of justice. They are precisely the extraneous facts we yoke the theory of justice to in order to serve our purposes.

Perhaps less obviously, Cohen is committed to rejecting the idea that the theory of justice articulates the end of a just society, if only because an end is a concept of practical rather than theoretical reasoning. An end is something to be aimed at or pursued in action. That the principles of justice cannot characterize an end is no criticism of them. For the ends are all ours. And who are we to blame justice for not meeting our needs?

§2.2: IS THE TELEOLOGICAL CONCEPTION NOT PRACTICAL ENOUGH?

While Cohen and Swift criticize the teleological conception for being too practical, others reject it as not practical enough. These critics are, in sharp distinction from Cohen and Swift, firmly committed to the view that political philosophy must help us cope with the pressing injustices that surround us. They are thus natural allies of the position I defend in this and the following two chapters. However, they reject the teleological conception on the grounds that it fails to play this practical role. The rub, as they see it, is the role the teleological conception grants the end of a just society.

Since Rawls is the main object of their criticism, we must see what in his work draws their ire. As we have seen, early in *A Theory of Justice*, Rawls not only divides the theory of justice into two parts but also suggests that the two parts are ordered.[9] Although nonideal theory deals with the "pressing and urgent matters" that confront us in our ordinary political practice, ideal theory gives us a systematic and deeper grasp of the problems nonideal theory handles that would otherwise be unavailable. Rawls presents this as a reason for beginning with ideal theory. We might express this claim by saying that ideal theory is "prior to" nonideal theory.

To evaluate this claim, it is crucial to understand what sort of priority Rawls has in mind, since he does not clearly indicate it himself. When mentioning the priority relation, he mainly orients the reader by employing temporal language. For example, he says that we should "begin" with ideal theory.[10] Elsewhere, he says that ideal theory is to be addressed before nonideal theory, which he tells us is to be worked out after ideal theory.[11] Similarly, he expresses the priority claim by saying that nonideal theory presupposes that the results of ideal theory are "already on hand" and that "until" ideal theory has been completed at least in outline, it lacks a goal.[12]

These temporal glosses might suggest that Rawls views the priority claim as a thesis about the proper genesis of the theory of justice.[13] As political philosophers, we have two tasks to complete corresponding to the two parts of the theory of justice. The priority claim addresses the following question: If we wish our theory of justice to be justified and rationally constructed, with which of these two parts should we start? It answers that matters pertaining to ideal theory are the proper starting point for the development of a theory of justice. We are to begin by investigating questions about the justice of a just society. Only later are we to turn to questions about the identification of, and response to, the pressing injustices that confront us in ordinary political life.

Indeed, when taken at face value, Rawls's temporal glosses might suggest something even stronger. If nonideal theory presupposes that the conclusions of ideal theory "are already on hand," then it looks like we must not only begin with ideal theory before turning to nonideal theory but finish ideal theory—"at least in outline"—before we can so much as make a start on nonideal theory. Since nonideal theory involves the identification of injustice and the proposal of remedies to overcome it, this strong temporal reading of the priority claim would seem to imply that we cannot be justified in identifying something as an injustice without employing some worked-out conception of justice as a standard. Even if we could identify something as unjust, it would seem to imply that we cannot know whether some alteration would constitute an improvement from the unjust status quo without having the end presented by ideal theory in view to guide us.[14] If philosophers wish to proceed in a rational and justified manner, Rawls's unguarded remarks suggest, they must arrive at a complete outline of an account of a just society before starting to theorize about injustice.

Critics argue persuasively that this genetic claim about method is wrongheaded. Elizabeth Anderson writes, "This [method] misunderstands how normative thinking works. Unreflective habits guide most of our activity. We are not jarred into critical thinking about our conduct until we confront a problem that stops us from carrying on unreflectively."[15] Anderson thinks the priority claim rests on a general picture of normative thinking as beginning from satisfied reflection on the successes of justice. But it is not a desire to reflect on the justice of the institutions surrounding us that draws us into political philosophy; we are rather driven to formulate a theory of justice precisely because our keen perception of injustice jars us out of complacency. This practical perception and the identification of injustice on which it rests thus necessarily antedate our theories of justice. Our normative theorizing about justice naturally and rightly begins with the identification of injustice and next proceeds to reasoning about the responses to this injustice. The priority claim rests on a false picture of the starting points of normative theory. The natural path in normative thinking begins with the nonideal and works up to the ideal.

Elizabeth Anderson also objects to the idea that comparative judgments about injustice presuppose a worked-out ideal theory. Often, we can know what is better without yet knowing what would be best.[16] In passages with a similar spirit, Amartya Sen points out that we can know that many things are unjust, and that reforms ameliorating or removing them are improvements, without having settled on a view about what it would be for a society to be perfectly just.[17] Sen's persuasive examples of obvious and egregious injustices include the subjugation of women, human trafficking, and mass starvation in the midst of plenty. We don't need a worked-out ideal theory to know that these evils are unjust and that we should address them if we can. For example, we need not have determined the details about the requirements of economic justice to know that sex trafficking is wrong and that things would be better (less unjust) if we stopped it. Anderson follows suit, pointing out that we can often settle a just claim on our conduct now in response to nonideal conditions without having completed our ideal theory even in outline.[18]

Charles Mills pursues a similar argument with a different emphasis. Mills agrees with Anderson that political philosophy begins in our ordinary political experience, but he points out that different groups have different experiences. The experience of political subjects who are victims of systematic oppression differs from that of political subjects who are not. For the former, the injustice of the present political order is the unavoidable and undeniable starting point of political reflection. For the latter, more privileged group, the present order is more ambiguous, substantially if imperfectly just. The priority claim, in effect, privileges the experience of the privileged.[19] It makes the experience of the privileged of substantial justice the legitimate starting point for inquiry, and it relegates the experience of the oppressed to second-class epistemic status. Because of depressing demographic facts about philosophy, it is no surprise that the priority claim would assume the status of an obvious and unquestioned truth. But this hardly speaks in its favor.

So while Anderson argues that the priority claim embodies a mistake about how normative thinking works, Mills suggests that the priority claim is no mistake. It accurately captures the experience of white male middle-to-upper-class normative thinking, and it functions to discount the experience of other disadvantaged groups. However, this disagreement aside, Mills agrees with Anderson that the priority claim is wrongheaded. For, if our concern in political philosophy is to address the pressing and appalling injustices that confront us in our ordinary experience, it makes good sense to take very seriously at the outset the experience of those who actually suffer the relevant injustices. And Mills certainly agrees with Anderson about the possibility of the direct identification of injustice.

These criticisms lead philosophers such as Mills and Anderson not only to reject, but to reverse the priority relation found in Rawls. On their view, political philosophy properly begins with our sense of the injustice of our society. If successful, it equips us to address this injustice well. Given that it begins in our experience of injustice, its proper starting place is nonideal rather than ideal theory. Having achieved a critical understanding of the systems of oppression in our society, we can then construct ideals of justice that function as effective remedies to these political pathologies. If, as practice demands, we are to stay in touch with reality, we must work outward from the injustice of the real to the justice of the ideal. Thus, Anderson and Mills reverse Rawls's priority claim, arguing that ideal theory should be viewed as posterior to nonideal theory. Ideal theory is, on their conception, the handmaiden rather than the queen of political philosophy.

These authors signal their allegiance to the reverse priority claim by reappropriating and granting new significance to the terms *ideal theory* and *nonideal theory*. Instead of treating them as names of two parts of one theory of justice, they use "ideal theory" to refer to a theory of justice like Rawls's, accepting the priority claim, and "nonideal theory" to name a theory like theirs that affirms the reverse priority claim. They offer us what is intended as a new and different way of doing political philosophy centered in our experience of injustice and proposed remedies to it.

§2.3: SOME HELP FROM ARISTOTLE

The authors we have considered stand to one another as reflections in a mirror that show the same object while reversing its orientation. They are united in rejecting the teleological conception and doing so on grounds of its relation to practice. But while Cohen and Swift reject it as wrongly practicalizing the theory of justice, Anderson and Mills reject it for wrongly failing to practicalize the theory of justice. To find our way through this hall of mirrors, a little guidance from the philosophical tradition might help.

Cohen finds, as well he might, a philosophical predecessor for his views in Plato. When drawing the connection, Cohen emphasizes that he thinks political philosophy is concerned with the nature of justice "in its purity."[20] Political philosophy provides an account of what justice is in itself, where that latter phrase is meant to extract justice from empirical facts, including the conditions of its practicability, such as the facts of human life or history. Plato appears, like Cohen, to directly reject the requirement of realism or practicability on an account of justice.[21]

For an alternative source of historical inspiration, we need go no further from Plato than his most illustrious student. Aristotle's *Nicomachean Ethics* articulates a conception of the relation of political philosophy to practice that is useful as a contrast with Cohen. To understand Aristotle's remarks about these issues in full would require grappling in detail with challenging and central questions of interpretation about book 6 of the *Nicomachean Ethics*, among the most difficult portions of that difficult book. This I neither intend nor am able to do. Instead, I draw together several provocative leitmotifs of Aristotle's discussion, guided selectively by what strike me as illuminating lines of interpretation in the secondary literature.[22] By doing this, I do not mean to affirm (or deny) details of Aristotle's account of political philosophy, either in form or substance. Instead, I mean only to draw from some of Aristotle's remarks a sense of the sorts of connections and propositions one would have to develop in order to maintain, pace Cohen, the practicality of political philosophy.

In book 6 of *Nicomachean Ethics*, Aristotle famously makes a division between the practical intellect and the theoretical intellect.

The activity of the theoretical intellect is contemplation of unchanging and necessary truth. It engages in scientific demonstration from first principles associated with science (episteme) and wisdom (sophia), the perfection of the theoretical intellect. The practical intellect, by contrast, is directed toward what is variable and so subject to change, whether through production (poesis) or action (praxis).[23] The perfection that stands to the practical intellect as sophia stands to the theoretical intellect as phronesis, or practical wisdom. As a perfection of intellect, it is concerned with truth, but the truth in question is practical truth, which Aristotle describes as involving a true account (logos) in harmony with right desire.[24] As the reference to "a true account" indicates, phronesis involves reasoning, but instead of scientific demonstration, the form of reasoning is deliberation or practical reasoning.[25] In deliberation, the reasoner brings into existence that about which they deliberate, taking the course of reasoning from starting points in an end back to what is in their power to effectuate here and now. This characterization applies to both craft (techne) that produces products and practical wisdom (phronesis) that issues in actions (praxeis) in Aristotle's elevated sense.[26] Aristotle tells us that politike is the same state as phronesis, insofar as it turns practical wisdom to deliberation about shared political life.[27] Politike, he tells us, is the highest deployment of practical wisdom.

Aristotle expects his audience to come to philosophy already as ethical and political thinkers and actors.[28] More than that, he expects them to be knowers: in virtue of their upbringing and their experience of practical matters, they have or can easily get the starting points of philosophical inquiry. In stylized form, Aristotle refers to that prephilosophical knowledge as knowledge of "the that" (for example, such and such is just), and he represents philosophy as rising from this to "the why." When orienting the reader to his project in *Nicomachean Ethics*, he says that the work is itself "some kind of *politike*," implying that the philosophical work toward understanding "the why" is itself an elevated exercise of the practical rather than theoretical intellect.[29]

Famously, he approaches this task in *Nicomachean Ethics* by articulating the *prakton agathon*, an end that guides the practically wise agent in deliberation generally, in politics and in household and private life.[30] He characterizes this end essentially in terms of the role it plays in practical reasoning. Indeed, in calling his investigation "some kind of *politike*," Aristotle suggests that the *Nicomachean Ethics* is somehow a use of the very same powers of practical intellect that citizens use when deliberating (well) about justice and the common good. Relatedly, he thinks of the structure of orientation to an end that he introduces in *Nicomachean Ethics* 1 not as something external that is imposed on the subject matter from outside, but as essential to its internal theoretical structure. For this reason, Aristotle views the pursuit of this good not as a personal purpose of the inquirer qua individual, but rather as a purpose constitutive of the very enterprise of this mode of philosophical inquiry, and so of the inquirer qua inquirer. Thus, he writes, "[T]he present inquiry does not aim at theoretical knowledge like the others (for we are inquiring not in order to know what virtue is, but in order to become good, since otherwise our inquiry would have been of no use). . . ."[31] Later he suggests that those who treat the subject matter of *Nicomachean Ethics* merely as an intellectual dispute, trafficking in arguments about the highest good without performing the required actions, misunderstand the nature of the inquiry and only play at being philosophers.[32] To be a political philosopher, Aristotle seems to think, is to be engaged in an exercise of the practical intellect. The philosopher reasons about justice not to contemplate it, but to see it done.

I do not mean to imply that any of these assertions are easy to understand. To understand them, we would need to explain how political philosophy, the theory of justice, could itself be the work of practical reason, perhaps of the very same powers of practical reason that we use in ordinary political deliberation. We would have to explain how it arises from a prephilosophical engagement with practice that contains an incipient knowledge about practice, and how its central concepts and the structure of the resulting theory are informed by their essentially practical role. Finally, we would need to explain how the political philosopher relates to the constitutively practical purpose of political philosophy, and so how the theory of justice the philosopher develops relates to political action. Nothing less will answer the antipracticalism of Cohen and Mason. In the remainder of this chapter and in Chapters 3 and 4, I will try to explain these points.

But first, another of Aristotle's insights in *Nicomachean Ethics* can help adjudicate the objections to the teleological conception of practically oriented critics like Mills and Anderson. When discussing the starting points of theory, and their relationship to the resulting theoretical structure, Aristotle writes, "Let us not fail to notice, however, that there is a difference between arguments from and those to first principles. For Plato, too, was right in raising this question and asking, as he used to do, 'Are we on the way from or to the first principles?' . . . For, while we must begin with what is evident, things are evident in two ways—some to us, some without qualification."[33] Taking inspiration from this thought, my argument will be that when it comes to the theory of justice, the beginning and the ending are different in character, and in consequence, as Aristotle tells us Plato used to say, we must distinguish between the way to and the way from first principles. The practical critics, I will suggest, emphasize rightly that in an unjust world injustice is both a practical problem and often better known to us. This insight has methodological consequences about the starting points of inquiry, some of which they have rightly emphasized, but it does not speak against the thought that there is a practical priority to the end of a just society. While the language of "[being evident] without qualification" does not come naturally to us, I will argue that there is a practical explanatory priority that the end has over reasoning toward the end.

On the view that I will defend, to say that political philosophy is practical is to say that the theory of justice bears a twofold relation to our political thought and action. As a systematic theory, it brings to self-consciousness, and organizes into a unified view, normative judgments that function in piecemeal and episodic ways in our political practice and practical consciousness. It thus flows from our sense of justice, understood as power of practical reason that we exercise in our everyday political life. In this way, the theory of justice does not proceed from esoteric and specialized judgments; rather, it makes explicit and carries to its rational conclusion thinking about justice that already plays a role in practice. In a sense to be further discussed in the pages that follow, political philosophy springs from ordinary political thought.

But the resulting theory stands in a second relation to practice. For political philosophy not only reflects on, but seeks to positively inform our political action. The theory of justice is a theory that is intended to guide our practice in the real world of politics. Its function is to enable us to engage critically with our institutions and the political status quo. If done right, it helps us to identify and respond to injustice and to clarify our political aims and commitments. To say that the theory of justice is practical is to say that it both flows from and seeks to inform the exercise of our practical intelligence in political action. There is a movement from practice to theory, as well as a return from theory to practice.

While not without content, this view about a twofold relation between theory and practice is compatible with any number of pictures. For, as stated in this schematic form, it leaves open the manner in which the theory of justice reflects on and informs practice. We arrive at a more determinate view by specifying the kind of reflection and the kind of informing we have in mind. The idea behind the teleological conception is that reflection on practice draws from our political thought the materials to fashion a conception of a just society, and this conception informs our political action by providing orientation to an end. With this orientation, transitional theory brings our reasoning back to action in the circumstance of injustice we confront. I turn now in earnest to developing this account.

§2.4: THE SENSE OF JUSTICE: STARTING POINTS

The theory of justice, as I understand it, begins from reflection on the operation of our sense of justice.[34] The sense of justice is a power of the practical intellect. It is a cognitive power, issuing in judgments about right and wrong, justice and injustice. To describe them as judgments is to say that they are made on the basis of reasons that serve as their supporting grounds, reasons that are typically available to the judging subject who makes the judgment on these grounds. These judgments are also practical. Speaking generally, justice is something to be done, and injustice something to be avoided (opposed, overturned, rectified). The sense of justice is thus a power to act on and be properly affected by considerations of justice.[35] These two aspects come together in the fact that when the power is operating well, judgments about justice and injustice provide us with considerations on which we act.

The sense of justice is situated in a broader array of moral powers. To understand how the sense of justice differs from other moral uses of the practical intellect, we need to have some sense of what makes justice a distinct domain of morality. Here I draw on the remarks from §1.2 about the idea of justice. Justice is strongly second personal. Duties of justice are directed duties, duties correlated with claims. Justice also has a stringency that is connected with the fact that unjust institutions must be reformed unless doing so will introduce greater injustices. The stringency of justice is connected also with the authorization to resist injustice in a variety of modalities, and the possibility of coercive enforcement. Finally, although also receiving expression in interpersonal relations, justice has an institutional focus. The sense of justice is the power to deploy this concept of justice in our reasoning about what to do with our shared institutions and practices.

By reaching our adult years, we have acquired a sense of justice and so are able to make the relevant judgments about justice, be affected by considerations of justice, and act on them.[36] The judgments of the sense of justice are, to begin with, pretheoretical in that they do not draw on a developed theory of justice. Though they are pretheoretical, it is important to point out that such judgments occur at all levels of generality.[37] To be pretheoretical, a judgment need not be about a described or actual case. Many judgments about justice are not only, or primarily, "intuitions" in the usual sense of that term. Ordinary judgments range from those about particular cases (the killing of Eric Garner), to general policies (broken windows policing), to huge and complex standing institutions (the prison-industrial complex and the system of mass incarceration), all the way up to abstract thoughts about, for example, what counts (or fails to count) as a reason for holding an institution to be unjust or about general features of injustice (for example, that there is only an injustice where someone is wronged).[38]

The sense of justice is something we employ constantly in our interpersonal life and as members of a political community.[39] We exercise the sense of justice when we hold political opinions on grounds of right and wrong, when we recognize and act to fulfill the valid claims of others, and when we do our part under legitimate institutional arrangements, accepting them as legitimate. We exercise our sense of justice in our judgments that various institutions and practices are good and by forming legitimate expectations about the way just institutions will treat us. We also exercise our sense of justice by pressing our valid claims on others who reciprocate by fulfilling the corresponding duties. These judgments about justice issue in action in a variety of ways, insofar as they lead us to fulfill the valid claims of others, license our activity of claim making, and lead us to accept and support just institutions and practices, either by doing our fair share to uphold them or by opposing changes that would undermine them. In a just society, our judgments of justice would primarily be practical in these ways.

But, as the practical critics rightly emphasize, in an unjust society, judgments about injustice are more salient than judgments about justice for a number of reasons. The stringency of justice entails that unjust institutions or practices call for change. Since change requires framing an alternative, and since achieving an alternative requires overcoming often daunting obstacles, injustice calls for the use of practical intelligence. To represent something as an injustice is to represent it as a problem to be solved through the application of our practical intellect to overcome obstacles or challenges, bringing about changes that will ameliorate or remove the injustice or at least pave the way for future relief.

But injustice is not just any kind of practical problem to be solved, for injustice involves legitimate grievance. As we have seen, wherever there is injustice, some agents are wronged. Furthermore, these wronged agents are wronged precisely by other agents: the valid claims of some on others are unfulfilled by those who have the corresponding duties. For this reason, to represent an injustice is to represent a practical cleavage, dividing agents along the lines of those doing and those suffering injustice. This is a crucial asymmetry between the representations of justice and injustice, for the representation of justice entails no such practical cleavage between doing and suffering injustice, and this affects the special way in which judgments of injustice are practical. In identifying an injustice, we make a division between agents, raising the question of how the one representing the injustice is related to this division. This affects what kind of a practical problem this is for the agent representing the injustice.

If one suffers the injustice, then the problem is that one is wronged by the institutions or practices in question and likely suffers harm as a result. Here a range of affective responses are proper to the situation, including indignation toward, or resentment of, those responsible for the injustice, along with a desire for the unfulfilled claims to be met and the harms removed. Sometimes one knows one is wronged before it is clear who is responsible. This is why the question of whom to be angry at for the wrongs one suffers is a practical question of great moment: it involves the proper attribution of responsibility for the harms one undergoes and an appropriately directed affective response. Furthermore, suffering injustice raises the practical question of what actions might be taken in light of one's unfulfilled claims, which usually license resistance to wrongdoing with various countermeasures.

Since the injustice one suffers is often general in its form, affecting many who are positioned in comparable ways, to judge one is wronged is typically to relate oneself implicitly to others who share one's situation vis-à-vis society's institutions and practices. The desire to remove the injustice one suffers is in its proper form a desire to remove the injustice suffered by others. It thus contains the seeds of solidarity. To see injustice aright is typically to see the wrong suffered by others as implicated in the wrong suffered by me, and to see justice for me as bound up with justice for them. This raises the practical problem of what responsibility I, as someone wronged, have to the others who share my plight, and they to me.

On the flip side, if one perpetrates or is complicit in injustice, then the problem is that one is contributing to the wronging of others. Here a different range of affective responses—although often not forthcoming for reasons to be discussed later—are proper to the situation, including guilt or shame for the injustice for which one bears responsibility, along with a desire to fulfill the claims and make amends for the harms one has perpetrated. Furthermore, since the injustice one does is often general in form, implicating many who are positioned similarly vis-à-vis the same institutions and practices, to judge that one does wrong is typically to relate oneself to others who share complicity in the same or similar injustices. The desire to remove the injustice one does is properly a desire to remove the injustice they do, holding them to account along with oneself. This raises the practical question of what steps must be taken to undo the injustice one contributes to and what costs must rightly be borne to make amends for the harms that one has caused.

If one is a bystander, then the problem is that others are doing and suffering injustice. Here a range of affective responses are appropriate, including indignation toward those doing wrong, compassion toward those wronged, and desire to address the situation. To describe this as a problem implies that it raises practical questions. One such question is whether intervention is appropriate and what obligation one has to try to right the situation as a bystander. Another is what forms of resistance to injustice are permissible for an ally to employ in light of the unmet claims of those wronged and the violations of duty by the wrongdoers. Note that when one has an obligation to oppose wrongdoers on behalf of those suffering injustice, if one fails to fulfill this obligation, one typically wrongs the sufferer of injustice in a secondary way and bears some responsibility for the wrong and resulting harms suffered.

Of course, it is possible to stand in more than one of these relations simultaneously, as when one does wrong in relation to some, and is wronged by others, and is a bystander to yet other injustices. Furthermore, one can be wronged while also being inducted into complicity with the very institution or practice that wrongs oneself and others. These situations introduce further practical complexities into the situation, some of which correspond to what Tommie Shelby has called "the political ethics of the oppressed."[40] That things can be, and usually are, complicated in just this way does not render the practical questions moot; rather, it contributes to their heightened complexity and sinister urgency.

Most injustices that engage our sense of justice are also already sites of contestation and struggle in society. Coalitions of agents, usually including those who are wronged and their allies, are often involved in ongoing struggle to resist and overcome the injustice. This activity is often opposed by some of those committing or benefiting from injustice, alongside various allies, who together are politically mobilized defenders of the unjust status quo. This takes the problem posed by injustice beyond the static nexus of doing and suffering injustice into a dynamic landscape that includes opposed sides engaged in a practical struggle. In representing one's own relation to the problem in question, one implicitly relates oneself to this dynamic terrain. Questions about the duty to rectify injustice in any of the three agentive modes often amount to asking whether and how one should contribute to the collective work being done by those opposing an injustice against others who support it. When such contestation is underway, the representation of something as an injustice thus implicitly raises the question, "Which side are you on?" This question has its own depths, including the complexities introduced by the fact that those pushing for just change may be imperfect and pursuing change in suboptimal ways, perhaps in coalition with still more problematic actors. Judgments about injustice thus reach out toward a messy process of ongoing collective struggle, relating one not only to the injustice but to the contested collective action opposing and bolstering it.

Since pretheoretical judgments of our sense of justice are the starting points of our reflection, and since judgments about injustice have a distinctive practical salience to our prephilosophical thought, we can see some of the points made by the critics of the priority claim vindicated. As I have stressed, we come to philosophy already political knowers, and we are able to make pretheoretical judgments about justice and injustice. Furthermore, in circumstances of injustice, our pretheoretical judgments about justice are often focused on what seem to us to be the problems of our social life. To the extent that our society fails to fulfill the valid claims of some or all members of society—and we are subject to injustice, complicit in it, or bystanders to it—this injustice is naturally an object of our practical concern and attention. Given the stringency of duties of justice, injustice calls for action, whether in the form of coping and self-protection, active resistance and opposition, altering our unjust course, or contributing as an ally to reform efforts. The starting points of political philosophy include prominently, if not exclusively, judgments about injustice that the practical critics rightly stress as starting points.

As the practical critics also rightly emphasized, in making these prephilosophical judgments about injustice, we are able—fallibly and roughly—to identify injustices before we have a developed theory of justice. Such judgments also often equip us to make at least provisional comparative judgments. For we judge not just that something is unjust but also, at least crudely, *how* unjust it is. If we judge rightly that slavery is terribly wrong, then we can also judge that ceteris paribus emancipation is far better. Furthermore, the practical critics are right that there is reason to attend particularly to the claims of those who experience and suffer from injustice, since they have standing to press legitimate grievances against the corresponding duty bearers for failing to fulfill their valid claims. If their perspective is marginalized, then injustice may be hidden from view.

Given these starting points, we can also see why the analogies for which Cohen and Swift reach shed more darkness than light. To make the case for his antipracticalism, Cohen likens political philosophy to arithmetic. Swift follows suit, broadening the analogy to include other contemplative disciplines, such as astronomy. But the primitive concepts involved in these contemplative disciplines are utterly unlike justice and injustice. To represent something as falling under the concept of number is not to represent it as good or bad. Indeed, to make an arithmetic or astronomical judgment is not even to represent something as calling for action. The basic concepts of such contemplative disciplines are not, as such, the concepts of reasons for action. Nor do these disciplines take as their basic material to be developed judgments bringing their basic concept to bear on practice. This explains why arithmetic and astronomical judgments need to be yoked by extrinsic facts to our practical purposes to become relevant to practice. Since their basic concepts are not practical concepts, to be made practical, they must be shown relevant to practical purposes by connecting them to purposes that come from outside their subject matter. Since judgments of justice articulate reasons for action, they are different. Astronomical and arithmetic problems do not raise in any special way the question of how one is implicated as an agent in the problem identified. And their solutions do not come through changing our relations to one another or to our shared institutions. The puzzles of astronomy and mathematics don't arise because of how we are living in relation to one another in light of our valid claims and violations, and they do not raise the question, Which side are you on?—at least not in the same way.[41]

Certainly, intellectual puzzles arise with respect to justice too, and political philosophy is sometimes motivated in part by the curiosity such puzzles elicit. But unlike that of arithmetic or astronomy, the resolution of the puzzles of political philosophy relates to practice, since these puzzles are ultimately about reasons for action. In an unjust society, the resolution of such intellectual puzzles about justice touches on the identification of practical problems and their solution through action in ways we will explore shortly. The point is that such practical problems call urgently for change.

In sum, justice, the basic concept of political philosophy, is a practical concept associated with necessity. The prephilosophical judgments deploying this concept, which political philosophy works up into theory through reflection, are judgments deploying this concept in practice. The reason for engaging in theory arises from the need to understand practice, which is oriented to justice as something to be done rather than something to be (merely) contemplated. The theory of justice inherits this practical orientation from the concept of justice and its deployment in ordinary life. The purpose of pursuing justice is not imposed by theorists on justice by what they personally happen to care about, since justice is itself a purpose. In an unjust society, the theorizing of the philosopher further implicates the philosopher in one of the three agential modes in the injustice that is theorized, and it reaches outward to collective struggle.

§2.5: THE ASCENT FROM PRACTICE TO THEORY

Supposing these practical materials are starting points for reflection, how does reflection proceed? At the start, our pretheoretical judgments about justice and injustice are necessarily episodic and unconnected. The piecemeal judgments about situations, policies, or institutions seem connected to one another. The judgments about the injustice of some institutions (for example, permanent felony disenfranchisement) seem related to the judgments about the justice of other institutions (for example, the right to vote) and related to further judgments about which we may be less sure (for example, the temporary disenfranchisement of the incarcerated). Furthermore, the low-level judgments we make seem somehow connected to the high-level, abstract judgments about justice, but it is obscure how. One goal of the theory of justice is to ascend through a process of reflection to a unified and self-conscious representation of justice that relates these different judgments to one another, displaying the connections and relations of dependence that hold between them.

The principles of justice are a crucial mediator between judgments at the same and different levels. Since justice is concerned with the claims people are entitled to press against one another, its principles function to specify the legitimate claims we have on one another, especially with respect to the ordering of our shared institutions and practices. As I conceive principles of justice, more and less general judgments relate to them in different ways.[42] The principles are themselves supported by general judgments we make about a variety of subjects—for example, about what features of institutions raise justificatory issues and what sorts of reasons, when rendered from those the institutions advantage to those the institutions disadvantage, do or don't suffice to meet these justificatory burdens.[43] These principles, in turn, explain a range of judgments at lower levels about the justice of various institutions, practices, and behaviors. They thus gather together lower-level judgments, showing their unified explanation by revealing how a variety of judgments, along with their supporting reasons, fall under general norms that explain and justify them.

The principles of justice also display the relation of our thought about justice to our thought about injustice. For the same principle, in virtue of specifying a range of valid claims, at once explains why an institution is just (when it fulfills these claims) and unjust (when it fails to fulfill these claims). Through their generality, the principles also extend our thinking into areas where our judgments about justice were uncertain. By showing us what explains our judgment in an area where we were confident, they help us resolve the matter in areas where we were formerly conflicted or felt confused that also fall under the purview of the principle. They can also extend our judgments in a different way, by revealing areas where we did not even recognize injustice because we did not grasp the commonalities between the relevant phenomena and others that we judged to be unjust.[44]

Let me reiterate: it is not that we are incapable of making any judgments about injustice before we grasp principles of justice, but rather that the principles raise to self-consciousness the basis of our judgments in their full generality, allowing us to relate our piece-meal and fragmentary judgments to one another both at the same level and between levels. By playing this mediating role between judgments made at different levels, the principles display the justificatory relations of dependence that hold between lower- and higher-level considered judgments. They show us how a range of concrete judgments we make are related to more general views about the claims individuals have on one another to order their shared institutions. The goal of reflection is to account for the sense of justice by revealing the dependence of some our judgments about justice on other judgments about justice, via principles that express, unify, explain, and extend them.

As Rawls famously emphasized, the process of reflection can reveal dramatic conflicts between our judgments.[45] When, for example, there are conflicts between principles and lower-level judgments, we face a choice. We must either abandon the lower-level judgment or revise the principle. Since the principle is supported by higher-level judgments, we have to see whether that higher-level judgment might be embodied in a revised principle consistent with the lower-level judgment. If it can't, we must decide which judgment we ought to give up. We will be justified in abandoning a judgment when we can provide a convincing account of the source of our error in making it and when we can say what seemed right about it—for example, by identifying a nearby true thought we conflated with the mistaken judgment.[46] By working back and forth from principles to judgment, we seek a reflective equilibrium between our judgments at all levels, as mediated by principles that reveal the structures of explanation and dependence that hold between them.[47]

It is important to stress that reflection is not a solipsistic process any more than the ordinary exercise of our sense of justice. Given the relational form of justice, we have strong reason to resist a

picture in which the process of reflection is one of a solitary individual arranging their judgments so that they might conform with
one another, as though we each have our own separate house of
judgments to order.[48] As we have seen, our pretheoretical judgments concern the claims we have on one another. In wanting to
understand justice, I want to understand my relation to other
agents who are sources of legitimate claims on me and on whom I
have legitimate claims in turn. The principles are public and such as
to be affirmed from each side of the reciprocal relations they
specify. We have seen that the judgments concerning injustice represent a practical cleavage between doing and suffering injustice,
mandate change to undo the injustice, and reach out toward ongoing struggle. The relevant change is usually to be achieved, if at
all, through political action alongside others with whom we share
(at least some of) the relevant judgments.

Similarly, our theoretical reflection is conducted in dialogue, and
sometimes in conflict, with the reflections of others. The basis of
our theory of justice is composed of judgments that are such as to
be shared with others, that pertain to our shared condition, and are
made for the purpose of action to be taken in concert with others.
The judgments themselves, being ostensible claims or the recognition of claims, already bring us into relation with one another. Both
the materials and the practical aim of the theory of justice necessarily bring us into practical dialogue, shared struggle, and conflict
with others.

For this reason, when, as philosophers, we try to raise these judgments to self-consciousness for the sake of action, the attempts of
others to do the same are always at stake. Just as our judgments
reach out toward ongoing struggle, so, too, do they reach out to the
ongoing attempt of other thinkers—including those involved in
struggle—to reflect on justice. For the other theorists, too, have a
sense of justice, and their theoretical endeavors, concerning the
same second-personal judgments and pertaining to the same

institutions, directly implicate and are immediately relevant to our own attempts. It follows from this that dialogue with other theories of justice is always relevant and will often be crucial. This is why we should view the ultimate aim of the process of reflection as what Rawls calls "wide reflective equilibrium." Of course, such dialogue can have many effects. It can get us to reconsider many of the judgments with which we work. It can also suggest to us different principles, or different methodological approaches, and much more.

§2.6: THE IDEA OF A JUST SOCIETY AS THE UNITY OF PRINCIPLES OF JUSTICE

Principles of justice often interact. Claims that would otherwise be valid are sometimes not valid when fulfilling them would lead to valid claims associated with other principles going unfulfilled. How the principles should be understood in relation to one another, how they should be combined, and under what conditions the claims associated with one principle take precedence are all central questions for the theory of justice.[49] This was already implicit in the pressure to revise judgments that contradiction put on our thought about justice, for some contradictions to be resolved through reflective equilibrium arise from the thought that institutions are just under one principle and unjust under another. Is this a situation where the conflict is real, and we must search for an alternative institution that satisfies the one principle without violating the other? Or is this a situation where what appeared to be a conflict is resolved once we understand the relation of the underlying principles to one another?[50]

Given the practical nature of justice as a purpose to be pursued, the principles must be not only theorized together but also pursued as a unitary end. As we have seen, if the institutions or practices of our society are unjust, then absent some special exemption, we must act to reform them so as to meet the relevant claims. If reforms introduce new injustices, or merely ameliorate existing injustice, we continue to be under requirements to act. For let us suppose we make an improvement in one area, meeting valid claims under one principle we were failing to fulfill before. But let us also suppose that some valid claims under another principle are still unmet in this area. In that case, injustice remains and our work is not yet done.

The same necessity of justice that motivated the first change now calls for other changes. Given the stringency of justice, those whom we are failing have the standing to hold us to move toward a set of institutions that fulfill the valid claims associated with all the principles of justice. We thus are led to a unified representation of the combination of the principles in a single totality by the necessity associated with claims of justice. This concept is an end to which we are driven in the course of our practical confrontation with injustice as the goal of struggle. This is the idea of a just society.

Sometimes philosophers of an urbane, antisystemic cast of mind say there is no reason to believe in advance that the specification of such a unified end will be possible.[51] These skeptics about the possibility of a unified representation of justice treat the situation as one where we should go in with an open mind and just see what we find. We have no reason to believe that justice will be so unified, and so no reason to try to arrive at a unified representation. To do so is to impose our wishes or longing for a harmonious world on the subject matter that we should be approaching in a dispassionate and clear-eyed way.[52]

If, as I have been urging, the theory of justice is the self-understanding of a practical intellectual power oriented to justice, then in constructing the theory of justice, we have every reason to try to arrive at a unified representation of a just society. This is not a purpose we "personally happen to have" that illicitly distorts our theorizing; rather, it is a constitutive purpose of the sense of justice, and so of the theory of justice that raises this sense to self-consciousness. For the sense of justice is concerned with the necessity arising from the legitimate and enforceable claims we have on one another. It is concerned with a mandatory purpose, the principles of which must have a certain unity and ordering if the claims that are grounded in them are to be met.

To declare at the outset, on the basis of one or two small-scale examples, that it will be impossible to fulfill this purpose is to declare at the start of our practical reflection, on exceedingly thin grounds, that a society without exploitation, oppression, marginalization, or any of the other forms of standing institutional injustice is impossible. From a properly practical point of view, this style of argument amounts to a hasty intellectual and practical defeatism. (I will discuss at length the real possibility of the failure of the theory of justice in the context of David Estlund's work on "hopeless" theories in Chapter 6.) As a theorist of justice, I have reason to try to avoid this kind of failure. Indeed, insofar as I have reason to build a future world in which injustice is overcome, I have reason to articulate an account of a just society as a unitary end for practice.

For this reason, I should precisely not go in and just see what I find, as though these were neutrally valanced options that intellectual integrity requires me to treat on a par. For to find that the idea of a just society as a unified end for practice is impossible is to find that our theory and our practice are doomed to failure. It is impossible to raise our sense of justice to practical self-consciousness and impossible to satisfy in reality the valid claims of others. While it is conceivable that we will fail in just this way, as both theorists and agents, our efforts are properly oriented to success rather than failure. When I engage in political philosophy, my initial assumption for the purposes of reflection should be that success in constructing a theory of justice answering the priority problem is possible. Of course, this does not tell us how we are to handle the examples of the urbane critics and the many probing challenges they raise. But this is the hard work of the theory of justice to which we must put our shoulder.

Supposing justice is an end, and supposing the just society can be represented, what kind of an end is it? And how does it relate to practice under conditions of injustice? Answering these questions is crucial for a satisfactory reply to the allegation of the practical critics that this idea is irrelevant to practice in an unjust society. We turn to these important questions next.

3

From Theory to Practice

To address the concerns of the practical critics, we must explain now how orientation to the end of a just society sharpens our practical intelligence in the confrontation with injustice. An adequate explanation will also illuminate the practical explanatory priority that the end discussed by ideal theory has over the end treated by nonideal theory. As we will see in Chapter 4, significant injustice poses its own distinctive philosophical problems concerning the relation of theory and practice. In this chapter, we lay the groundwork for that later discussion.

§3.1: WHAT KIND OF AN END IS A JUST SOCIETY?

The first step is to see what kind of end a just society is and how it figures in our practice. Since we live in an unjust society, this is a question about the relationship of ideal theory and nonideal theory. John Simmons, an advocate of the teleological conception, has likened the role played in nonideal theory by the end of a just society to knowing the destination toward which you are traveling. Simmons introduced this analogy as a criticism of Amartya Sen. Guided by a social choice methodology structured around pairwise comparisons of outcomes, Sen argued that the fundamental practical task for thinking about the response to injustice was the making of pairwise comparative judgments between the present arrangement and feasible alternatives (and between the alternatives).[1] His argument was that all we really need to know about any pair of alternatives is which is more just. He claimed that for these purposes it was unnecessary to know what arrangements were fully just, since we could simply compare any two candidates directly. He likened this to comparing the heights of mountains: to know which of two mountains is taller, it is unnecessary (and irrelevant) to know what mountain is the tallest in the world.

In a seminal article that defended a version of the teleological conception, Simmons replied by arguing that Sen's analogy ignores the way that the just society functions as an end for our practice. A better analogy for our practical activity than measuring the height of mountains, Simmons suggested, would be driving to the highest mountain.[2] To know whether to head this way or that way, you need to know your destination. If a just society is an end toward which we must move, then it will be of the utmost relevance to the choice between contending alternative ways forward, which will not be a purely comparative exercise. To reach the highest mountain, we can't simply direct the car to whichever path has the highest incline at each point. We have to know where we're going.

We will raise problems for Sen's view shortly. For now, we can note that even if Simmons was right to introduce orientation to an end as a relevant consideration that Sen misses, his metaphor is misleading. To see how, we need to dwell for a moment on different sorts of ends. The end of a journey is what we might call an end in the sense of a terminus. Suppose I'm driving from Chicago to New York City. When I'm halfway there—say, at the border of Ohio and Pennsylvania—I'm in no way yet in New York City. Being halfway to New York City is not a way of being halfway in New York City. Another point about traveling to a destination is that when you reach your destination, the journey is over. The destination no longer figures in your practical thought as a destination, because you've already arrived. The metaphors of justice as a destination involve a kind of end where the process by which we reach it is not yet being at the end (even in part), and where the activity pursuing the end comes to a close when the end is achieved.[3] The end is, in this sense, separate from the pursuit of the end and guides it as the end point of the process.

Other ends share some but not all of these features. Take the end of building a mansion. When I'm halfway done building the mansion—say, when I've built the north and west wings—the mansion is at that point halfway built. To be a certain way into the process is to have realized the end to some degree. (The same would have been true of traveling had we specified the end as "traveling to New York City" rather than being in New York City.) But, like driving to a destination, building a house pursues an end that is a stopping point. Once the house is built, the job is done. To reach the end is to finish the activity. As with the car trip, in this case, to realize the end is to bring the activity pursuing the end to completion. Let us follow Sebastian Rödl and call such an end a "finite end" to signal that it has a stopping point at completion.[4]

Other ends are not like this. Consider health. Health contrasts with a terminus like a geographical destination in that to make progress toward health is to be healthy to some degree. Health is a kind of end that exists within the pursuit of it. But it is also true that there is no such thing as being healthy to completion; someone who is already healthy will have reasons of health to perform healthy acts. Thus, health as an end does not exhaust its power to explain our actions once health has been realized. To realize the end of health is not to bring a process to completion. Health is, we might say, an inexhaustible source of reasons for action. In light of this inexhaustible quality, Rödl calls this an "infinite end."[5]

We might wonder what the concept of an end is under which both finite and infinite ends might be brought. Perhaps we are using a common term here only by analogy. But there is a more general concept of an end under which they both fall. In this more general sense, an end is that for the sake of which we deliberate and act intentionally: as we merge onto I-80 for the sake of reaching New York, lay the foundation for the sake of building the mansion, and eat nutritiously for the sake of health. An end in this sense is a unitary standard to be pursued, in the light of which our current situation can be judged. A finite end is one where the pursuit of the end is the end point of a process. The end serves as the external standard guiding the activity pursuing it, by providing it with something to bring about. An infinite end is one that is immanent in the activity pursuing it. When the activity is defective, one seeks to realize the activity more perfectly or fully. Furthermore, there is no end point to the activity, since activity manifests the end and will continue to manifest the end even when perfected.

Let us consider now the pursuit of justice. What sort of an end is involved here? To pursue justice is to be partway toward this end. Although we do not live in a just society now, there are many goods of justice that we do have. Even in the most unjust society, people think and act in terms of justice, fulfilling the valid claims of others. Furthermore, our own highly flawed institutions secure many goods of justice, albeit to a highly imperfect degree. To be pursuing justice is already to be evincing justice by responding to considerations of justice in numerous ways. In this situation, we have partial justice and we want it in full. It is thus not like the terminus of a destination, but more like building a mansion or health.

But is justice a finite or infinite end? It is clear that justice is an end that is never completed. Were we to live in a just society, we would be guided by ideas of justice and act on their basis. Indeed, justice would then figure considerably more in our lives, thoughts, actions, practices, and institutions. Justice is thus an infinite end like health rather than a finite end like painting a house. When our activity is defective, we seek to realize justice more perfectly. Furthermore, there is no end point to just activity, since just activity manifests the end of justice and will continue to manifest the end even when perfected. The work of justice is never over and done.

Given this, we can expect justice to figure as an end in two ways. First of all, since the response to injustice presupposes that the society in which we act is not yet fully just, the end of a just society is a goal to be reached through a process of political change. The same end that under conditions of justice would figure as something to be manifested and reproduced through our dispositions, institutions, and actions under conditions of injustice figures instead as something to be produced. The response to injustice thus includes orientation to the end of a just society as something to be brought into being through political action. Picking up on the language of Pablo Gilabert, let us call this the "dynamic dimension" of the pursuit of justice since it involves a dynamic process of change.[6] It is this dynamic dimension of the pursuit of justice that makes the term "transitional theory" an appropriate name for nonideal theory on teleological conception.

Secondly, since the pursuit of justice already involves justice now, albeit an imperfect justice, we can expect the principles and justifications that characterize the justice of a just society to have some reality and application even to circumstances of injustice. What form of reality and application is a large topic we will broach presently. But speaking schematically, we can say that there will be claims of justice to be fulfilled now, and many apposite considerations relevant to the end of just society already figuring in the valid claims we have on one another in circumstances of injustice. This means that questions of principle are always already at stake in the response to injustice. The pursuit of justice is itself a principled affair with its own intrinsic significance as a manifestation of justice. Let us call this the "immanent dimension" of the pursuit of justice. The end of justice is immanent in the pursuit of justice, as the end of health is immanent in the pursuit of health. Justice figures both in thought about what we are moving toward and in thought about where we are now.

The recognition of the immanent dimension of the pursuit of justice helps address a nagging sense that Simmons and those who follow him instrumentalize justice, reducing all questions about the pursuit of justice to the contribution of our actions to some future end, as though nothing of principle and intrinsic importance is at stake in current struggles for justice and hard-won political victories.[7] It is true that Simmons acknowledges the independent importance of questions about what means are permissible to take in the pursuit of justice, and also raises perceptive questions about the kinds of trade-offs that can be made in the principled pursuit of justice. But, nevertheless, the way he characterizes the end toward which nonideal theory is oriented makes it hard to keep in view the intrinsic significance of the justice we have now and of the further gains we might win through struggle. For they are theorized merely as waystations on (constrained) paths to a different destination.[8] But one can retain the dynamic orientation toward the end of a just society for which Simmons pled, while acknowledging the immanent significance of the struggle to get there.

Before discussing the dynamic and immanent dimensions of justice, I will explore the role justice as a unity of principles plays in identifying injustice and gauging its severity (§3.2). For these functions set the stage for the dynamic and immanent roles, since both roles involve the confrontation with injustice. Already, we will see that this preliminary material provides ample resources to criticize purely comparativist approaches like that of Sen. I will then consider first the dynamic (§3.3) and then immanent (§3.4) dimensions of the pursuit of the end of justice, turning finally to their relationship to each other (§3.5).

§3.2: IDENTIFICATION AND WEIGHTING OF INJUSTICE

The idea of a just society is the idea of a unity of principles of justice together constituting one end to be pursued in practice. One way that this idea enters into our thought about injustice here and now is by helping us to identify injustice. As we have seen, the principles of justice reveal the relation of our judgments about injustice to those about justice. For the principles specify the valid claims of individuals on their shared institutions and practices, and so simultaneously explain what it is for institutions and practices to be just (when the claims are met) and what it is for them to be unjust (when the claims are unmet). Furthermore, they unify a broad range of judgments of both kinds by bringing them under a single principle and also extend our judgment into new areas about which we were uncertain or where we were previously unaware of injustice.

By specifying the various dimensions of justice and articulating the requirements that institutions will have to meet in order for people's valid claims to be upheld, ideal theory equips us to spot ways in which institutions fall short.[9] Clarity about these principles equips us to make more general, systematic, and careful judgments about injustice when we find it. For when the institutional requirements are not met, we know injustice exists, and our nuanced understanding of the dimensions of justice, with their associated valid claims, equips us to make systematic judgments about the grievances people have in light of these institutional failures.

In addition to helping us identify injustice, the idea of a just society also provides a threshold that allows us to make judgments about the severity of injustice. David Estlund has rightly emphasized that the principles of justice mark a threshold between justice and injustice that is essential to many judgments about the severity of injustice.[10] This is a nuanced point, for the mere existence of the threshold does not settle questions about the severity of the injustice, but it is a precondition for settling them. I will deploy and expand on Estlund's point by arguing that these judgments about severity are important for practice, informing our thought about practical priorities and the principled responses to injustice.

Estlund makes these remarks in the context of criticizing Amartya Sen, who argues for the importance of pairwise comparisons of the justice of various outcomes. For Sen, as we have seen, practice requires only a *comparative* concept of justice. The practically relevant judgments of justice are of the form "Outcome X is more (or less) just than outcome Y." Sen holds that we can dispense with the noncomparative judgments that partition justice and injustice—namely, "X is just" or "X is unjust."[11] These are, of course, the sorts of judgments presupposed by ideal theory that articulate the end of a just society.

Estlund rightly points out that if all we had were such comparative judgments, then it would be impossible to understand a large swath of our ordinary thinking about justice and injustice. For example, if I had only the comparative concepts, then I could not judge that "Slavery is unjust" or "Democracy is just," for these judgments use the concepts of justice and injustice simpliciter. I could only judge, say, "Slavery is less just than free labor" or, equivalently, "Free labor is less unjust than slavery." This is already strange, since these are ordinary judgments in which we have great confidence.

If we dispense with the partition between justice and injustice simpliciter and focus solely on comparative judgments about which outcome is to be preferred by the lights of justice, then the comparative concept of "more or less just" is equivalent to the comparative concept of "more or less unjust." For without a dividing line between justice and injustice, they are variant idioms for registering whether one or another alternative is preferred with respect to justice. To be sure, they use reverse orderings: to say that X is more just than Y is to say that X is preferable to Y from the perspective of justice, whereas to say that X is more unjust than Y is to say the opposite. But there is no conceptual difference being marked by using one term rather than the other, since a simple translation from one idiom to the other is available.

The contrast we developed between justice and injustice highlighted their asymmetry, since justice simpliciter is a situation in which people's valid claims on their fellows to order shared institutions and practices are met, and injustice a situation where valid claims are unmet and so some are wronged. In dispensing with justice simpliciter and the attendant asymmetry between justice and injustice, Sen dispenses with this contrast as well. Perhaps he would reject the judgment that wherever there is injustice some are wronged. But supposing he retains this judgment, perhaps he will render it too in comparative terms, saying that the only practically relevant question is which arrangement wrongs people less. Perhaps he will treat institutions that wrong no one as a special kind of comparative limit case to which none is better from the perspective of justice. In that case, it would be analogous to the highest mountain. His point is, then, that knowledge of this limit case is irrelevant to comparative judgments about injustice and so irrelevant to practice.

It is worth pointing out that cracks in Sen's analogy are already beginning to show here, insofar as height is a measure with no conceptual upper bound and where no point on the scale stands in a special relation to any other point. In the case of justice, by contrast, injustice is a defect consisting in people being wronged, and justice is the absence of this defect. It thus appears that justice is uniquely singled out from all the unjust states. Furthermore, it is singled out in such a way as to bear a special, asymmetric relation to injustice. For by differing from just arrangements, unjust arrangements are precisely and thereby bad. Sen's comparativism obscures and downplays this striking asymmetry.

This downplaying of the practical relevance of justice simpliciter makes for further trouble. Hewing solely to comparative judgments Sen favors in either of the two interchangeable idioms ("more just than," "more unjust than"), let us ask whether we can introduce only an ordinal ranking, or also an interval scale.[12] An ordinal ranking orders the items with respect to one another, establishing a rank ordering by telling us which are preferred to which others.

It does not contain any information about how much more any outcome is preferred to any other outcome. For example, suppose we have the status quo Z and two possible departures from the status quo, X and Y. With an ordinal ranking, we might be able to say that X and Y are each preferable to Z and, furthermore, that Y is preferable to X. But we would not be able to make any judgment about the comparative distance between Z and X, and Z and Y. An interval scale, by contrast, not only ranks the outcomes but also gives us information about the comparative distance between different ranked items on the model of the distance between points on a line. With an interval scale, we might be able to judge in the preceding case that the move from Z to Y is twice as far as the move from Z to X.

The problem is that neither ordinal ranking nor an interval scale would allow us to make judgments that some institution was "nearly just" or "far from just," since this would suppose a partition between justice and injustice, as well as a sense of distance from that partition. I also could not judge, "Slavery is profoundly unjust" or "Tenure is mildly unjust." For to judge that something is profoundly (or mildly) unjust, I need to be able to judge how far it falls from a condition of justice simpliciter. Now, you might think that an interval scale would supply us with the information required to make these judgments because it gives us comparative information on the distance of different arrangements from one another and the severity of injustice is a matter of distance. But such comparative judgments of distance don't tell me anything about the severity of the injustice of any of the elements under comparison. With an interval scale, all I could say are things like "Although serfdom and free labor are both improvements over slavery, free labor is twice the improvement that serfdom is." Whether any, or all, of them are profoundly unjust, or very nearly just, or mildly unjust, or severely unjust, I could not say. For these concepts have no application in a purely comparative framework. These judgments all presuppose an asymmetry between justice and injustice, and noncomparative roles for each concept, with justice setting the benchmark against which the severity of injustice is measured.

To see what we lose in losing judgments of severity, note that judgments about the severity of injustice are crucial for thinking in principled ways about the response to injustice in two ways. The first is that judgments about severity play a role in determining the urgency of the claims of those wronged. Different timescales for processes of change ameliorating an injustice may be justified on different assumptions about the urgency of the underlying claims. If the injustice is mild, perhaps changes that we anticipate will address the problem over the long term may be sufficient. But if people are subject to grievous injustice now, then strategies that rely on demographic effects and take generations to accomplish their results may be unjustifiable. The second is that judgments about severity play an essential role in determining what sorts of principled responses to injustice can be justified. I have pointed out that it is a general feature of justice that we are licensed to actively oppose injustice. But the form that this justified opposition can take depends on the nature and severity of the injustice. Mere interval-scale judgments will never provide this crucial information, for it may be that all the intervals are incredibly close to one another as judged in relation to justice simpliciter, so that the fact that X is ten times farther from Z than Y has literally no consequences for what sorts of response is licensed in situations X, Y, and Z. We cannot have a violent revolution because the current situation with parking meters is mildly unfair, and this will be true even if the postrevolution parking meter reforms are ten times more of an improvement over the tepid parking meter reforms Y that are possible without a revolution. A systematic approach to the principled response to injustice must draw on judgments about severity in articulating its theoretical claims about justified resistance.

Thus, one principled way that thought about the end of a just society informs our reasoning about the response to injustice is through judgments about the severity of injustice. The urgency of the claims of the wronged and the modes of resistance to injustice that are permissible are determined in part by reference to the distance between the current situation and justice simpliciter. Again, this is not to say that we have no sense of this distance pretheoretically; we do, of course, but this sense depends on undeveloped judgments about the relation of an injustice to justice simpliciter. So if we wish to reason in systematic and principled ways in nonideal theory, we must make reference to the idea of justice developed by ideal theory. By specifying the absolute threshold in reference to which we make judgments of severity, ideal theory helps to determine the grievousness of injustices and so too the forms of resistance that can be used to legitimately respond to them.

It is worth mentioning the compatibility of all this with an important insight of Sen's. Sen rightly points out that the ability to identify the idea of a just society, and so a "grand partition" between justice and injustice, is not sufficient by itself to make judgments about the ranking of injustices that fall on the wrong side of the partition.[13] For there will be many different ways of falling away from justice, along many different dimensions. The scale will not be monodimensional, and so judgments of severity will be complicated in ways that cannot be read from our specification of the ideal. As Rawls and others have pointed out, ideal theory provides some guidance in the form of prioritizing and weighting different considerations in a just society, which will presumably be relevant for thinking about the severity of various departures from justice, at least in a range of cases.[14] Furthermore, the understanding and rationale of various aspects of justice provided in ideal theory will inform our reasoning about the relative seriousness of different departures from justice. Democratic theory, for example, helps us understand what is at stake in rights of democratic participation and so can help us to think about the severity of various failures to realize democratic institutions. But, although relevant, Sen's basic point remains that judgments of severity cannot be read straight off from the specification of an ideal.

This point is compatible with my argument. For all I have been claiming is that the partition between justice and injustice is necessary if we are to make judgments of severity, which is obviously compatible with thinking that knowing what constitutes justice is insufficient for making systematic judgments of severity. Nonideal theory addresses, among other things, the severity of departures from justice, the urgency of the underlying claims, and what principled forms of response are justified to these departures. In doing so, it presupposes and draws on the account of justice provided by ideal theory as the condition from which departures are judged to be of some degree of severity. But there is independent work for nonideal theory to do in thinking about the relative severity of injustice along different dimensions, and the responses to these injustices that are licensed by justice. While guided by some reasoning from ideal theory, these are inquiries that must be carried out at the level of transitional theory.

It may well be that judgments about severity, although presupposing justice simpliciter, are nonetheless very local and that nothing bordering on a uniform approach to weighing injustice can be applied to all nonideal conditions. If so, this interesting and important result of nonideal theory only increases the need for nonideal theory to examine local contexts in light of their departures from a threshold of justice simpliciter. It in no way speaks against the significance of the grand partition—to the contrary, it speaks strongly in its favor.

In sum, a problem with the comparativist approach is that it throws out many ordinary judgments about justice and injustice that provide starting points for our reflection on the sense of justice. It thus threatens to distort at the outset our ascent from practice to theory by allowing the requirements of formalism to suppress a range of ordinary judgments that are natural starting points for reflection.[15] It also seems to elide, or at the very least downplay, the crucial conceptual and practical asymmetry between justice and injustice. As a result, it renders essential judgments about the comparative severity of injustice unintelligible. Practice can do neither without the concept of justice simpliciter nor without "the grand partition" between justice and injustice this concept marks.

§3.3: THE DYNAMIC DIMENSION

One familiar mode of practical reasoning is deliberation that begins from an end and works backward, ultimately bringing the reasoning back to actions that are within an agent's power to effectuate.[16] If nonideal theory responds to injustice in part by dynamically deliberating in pursuit of justice, then the end specified by ideal theory will be of obvious practical importance for nonideal theory. For, in deliberation, we choose the means as ways to realize the end. If we vary the end that we pursue through deliberation, different actions will become the requisite means.

Since political agents already exercise practical intelligence in the absence of ideal theory, although in a piecemeal and fragmentary way, the point is not that ideal theory provides a practical light that did not exist before. Political agents already pursue claims of justice in their practical activity and so already pursue ends through deliberation. Instead, ideal theory further determines and specifies the already existing ends in question, relating them to one another, so as to provide orientation toward a unified idea of just society as an end to be pursued in our action. This unification and specification of an end alters the practical field, allowing for a more determinate and adequate application of a range of dynamic concepts that figure in deliberation.

One such dynamic concept is that of an obstacle.[17] An obstacle is something that must be circumvented or overcome in deliberation. In the context of transitional theory, an obstacle is that which blocks possible routes of change, thereby holding in place the current unjust status quo by precluding, or rendering more difficult, action challenging the status quo. But different ends face different obstacles, so this concept applies only where we have an end in view for the purposes of deliberation, and some range of possible routes of change that might reach it. Since injustices will usually be produced and reproduced in part through the activity of political actors, the obstacles to progress toward an end often involve the coordinated activity of agents.[18] By specifying the end, we provide essential materials for specifying the political forces of opposition, for different obstacles in the form of organized interests will loom for different dynamic routes of change in pursuit of different ends.

Specifying an end is also relevant for thinking about what powers and resources agents will have to acquire or deploy in order to bring about their end. Pablo Gilabert has recently articulated the crucial concept of dynamic powers, which are the powers agents have to act so as to transform their circumstances so as to be able to do further, more ambitious things later.[19] Dynamic routes toward an end relate to capacity building for the purposes of political transformation. Depending on the nature of the end, different agents will need to acquire, develop, and consolidate different capacities, and they will need different resources to exercise these capacities and so bring about the end. The more the end is specified, the greater determinacy our thought about these concepts will have.

We can say much the same about the concepts of opportunity and hazard. An opportunity is a temporally bounded set of circumstances that allow agents to pursue an end by opening up favorable possibilities for action. Whether or not something is an opportunity, and how much of one, will depend on the end being pursued.

A hazard, by contrast, is a concept that applies when we consider both possible routes of change toward an end and the risks involved with various courses of action judged against the baseline of the status quo. Without some dynamic perspective that involves the specification of an end, this concept lacks application. But it is of the first importance for deliberation, for to deliberate intelligently we must decide which hazards are worth risking and which should be avoided. As we further specify the end, we make it possible to more determinately specify the hazards in pursuit of this end. Vary the end, and something that is an opportunity in one case will be a hazard in another. A window of opportunity for market socialism may be a period of looming hazards for capitalism. If we have not determined the end specifically enough to distinguish between them, then the corresponding practical concepts will lack determinacy. In this case, it is especially clear, since those are different and opposed political projects. But even ends that stand in more complicated relations will face different dynamic terrains, involving distinct windows of opportunity and hazard.

We should note that there are different levels of specification that the idea of a just society can take in ideal theory. Merely to specify the principles and their combination is already to determine the end to a great extent, for it allows us to think holistically about different aspects of justice, informing our judgments about severity under conditions of injustice, and so informing our thought about trade-offs, and helping us understand what institutional changes might constitute an improvement over the status quo.

However, for reasons that will only emerge fully by the end of Chapter 5, institutional proposals for realizing the principles of justice have a definite place in ideal theory as well. We can think of such institutional proposals as further specifications of the idea of a just society, concretizing the end so that it can play a greater role in practical reasoning, not only as a unified set of standards but as a concrete institutional reality. We can think of such institutional proposals as themselves coming in degrees of specificity. The greater the specificity, the greater the determination of the concepts pertaining to deliberation.

However, it is easy to fetishize concrete institutional proposals in inappropriate ways.[20] First of all, institutions are often necessary in order to render determinate claims of justice, and there may be uncountably many satisfactory ways of doing this. Which of these should be pursued may well be impossible to choose until one is close enough to the end to view the dynamic landscape of shifting opportunity structures. Furthermore, insofar as institutional proposals depend on the adequate performance of the relevant institutions under different empirical scenarios, it is often impossible to obtain the necessary information to select institutions without democratic experimentation under realistic conditions. Especially when proposals differ drastically from present institutions, we often lack the information necessary to convincingly assess them.

For all these reasons, the end specified by ideal theory will tend to become more institutionally concrete as we approach it: in this way, ideal theory too must change with the shifting practical landscape as more concrete institutional proposals become possible to evaluate and the end acquires greater determinacy. At a sufficient distance, institutional proposals in ideal theory must often take an exploratory tone, extrapolating out from the present in responsible ways with due humility, often less to write recipes for future cooks than to suggest that recipe options exist with which future cooks may experiment.

§3.4: THE IMMANENT DIMENSION

The struggle to overcome injustice is significant even apart from the dynamic contribution such changes make to bringing about a future just society. The response to injustice here and now is a principled affair that already engages ideas of justice. This is because the end of a just society is immanent in activity pursuing it. It plays a role in explaining the principled response to injustice and the intrinsic significance of this response. I distinguish the following places where thought about the end of a just society is immanent in the response to injustice by (i) explaining the intrinsic significance of satisfying present claims, (ii) informing our thought about the value of partially realizing or approximating justice, (iii) illuminating principled modes of resistance to injustice, and (iv) explaining how justice is manifested in the act of struggle itself.

i. The Intrinsic Significance of Satisfying Present Claims

To view satisfying the claims of the people who are wronged as merely stepping-stones to a fully just society is to treat these claims in an instrumental fashion, and so to fail to view them as claims of justice. When we amend institutions or practices so as to ameliorate or remove an injustice, it is right that we do so, even apart from the further vistas of transformation that such changes may (or may not) open up. For people have valid claims on us now in conditions of injustice that call out to be fulfilled, and when we fulfill them, we do right by those people. For example, ending mass incarceration is not only about achieving a future society where all can at last be free. Transformation requires a long view, so it may be that the later claims we aspire to satisfy in a fully emancipated society are not even the claims of the same people. We should by all means think about future justice, but without forgetting the claims of those who suffer injustice now. For some are wrongly unfree now, and if we free even some of them, what we do is good because it satisfies their urgent unmet claims on us.

The end of a just society sheds light on this immanent value in the amelioration or removal of injustice. In specifying the valid claims that people have, the principles of justice help to explain why removing an injustice is intrinsically and not only instrumentally good. It will often be the case that when institutions are altered to better meet the claims of some at present, the principles of justice straightforwardly explain why this is good. For example, suppose that a just society is a democratic society. In that case, the explanation of why winning the franchise for those who have been denied it historically is intrinsically good involves the appeal to democratic principles. Furthermore, the deeper rationale of those principles, connected to high-level judgments about justice, will shed light on the deeper grounds of the intrinsic goodness of the change in meeting the unmet valid claims of the previously disenfranchised on us more adequately. Here our understanding of democracy helps us to understand the justice of expanding the franchise. Even were the society never to become a full democracy, this change is and would be just.

ii. Partially Realizing Justice

A related way in which the end of a just society is immanent in the response to injustice involves thinking about the desirability of various improvements, not only as waystations on dynamic routes toward a fully just society, but also as intrinsically significant partial realizations of a just society. When we cannot have justice in full, it often makes sense to realize it partially. Or if we cannot realize some aspect of justice in part, perhaps it makes sense to at least approximate its realization. These changes are intrinsically significant whether or not they pave the way for eventually winning a larger justice. But, of course, on different specifications of the end, different things will count as partial realizations. Or if I wish to approximate something, then what counts as an approximation, and our sense of how proximate it is, will vary with the specification of the end. To make these judgments about partial realization and approximation in a systematic way, knowledge of a just society provided by ideal theory is crucial. This is another way that thought of the end can be immanent in our response to injustice. A principled response to injustice will often involve trying to win some part of justice, or at least approximate it, and so draw on an account of that which is to be partially realized.

Partial realization has its limits. The value of meeting requirements of justice sometimes depends on the fulfillment of other requirements as background conditions. In circumstances of injustice, by meeting some requirement of justice that would be satisfied in a just society, we might not improve the situation, or we might even make it worse.[21] For example, it may be that given background democratic equalities, in a just society our discourse in political deliberation would be structured by norms of civility and public reason.[22] But in situations with entrenched imbalances in democratic power, hewing to principles of civility can be a way of enshrining and protecting democratic inequality.

Far from undercutting the relevance of the idea of a just society, this point only emphasizes how essential ideas about justice are for settling this question. For we can only so much as formulate this question if we have in view the different requirements of justice that would be met in a just society and are then able to ask what relations of dependence they have on one another. Even where the answer is that some requirement of justice would be counterproductive to fulfill under present circumstances of injustice, such reasoning paves the way for thinking about what departures from the ideal might be justified.[23] Here, too, thought about the end is immanent in the principled response to injustice. For a partial or approximate realization of justice can be good in itself even apart from its contribution to reaching something better still in the future.

iii. The Principled Character of Modes of Resistance

A third important point concerns strategies of opposition to an unjust status quo. These strategies will often license behavior that would not be justified in a just society. Insisting on behavior that would satisfy the requirements of justice in a just society, we will be wrongly stifling the forms of principled resistance justified by the severity of the injustice that confronts us. But in understanding the rationale for different modes of opposition, it is crucial that we understand both why the behavior they license would not be permissible absent injustice and how these modes of opposition might nonetheless be seen as expressing allegiance to justice by other means. For these aspects can explain both the rationale and limits of principled resistance to injustice.

For example, to understand the limitations on the justification of civil disobedience, we must understand the requirement to obey legitimate laws in a democracy to see first how systematic injustice of certain kinds and severity undermines this requirement. Furthermore, only with the help of a deeper understanding of democracy can we see how civil disobedience can under certain conditions be a profoundly democratic act, speaking to the deeper, underlying democratic values articulated by ideal theory in a context where they are frustrated through official processes of collective decision-making.[24] Thus, our thinking about a democratic society is immanent in our thought about civil disobedience, even as it contravenes requirements that would hold in a democratic society. By coming to a richer understanding of democracy by ordinary means, we come to a richer understanding of the rationale for democracy by extraordinary means—including its ethics and limits.

This is another way the end of a just society is immanent in the principled response to injustice. Were the only relation to justice dynamic, then our reasoning about strategies of resistance to injustice would be solely instrumental, and the only question would be how to get from here to there. When it comes to justice, however, thought about the end is immanent in thought about the means, for considerations of justice are already at play now, and the responses to injustice prefigure various dimensions of justice. Strategies of resisting injustice are both limited and informed by our understanding of justice as an end.

iv. Justice as Realized through Struggle

This reflection on justified resistance brings us to our final, intimately related topic: the way justice is prefigured—and to some extent even realized—*in* struggle. Of the four aspects of immanence, this is the most conceptually difficult and perhaps the most profound. I am painfully aware that I can do no more here than make a start. To lay the groundwork, we must take a closer look at the relation of unfulfilled claims to justified resistance.

When one has an unfulfilled claim of justice, correlated duties are being violated by other agents. In this situation, one typically has standing to resist the violation and seek fulfillment of the claim. In §1.2, I mentioned this as one of the marks of duties of justice that sets them apart from other classes of moral duty. Of course, what sort of resistance is justified will depend on the nature of the underlying claim and the severity of the injustice involved in its violation. But whatever form it takes, the standing to resist flows from the unfulfilled claim: if one does not have such a claim, the resistance to one's (legitimate) treatment is not justified. Part of what it is to have a claim of justice on others is to be licensed to resist the violation of the corresponding duties and to push for fulfillment of the claim.

Let us consider acts of civil disobedience—for example, the lunch counter sit-ins during segregation, used by African Americans to protest legal exclusion from white businesses. When black diners sat down at whites-only lunch counters, they justly asserted their claim to equality before the law. This license to justly break the law flowed from their underlying claim to equal treatment and inclusion in the economic and civil institutions of society, and from the corresponding violation of the duties of their white fellow citizens to provide them with equal and dignified treatment. This violation was severe enough to justify a range of dramatic forms of resistance. Such acts of justified resistance, authorized by the underlying claims of justice, were assertions of these very claims in the face of the injustice of segregation.

Claims asserted in resistance to injustice have a kind of practical reality. For the same claim to equality that put their fellow citizens under correlated duties they were failing to meet also authorized the creative resistance to segregation the civil rights protestors employed. Admittedly, this sort of practical reality is not the best kind; the straightforward recognition of the claims and fulfillment of the correlated duties is much better. Nonetheless, it is a kind of practical reality as the enacting of a claim in response to violations of the correlated duty. In the face of unjust inequality, the civil rights movement actors asserted their equality.

In this sense, we might say there is freedom in the struggle for freedom, and equality in the struggle for equality, for the claims to freedom and equality are being acted on by those struggling for freedom and equality. Claims asserted in the face of injustice are illuminated by the principles of justice in the ways we have seen. It will often be the case that the freedom that is asserted in struggle is the same freedom that would characterize relations of citizens in a just society. When this is so, this freedom in struggle is a prefiguration of the freedom of a just society. The same freedom that is now asserted in struggle will then be respected and protected by the institutions and practices of society.

Furthermore, when one is wronged by the institutions and practices of society, one's standing as the source of the relevant claim goes practically unacknowledged. I am in relation to others as the source of claims on them, but this relation is not acknowledged by them and made the basis of action to satisfy the claim and rectify the situation. Furthermore, it is possible to at least partially assimilate this perspective on oneself, conceiving of oneself as unworthy of recognition as the possessor of the relevant claims. This is one way injustice can deform those who are wronged. By asserting my claim in resistance to injustice, I put myself forward as someone who is worthy of practical recognition. I conceive of myself as having a standing to make a claim, and by exercising that standing, I represent my claim as worthy of being upheld.

Tommie Shelby, in the most profound contemporary discussion of this phenomenon of which I am aware, calls this *self-respect*.[25] Shelby also speaks of the duty of self-respect, which one fulfills by resisting assaults on one's self-respect. In these discussions, he makes the point that upholding self-respect through resistance is a good of justice and in some cases even a duty. This self-respect is the same standing that I would conceive myself as having in a just society where my equality and worth were affirmed by all and recognized by the institutions and practices we share. In this way, too, my self-respect prefigures the standing I would conceive myself to have were the world aright.

Furthermore, when claims are asserted by those who are wronged in concert with others who suffer the same injustice, the struggle is reciprocal. It involves a mutual practical recognition of the claims and the others' standing to assert these claims in opposition to the shared injustice. Acting in solidarity, each group asserts not only its own claim but also the claims of the others who are wronged. In doing so, they recognize, affirm, and act on those claims, and they have their claims recognized, affirmed, and acted on in turn. This mutual practical recognition of the standing to make claims is a good of justice that is immanent in struggle. Furthermore, in some cases, those who are wronged may have a duty to resist injustice alongside their fellow sufferers of injustice. If so, they do right by one another by engaging in shared struggle, fulfilling duties to one another that arise from their unfulfilled shared claims. Since, in a just society, such mutual recognition would structure the relations of members to one another and have practical effect through the fulfillment of the duties corresponding to such claims, here, too, we see in struggle and solidarity a prefiguration of the nature of the just society.

Similar points can be made also about struggle for those who stand in either of the other two agential relations to injustice. By struggling against the injustice they formally perpetrated, the wrong-doers acknowledge the claims they failed to take up before. By taking active steps to resist the injustice alongside others, through their actions they now reject complicity and may begin to make amends. In doing this, they prefigure the right relations of mutual recognition and the fulfillment of claims that will be a matter of course through the institutional arrangements and practices of a just society. When bystanders join in the struggle for justice, they also publicly acknowledge the standing and worth of the claims of the wronged. Often, they, too, avoid the complicity that arises from inaction and so fulfill duties that arise from the underlying claims of the wronged. In doing this, they prefigure the right relations of a just society, and this partly explains why what they do is right.

The topic of bystanders and wrongdoers points the way to further questions about the ethics of struggle, which we will return to in Chapter 4. The question of how we relate to each other in struggle reveals that the values we seek to realize through struggle are already at play in the relations between agents. This means, too, that the injustices we wish to remedy can also be reproduced in the struggle against those very injustices. As we will see, this opens onto huge and difficult topics, including the proper relation of theory to practice.

But enough has been said for now to limn the topic of justice in struggle. We should note that unlike the first two aspects of immanent justice I have mentioned, justice realized in struggle is not conditional on the partial success of the resistance to injustice. For one can realize the values of justice in struggle even when one is defeated and injustice abides. Although the possibility of change is usually the most important practical consideration, the justice immanent in struggle helps to explain why it can be permissible and worthwhile to resist injustice even when there is almost no hope of success at present and failure has its costs.[26] For self-respect, mutual recognition, and solidarity are goods of justice, and there is a kind of freedom in the struggle for freedom.

§3.5: RELATIONSHIP OF THE DYNAMIC AND IMMANENT ROLES

In its dynamic role, the end of a just society serves as something to be produced by traversing pathways of change. It is something to be reasoned toward, working outward from present conditions. It enables deliberation by helping to render determinate our thought about means to take toward this end, in part by specifying a range of end-relative concepts that inform practical reasoning in pursuit of change. In its immanent role, the end of a just society informs our response to injustice by helping us to understand the ways in which justice is already at stake under conditions of injustice. Furthermore, the end of a just society sheds light on principled strategies of resistance and reveals ways in which there is substantial justice realized in struggle itself.

The dynamic and immanent roles of the idea of a just society in our practical thought are tightly related. There is not one end that figures in the dynamic role and a separate one that figures in the immanent role; it is the same end playing both roles. Furthermore, in an unjust society, the same end plays both roles simultaneously with respect to the same actions responding to injustice. We can then expect that these two roles will inform and interact with each other.

The immanent role clearly conditions and informs the dynamic role. The pursuit of justice is itself a principled affair. Although the end does indeed justify the means, it does not justify all the means, as it would were the only role for justice dynamic. Questions of justice arise in the pursuit of justice. Some routes of change toward justice are closed by the very justice toward which they are routes. For example, the same ground that explains why torture is unconditionally impermissible in a just society explains why one cannot torture political opponents in the pursuit of a just society.

In other cases, pathways with a greater likelihood of producing real change may be foreclosed because they call for the greatest sacrifices from those who are already oppressed and who are powerless in the political process. Here we need to inquire what obligations of justice different groups have in light of present injustice, and who can be made to bear what costs in transition, keeping in mind that it is often obscene to expect those already suffering the greatest injustice to bear the full cost of a transition to a greater justice.[27] In this case, the present unfulfilled claims of some take precedence over the goal of achieving a future justice that will require wronging them still more gravely in the transition.

Even where something is permissible to employ as a means in the dynamic pursuit of justice that would not be permissible in a just society, the immanent role of justice informs our thinking about the costs that are involved. In some cases, the immanent role of the end of a just society allows us to see these otherwise impermissible means as responsive to the principle in the special circumstances of injustice. For example, we have already seen how our understanding of the value and nature of democracy helps us to understand the crucial idea of democracy by other means. But in other cases, when terrible necessities are imposed by severe injustice, we may be justified in pursuing a value in ways that contravene that value. For example, we may be justified in pursing democracy through undemocratic means. Even where this is the case, the immanent role of justice helps us to reckon the costs from the perspective of justice involved in employing such unsavory means and to appreciate the weighty values on each side so we can think seriously about the question. It also allows us to select from a range of bad options those most compatible with our principles.

So far, we have been speaking about the ways that the immanent role conditions and informs the dynamic role. But the dynamic role also informs and conditions the immanent role. As Pablo Gilabert has argued, sometimes it is necessary to forgo a change that would be good in the present in order to achieve a greater justice in the future.[28] This will especially be the case where making a change in the present that ameliorates an injustice also locks in a status quo that forestalls further change—for example, by sapping the resolve of some for more ambitious change and simultaneously empowering a set of actors who will unjustly oppose further change. Here, we might say, the dynamic consideration takes precedence over the immanent ones.

Having noted the possibilities of mutual limitation, the more typical case is one where the two roles point in the same direction and so support rather than limit each other. The way to pursue the end of a just society is often simply to ameliorate or overcome some given injustice by instituting changes that are good because they are more just than the current status quo. Sometimes ameliorating an injustice removes obstacles to winning further changes or builds capacity for agents of change. This is a case of productive synergy. But even more often, we lack any reason to believe that making a change for the better will affect the prospects of future change one way or another. When a greater justice is possible now without affecting dynamic routes to further change, to institute a change that is good because it is (more) just is thereby to make progress toward the end of a just society. We have more justice now and are one step closer to having a just society. What would be good immanently is also good dynamically. What's not to like?

My point in adumbrating these various outcomes is to indicate various possible ways the two roles for the end of just society may interact in transitional theory. I have not tried to say how one might develop nonideal theory so as to arrive at a view about which of these various relations hold in any given case, or how we are to think about the various trade-offs where permissible. To discuss this topic adequately, one would need to put flesh on the skeleton of the theory of justice. All I have done here is identify the rich topics with which transitional theory must engage, noting some ways in which transitional theory must draw on realistic utopian theory. My goal throughout has been to clarify the abstract idea that justice, as an infinite end, plays two related roles in transitional theory.

§3.6: THE PRIORITY OF REALISTIC UTOPIAN THEORY OVER TRANSITIONAL THEORY

With these two roles in view, we are in position to see that although Rawls overstates the point in a way that is unhelpful, there is more than a grain of truth in his claim that without the idea of a just society explored by realistic utopian (ideal) theory, transitional (nonideal) theory lacks a goal with which its concepts might be rendered determinate, systematic, and critically intelligent. He was wrong to put the point in genetic terms, thereby seeming to mandate an implausibly rigid order of entry into theory and perhaps even to imply that piecemeal judgments about injustice were impossible. But in a deeper sense, he was right, for there is a practical explanatory priority of ideal theory over nonideal theory in senses corresponding to our two roles.

While we can certainly make various fragmentary and piecemeal judgments of a nontheoretical kind, the theory of justice organizes and further develops these judgments to specify the end of a just society in realistic utopian theory. By identifying valid claims under principles of justice, our understanding of this end sharpens our ability to identify injustices. By specifying a threshold from which injustice is a departure, it also renders more determinate judgments about the severity of injustice.

Starting from this basis, transitional theory further organizes our practical thought about the response to injustice. In doing so, it draws on an understanding of the end specified by realistic utopian theory as something to be produced through political action that traverses routes of change. We can see the relevant form of practical explanatory priority associated with the dynamic role in the general fact that the specification of an end has practical explanatory priority over the specification of means toward that end. For means are means only in relation to an end, but the reverse is not true. By rendering the ends of practice more determinate, ideal theory thereby sheds an explanatory light on the dynamic questions dealt with by nonideal theory. Given the relation of explanatory priority that an end has over the end-relative practical concepts we canvassed, without ideal theory, nonideal theory has nothing to draw on but undefended and unarticulated partial understandings of justice.

Furthermore, the end of a just society informs our thought about the response to injustice immanently, for the pursuit of a greater justice is itself a principled affair. Understanding the principles of justice illuminates what claims people have now and why meeting them is just. The values they articulate and defend inform our sense of what routes of change are impermissible to pursue. Understanding these principles and the end they together constitute also allows us to think more critically and systematically about approximating or partially realizing them. For the concepts of approximation and partial realization are asymmetrically dependent on understanding that to which they are proximate and partial. The end of a just society also helps us to understand strategies of resistance that deviate from the principles in various ways, as our understanding of justice by extraordinary means asymmetrically presupposes some understanding of justice by ordinary means. Finally, realistic utopian theory helps us to understand justice in struggle, as thought about what is prefigured or adumbrated in that struggle depends asymmetrically on a conception of that which is prefigured or adumbrated.

All of this is not to denigrate our pretheoretical understanding of injustice, and it is not to mandate a particular order of inquiry. We come to political philosophy already knowers, including about injustice; were this not the case, political philosophy would be impossible. Furthermore, we can approach an issue from many directions. It is often possible to make significant progress in nonideal theory by presupposing some perhaps unarticulated background views about justice. This is not ruled out by the practical explanatory priority of realistic utopian over transitional theory.

The form of practical explanatory priority is also compatible with transitional theory having priority in a different sense. Given the stringency of justice, the problems presented by injustice are salient practical priorities for us. They are prior in the sense of urgency. Thus, under conditions of injustice, transitional theory is without a doubt the most important part of the theory of justice. Furthermore, just as practical reasoning is done for the sake of action, the theory of justice exists for action. As we will see in Chapter 4, under conditions of injustice, transitional theory is the part of the theory of justice where theory meets practice. In other words, transitional theory is where the action is.

Agents of Change

§4.1: CONUNDRUMS OF THEORY AND PRACTICE

On the teleological conception, the theory of justice is practical and so exists for the sake of action. This feature was on dramatic display in our use of deliberation as a framework for the dynamic role of justice, for deliberation begins with an end and terminates in action. This suggests that the theory of justice does not stop short of action.[1] This idea is difficult to understand. It is time that we faced up to pressing questions about the relation of theory and practice on this picture.

One set of questions arises from the fact that theory is general, while—as Aristotle loved to emphasize—action concerns particulars. We act here and now, confronted by shifting arrays of opportunity structures in an evolving practical landscape populated by agents, obstacles, institutions, and events. The theory of justice is general by its very nature, since theory is general. What, then, can it mean for the theory of justice to exist for the sake of, much less reach all the way to, action?

A second set of questions arises about the identity of the subject who theorizes and the subject who acts. For the political philosopher is one person, we might think, whereas political agents are other people. If they coincide in any particular case, the philosopher appearing for the moment as a political actor, then the philosopher acts in a different capacity, not qua philosopher but qua citizen or human being. But how can theory exist for the sake of practice when theorists and practitioners are different people? Who is the practical subject of the theory of justice who both possesses the knowledge in question and acts on it? For the sake of whose action does the theory of just exist? Of whose action does it not stop short?

Before we turn to these questions, let us note one more feature of nonideal theory. On the teleological conception, nonideal theory is transitional theory. If ideal theory articulates the end of a just society, transitional theory operates in circumstances of injustice with a view to transitioning from injustice to justice. The action for the sake of which transitional theory exists is precisely action overcoming injustice. Since injustice is what transitional theory theorizes, transitional theory exists for the sake of action that overcomes the very conditions that make transitional theory necessary and possible. In other words, transitional theory works toward a world in which there is no practical need for transitional theory. Since the theory of justice is practical, under those conditions transitional theory will no longer be part of the theory of justice. So, on the teleological conception, the very division of the theory of justice into ideal and nonideal components is not an immutable feature of political philosophy, but a product of injustice. By moving toward a just society, transitional theory strives toward its own practical self-annihilation.

Supposing that we are in circumstances of injustice, we can expect the answers to our two sets of questions—about the generality of theory and about the practical subject—to take a special form. For the relationship of theory to practice is presumably affected by the same conditions of injustice that force the division of the theory of justice into ideal and nonideal components. Where there is a division of the theory of justice into two parts, we can expect that the relation of theory and practice will be different than if the theory of justice were simply realistic utopian theory. We must try to understand how. Let us start by very briefly mentioning a few of the elements of transitional theory as practical opposition to existing injustice.[2]

The identification of injustice, as we have seen, draws on principles of justice. But it also draws on empirical knowledge of the phenomenon in question. The diagnosis of the underlying pathology consists in an account of the processes reproducing the injustice as a stable status quo, deepening our understanding of it as injustice. For how a state of affairs is reproduced is often relevant to judgments about whether, and on what grounds, it is unjust—and how severe an injustice.[3] Our diagnosis also helps to specify many practically relevant concepts, including obstacles to be overcome and perhaps both perils and opportunities.

Nonideal theory also proposes institutional changes that would disrupt the processes of reproduction, working to overcome or ameliorate the injustice. These institutional alterations must be viable in the sense that were they instituted they would both disrupt the reproduction of the injustice and be possible to maintain over time—or, better yet, open the way to further transformations. As we have seen, they must also be permissible from the perspective of justice given their other effects on the system and their impact on the feasibility of future transformation.

Nonideal theory must also identify a path of transformation through which the change could be effectuated and, crucially, a potential agent of change who either has or could acquire the capacity to introduce the proposed remedy. It also involves the identification of principled strategies of resistance to injustice with which this agent of change can work in overcoming opposition to the change that draws on a theory of political agency and accounts of various modes of principled resistance.

This chapter builds toward an account of the relation between theory and practice under conditions of injustice by exploring the task of identifying paths of transformation. In particular, I will focus on the identification of an agent of change. This is not to say that the other functions do not raise their own issues. I focus on this one only because it is a place where the relationship of theory and practice takes a distinctive shape in nonideal theory. Furthermore, I will argue that his failure to grapple with the problem of agency is what prevents Rawls from coherently solving this problem. Discussing the problem of the agent of change is also a necessary preliminary to addressing the question of the subject of theory and praxis, as well as the question of the relationship of transitional theory as something general to action as something particular.

§4.2: THE CITIZEN AS UNIVERSAL PRACTICAL SUBJECT

It is very natural for philosophers to fall into a universalizing mode of discourse in nonideal theory. To see how, it will help to work with an example. (A word of caution is in order, since any example I select will have a political orientation that is inessential to the points I am making.) Suppose a philosopher is giving an excellent talk in non-ideal theory.[4] Using social science in conjunction with principles of justice and conceptual clarification, she works to identify an injustice in the US workplace consisting of the exploitation and domination of low-wage workers. She next provides a diagnosis of some of its underlying causes, locating them in labor law and the structure of authority in the firm. In doing so, she identifies corporate managers and boards as the agents who are violating duties corresponding to the claims of low-wage workers at their firms, imputing responsibility to them for this wrongdoing as agents of oppression. Drawing again on social science, she next identifies radical labor reforms that would effectively remedy the injustice, criticizing alternative policies as either causally insufficient or normatively problematic. When it comes to implementing the proposed political change, let us imagine that she employs a first-person plural without any further specification, saying what "we" should do to address the injustice.

The proposal put forward appears to recommend a course of action. It says what is to be done to overcome injustice. But everything done is done by someone; every change that is effectuated through action is effectuated by some agent or agents. So who is the envisioned agent of change here? Who is to bring about the recommended policy changes, and by what channels? This first-person plural seems to name the practical agent on whose behalf, or from whose perspective, the reasoning about what to do is being conducted. But who are we?

In this case, the most natural answer is that we are the members of the political community. Certainly, if the author's arguments are successful, the political community is failing low-wage workers by allowing firms to exploit them. And the members of the political community are under a requirement of justice to remedy this problem. The proposed changes are, after all, changes to the laws and the underlying economic structures of the political community.

Sometimes philosophers explicitly assert that this is how the practical subject (or "addressee") of political philosophy must be understood in a democratic society "like ours." John Rawls addresses this question in his *Lectures on the History of Political Philosophy*, which were originally intended as an introduction to students at Harvard University, orienting them to political philosophy as it was to be practiced in the contemporary United States and other constitutional democracies. Rawls raises and answers two related questions. The first is to whom political philosophy is properly "addressed." The second question is how political philosophy enters into and might affect the outcome of politics.

In answer to the first question, Rawls writes, "Surely, in a democracy the answer to this question is: all citizens generally, or citizens as the corporate body of all those who by their votes exercise the final institutional authority on all political questions, by constitutional amendment, if necessary."[5] Here and in the text that follows, Rawls says that the addressee of political philosophy in a constitutional democracy must be the body of citizens as a whole, who exercise through their vote the final institutional authority in a democracy. In systems that have judicial review, he goes on to say that it may also be addressed to a constitutional court, another constitutionally empowered political actor.

David Miller echoes Rawls's view, tying it to a view of political philosophy as practical reasoning and making explicit that the addressee is to be conceived as an agent. He writes, "I start from the assumption that political philosophy is a branch of practical reason— it is thought whose final aim is to guide action, as opposed to having a merely speculative purpose . . . [I]n Rawls' view (and in mine), political philosophy in democratic societies should be aimed at citizens generally, setting out principles that they might follow when supporting or changing their institutions and practices."[6] Political philosophy, Miller thinks, is a branch of practical reason that aims to guide action. So far, so good. But whose action? In democratic societies, like the contemporary United States and the United Kingdom, it should be aimed at "citizens generally." For Miller, as for Rawls, citizens in general are the practical subjects whom the reasoning involved in political philosophy is to guide in the first instance.

Rawls answers his second question about how political philosophy might influence this universal agent by pointing out that since there is no state ideology or position of authority for philosophers in a constitutional democracy, they can only affect their addressees in certain ways.[7] Political philosophy can reach the citizen body by influencing the background culture of ideas and arguments that they encounter in public discourse or in the course of their education. His picture seems to be that political philosophy puts deposits into a general cultural repository from which citizens in general can draw in their practical reasoning about politics.

This is connected with another of Rawls's views. Rawls articulates four roles that political philosophy may play for citizens in general in the public political culture in a society "like ours."

Significantly, he calls the first role that political philosophy can play "the practical role." One expects that in explaining the practical role of political philosophy, Rawls will explain how theory relates to practice. He writes about this practical role as "arising from divisive political conflict when its task is to focus on deeply disputed questions and to see whether, despite appearances, some underlying basis of philosophical and moral agreement can be uncovered, or differences can at least be narrowed so that social cooperation on a footing of mutual respect among citizens can still be maintained."[8]

First of all, note that Rawls frames the practical role of political philosophy as responding to "divisive political conflict" that besets our political community. Second, note how Rawls thinks philosophy responds to this conflict. He tells us that it focuses on the disputed question and tries to find underlying bases of agreement that can transcend this disagreement. It finds beneath superficial disagreement deeper sources of agreement that can persuade the parties to the conflict, resolving the practical conflict through intellectual work that achieves concord through rational persuasion. This is connected to his view about the addressee of political philosophy, or, in Miller's language, the agent whose practical reasoning the theory of justice is to guide as part of the public culture. The philosopher responds to divisive conflict in the political community by writing to the citizen body in general, uncovering suppressed bases of agreement that can be affirmed and acted on by all citizens, so that social cooperation can proceed on a footing of mutual respect. After annunciating this view of the agent to whom the theory of justice is addressed, and the role such a theory is to play in our shared public life, both Rawls and Miller go on immediately to suggest that any other view on which the practical subject might be less than "citizens generally" (or another constitutional body, such as the Supreme Court in a system with judicial review) is sinisterly undemocratic. If political philosophy is to be public and democratic in character, then it must speak to citizens in general.

Many problems lurk in this analysis. To start, why is the practical problem that political philosophy confronts disagreement? Surely, we might think, under conditions of injustice, the practical problem political philosophy confronts is injustice rather than disagreement. Disagreement, after all, wrongs no one, unless it causes injustice. But perhaps Rawls is thinking that since citizens in general hold the ultimate constitutional power in a democracy "like ours," the reproduction of injustice must depend on disagreement about whether institutions are in fact unjust in these ways. For if citizens in general agreed that something was unjust, then they would surely exercise their ultimate constitutional power to rectify it.

One wonders whether this is a plausible diagnosis of the reproduction of every injustice: that it is reproduced primarily by the opinion of a majority of citizens who exercise their constitutional powers to maintain it. Aren't there other empirical possibilities, perhaps ones that acknowledge the causal influence of more specific political actors? Might a better resolution of the problem come from some course of action other than the attempt to convert citizens in general through the uncovering of suppressed sources of agreement? Surely it is wrong to settle these questions of diagnosis and strategy by methodological fiat rather than real analysis. As we will see shortly, these questions point to reasons for doubting Rawls's and Miller's doctrine of the universal democratic addressee for nonideal theory that have nothing to do with secrecy and concealment. Indeed, the doctrine is untenable, at least in the naked form they propose.

§4.3: AGENTS OF CHANGE AND AGENTS OF INJUSTICE

Here is a simple observation that harks back to our initial discussion of the practical character of injustice in Chapter 2. The diagnosis of a problem to be addressed in nonideal theory often involves the identification of several groups, including, on the one hand, those suffering an injustice and, on the other hand, agents of injustice.[9] By introducing the nexus of doing and suffering injustice, injustice introduces practical divisions into the body of citizens. For injustice divides the practical world into asymmetric relations of wronging and being wronged. Furthermore, these cleavages are precisely what constitute the practical landscape as it is delineated in an account of the reproduction of the injustice. Since the agents of injustice are often politically mobilized defenders of the status quo, the forces they can bring to bear are among the obstacles to a solution that must be overcome through political action. In this case, the activity of the wrongdoers is part of the problem for which the proposed remedy is a solution.[10] The whole question of a remedy is how, through institutional changes, we can make them stop.

For an illustration, let us return to our imagined case, where the relevant agent of injustice is that segment of the corporate community dominating and exploiting low-wage workers. What was being proposed as a solution to this problem by the philosopher were radical labor reforms—labor reforms that would make it much more difficult to dominate and exploit low-wage workers. Let us elaborate the case slightly by supposing that the philosopher's empirical theory about the reproduction of this injustice includes a large role for the political activity of the corporate community and that her analysis predicts this will constitute the main obstacle to forward progress.

Drawing on knowledge of the current functioning and history of corporate lobbying in the United States in reproducing this unjust status quo, she tells us that we can anticipate that a sizable portion of the major firms employing low-wage labor will fight the proposed legal changes tooth and nail with a mix of hired and in-house lobbyists.[11] We can expect that their activity will be supplemented by business organizations like the Chamber of Commerce and Business Roundtable, who make it a policy to oppose even modest labor reforms. In fact, she tells us, we may anticipate that the issue will serve as a "business unity issue," as labor issues often do, drawing a very wide range of firms into the fray, even those not directly affected by the proposed reforms.[12] We can also anticipate that wealthy elites, many of whom are corporate board members or the family members of board members, will use their political organizations, campaign contributions, and other modes of influence to oppose change. For the opinions of economic elites diverge sharply from poorer people around questions of workers' rights and other aspects of justice in the workplace, especially as these affect low-wage workers. Furthermore, the opinions of economic elites have an outsized effect on the political system.[13]

On this analysis, the activity of the corporate community will constitute the organized opposition to any forward movement on this issue that the agent of change must confront. This suggests that change will have to be pursued by other agents who act in opposition to the corporate community. Presumably this would at least include the labor movement, broadly construed to encompass currently unorganized workers, whose contentious activity in the United States has in the past been the source of major labor reforms. (Why workers' organizations are obvious candidates for being an agent of change is something we will return to shortly.) This already signals trouble for the Rawls-Miller approach, for it suggests that the theory ought to be addressed to an agent of change that is more determinate than the body of citizens, including as it does both the corporate community and whatever agents might push for labor reform in opposition to the corporate community. Thus, the idea that in transitional theory we must always view ourselves as addressing a "we" that is indexed to the political community is mistaken. The reason why has to do not with concealment but rather with the analysis of the reproduction of the injustice and the practical obstacles, including organized activity of groups within the political community, along with thoughts about who are plausible potential agents of change to oppose them.

But perhaps I've been too quick with my dismissal of the "we" indexed to the entire citizen body. Granted, if understood to mean "all citizens," it would seem to be overly inclusive in the ways we have seen. However, Rawls's and Miller's remarks aside, we need not understand it in this way. For since we live in a democratic republic, the people have representative government, which (so they say) acts on our behalf and in our name and is not to be identified with the interest of any particular group.[14] So perhaps the "we" refers to the government acting on behalf of the people. It is a recommendation about what our government is to do. Unless, after all, we are imagining a change brought about through revolution, the labor reforms in our imagined case will be enacted by our representatives in Congress, if they are enacted at all. After all, in a representative democracy, citizens exercise their ultimate power not by voting on legislation (in the main) but by electing representatives who pass legislation for them.

However, under conditions of serious injustice, the mere fact that government action is required for some political change to come about does not automatically make the government the agent of change, at least not in the first instance. Indeed, the resistance of government to altering an unjust status quo may be one of the main obstacles to overcome in bringing about change. The functioning of representative government may itself be a major source of injustice, to the extent that it fails to be responsive on terms of equality to all citizens and serves to defend an unjust status quo. As should be plain from our example, the activity of agents of injustice often reaches deeply into the functioning of the political system, subverting its operation and stably reproducing the injustice.

After all, the analysis of what sustains the unjust status quo may in part lie with the nature and dynamics of party politics in the United States.[15] The question might initially be how one of the two parties can be forced to deal with an issue that its members have intentionally kept off the legislative agenda for decades. Or, more ambitiously, the question might be how one of the two parties can be reformed such that it comes to embrace the cause in question.[16] Or, most ambitiously, the question might be how to form a third party that pursues interests neglected by all current parties. In the first case, it is probably not right to describe the party as the agent of change at all. To do so would be to describe its members as the source of a change, when in fact they were an obstacle to that change whose resistance had to be overcome. In the second case, posttransformation the party will have been brought into a coalition serving as the agent of change. But, initially, the question is how to overcome the party's opposition in such a way as to transform its character and make it an agent of change. In the third case, current representatives are not even candidates to be among the agents of change, unless we imagine the third party forming as a splinter from currently existing parties.

This observation raises problems for the use of a first-person plural referring to the political community as a whole, whether it ranges directly over all citizens or does so through a more sophisticated representative mode. The problem is that the pronoun, on this interpretation of its scope, does not discriminate between potential agents of change and the organized opposition they confront, an opposition that works in part through government structures. But when there are identifiable wrongdoers, such discrimination is an essential preliminary in identifying a real practical subject of change and the obstacles it must overcome. What all this suggests is that in contexts of significant injustice and oppression, we may need a more discriminating concept of the "we" of political action, a concept that does not necessarily represent the whole of the political community. For, under conditions of oppression, the nonideal theorist is likely, in identifying the agent of change, to end up identifying an agent who is of necessity a partisan in a struggle against agents of injustice.

To be clear, I do not mean to be policing language. The use of the first-person plural to refer to the political community as a whole has legitimate uses in a nonideal context. For example, it can remind us that the injustices belong to the political community to rectify, and it can rhetorically imply (which is true) that this moral responsibility falls on the shoulders of everyone, including those directly responsible for the injustice. Such statements can have numerous practical roles, including speaking truth to power, rallying those most affected to action, swaying bystanders, and persuading some wrongdoers to change their ways. It can also be quite useful at a certain stage of our thinking, when we reason as a concerned citizen about injustice without having gotten clear enough about the problem yet to identify possible agents of change. My point is not that there is no point to using a broad first-person plural in a political context of significant injustice, but rather that its uncritical use can cover over the problem of the agent of change, a problem that must be addressed in nonideal theory. We cannot simply assume that the practical subject is the universal citizen body. Indeed, the question of who the practical subject is that might oppose a given injustice is a central and fraught topic for nonideal theory.

In a conciliatory gesture, we should remind ourselves that even in transitional theory there is an element of truth to Rawls's and Miller's view. Firstly, it is worth pointing out that transitional theory identifies true judgments about injustice and works to identify truths about what would ameliorate or overcome it. These claims, in virtue of being true, should be accepted by all, including those who are implicated in doing injustice. While that may not be realistic to expect, it is in the nature of the claims advanced in nonideal theory that they should be accepted and so have the proper form to be affirmed by all sides. But merely noting this is not sufficient to identify the practical role of political philosophy or to identify the agent of change whom such theory is meant to guide.

We can also note that since nonideal theory works toward overcoming injustices, it works toward a condition where the practical cleavages presented by injustice will be overcome. Thus, even nonideal theory, where the practical subject is fragmented, works toward a condition of universality.[17] In doing so, it works toward a condition where transitional theory will no longer be necessary. It also works toward a situation where the practical cleavages introduced by injustice will no longer disfigure either the citizen body or the theory of justice. Since the end is immanent in pursuit of the end, this less divided condition will have some role in transitional theory by conditioning our identification of the injustices we confront, informing our account of the various legitimate modes of resistance and political transformation, and showing us justice of the prefiguration of universality and mutual recognition.

Perhaps there is yet another profound truth being expressed by Rawls and Miller. Pending the resolution of some difficult issues in democratic theory, Rawls and Miller may be right that just institutions will involve democracy of an egalitarian sort. If so, a just society will have robustly democratic arrangements, where citizens address the collective problems they face on terms of equality, participating as equals in the decision-making processes of their society. Perhaps they are right as well that some form of a doctrine of public reason is defensible as part of an account of democratic reasoning among equals who attempt to support their views in the public forum on the basis of justifications that are available and open to all. Perhaps for these purposes representative arrangements will be both necessary and justified, and there will be duly constituted public authorities necessary for interpreting and executing laws and policies.

If this is correct, then the disagreement that is integral to democratic processes of self-government in a just society might well take the form that is amenable to Rawls's and Miller's approach. Political philosophy would in the first instance be addressed to all citizens, both directly and as organized through their representative institutions. Perhaps in these circumstances, political philosophy would play a practical role primarily by overcoming divisive conflict through appeal to sources of agreement open to and shared by all.

Showing this would require many arguments, but my point is that it might be true. Were it so, transitional theory would work in conditions of injustice toward a situation where political philosophy related to practice and the resolution of conflict in just the way described by Miller and Rawls. Given both the immanent and dynamic dimensions of nonideal theory, this would have some consequences for how we view transitional theory. But it certainly would not prescribe the use of a universal practical subject in nonideal theory, even for a "democratic society like ours."

§4.4: WHO IS THE AGENT OF CHANGE?

These observations show how important the concept of the agent of change is to transitional theory. Let us now try to formulate a workable account of the concept suitable for the teleological conception.[18] An agent of change is one who acts to disrupt an unjust status quo, overcoming the obstacles to effectuate change that ameliorates or removes the injustice. The relevant action is intentional in that we are speaking not, for example, of unforeseen consequences, but rather of the intentional pursuit of change. Since agents of change are usually collective agents, in at least the thin sense of people acting together, the relevant kind of intentionality will be whatever sort characterizes collective action.[19] Furthermore, these intentionally undertaken actions must be voluntary rather than forced by the actions of other agents. For if an agent must be forced to act, then this unwillingness to take the relevant steps is part of the political problem that some agent of change must overcome.[20] In short, the agent of change is one who acts intentionally and voluntarily to overcome an injustice.

In transitional theory, we respond to current injustice by making proposals about change that is not yet accomplished and sometimes not yet underway. The agents we address are thus potential agents of this change. To identify potential agents of change, we must attend first of all to the feasibility of different actors overcoming resistance to bring about the proposed changes. Pablo Gilabert, developing a line of argument originally worked out in concert with Holly Lawford-Smith, has presented the most systematic and relevant analysis of political feasibility.[21] Feasibility as Gilabert and Lawford-Smith present it involves a four-place relation between an agent, an action, an outcome, and a context. It is feasible for an agent X to perform action φ to bring about outcome O in circumstance Z.[22] Furthermore, feasibility judgments come in two varieties: binary and scalar. We are interested primarily in the latter.[23] Scalar judgments of feasibility admit degrees of feasibility that register the probability of success in bringing about O conditional on the agent in question trying to act so as to achieve this outcome. What is easy for one agent to accomplish, given their resources and powers, is a shaky prospect for another agent lacking these means. And what is highly feasible for a given agent in one political context of action may be nearly infeasible in another when the circumstances have shifted.

Furthermore, in light of the dynamic dimension of transitional theory, the feasibility we are interested in will usually be what Gilabert has called "dynamic feasibility."[24] We are interested not only in what agents might do at present, but in how they might act so as to transform the future contexts of action. This includes, crucially, how they might act to gain capacity over time for accomplishing future action—for example, by building alliances and coalitions with other agents seeking change or developing institutional capacity or resources.[25] Thus, when thinking about feasibility, we are usually considering what we have called dynamic routes to the proposed change. This is especially so when we consider ambitious challenges to highly entrenched injustices. In identifying potential agents of change, we ask which agents can most feasibly pursue dynamic pathways to change, beginning in the present and working outward.

However, it is clear from our discussion that dynamic feasibility is not enough, for not all potential agents who could feasibly act so as to overcome an injustice are plausible agents of change. Since the relevant action is intentional *and* voluntary, in identifying plausible agents of change, one must also attend to questions of motivation, for feasibility is conditional on an agent trying to bring about the change, and it is unrealistic to think that all agents will voluntarily do this.[26] A plausible potential agent of change is one who is, or might realistically come to be, willing to pursue change to address the relevant injustice. This is what, in our example, ruled out the corporate community as a plausible potential agent of change for radical labor reform, as effective as it would otherwise likely be in this endeavor. In other cases, where moral suasion is realistic, current perpetrators of injustice or uninvolved bystanders may eventually be part of plausible potential agents of change.

Let us pause here to dwell for a moment on the motivation to pursue change, asking why it might be true that the corporate community is not a realistic target for moral suasion to the cause of radical labor reform.[27] Why is it unrealistic to assume the corporate community, including the Chamber of Commerce, the National Association of Manufacturers, and top executives and corporate board members, could be persuaded to abandon their opposition and push for radical labor reforms that would secure justice for workers? The question is empirical and would be addressed by the theory of the reproduction of the relevant injustice, which will include an explanation why agents who work vigorously to maintain an unjust status quo do so. Here are some possible, mutually inclusive explanations that might hold in this case.

The first is that corporate elites are not working class and so do not suffer the same injustices as low-wage workers, and they do not have a vivid sense of the harms and indignities low-wage workers suffer as a result of unaccountable corporate power and exploitation. Furthermore, given the self-segregation of the affluent, they are unlikely to have close personal relationships with low-wage workers, whom they interact with primarily in hierarchical contexts. This might explain in part why they might not take as seriously as they should the claims of low-wage workers and why they might tend to see other considerations outweighing those claims. A problem of ignorance, this could be rectified by education and communication, and so this obstacle is perhaps not by itself insurmountable, provided agents of change could get the corporate community to listen.

The second is that the corporate community benefits from the injustices in question, for the profits from exploitation of low-wage workers flow to firms that employ or subcontract low-wage workers. These profits increase the value of the stock held by board members and executives. They also fund the salaries of executives as well as the activities of the Chamber of Commerce and the National Association of Manufacturers. Such serious material incentives can produce shamelessness as well as motivated reasoning. Shamelessness involves knowing that some behavior is unjust but brazenly carrying on with it. Motivated reasoning involves responding to evidence in rationally suboptimal ways that align with one's interests. If they play a large role in our account, these phenomena might give us reason to doubt that uncovering sources of agreement shared by the corporate community will be a realistic strategy for inducing them to pursue radical changes to labor law.

The third is that the exploitative practices of the corporate community have ideological support in a pro-business ideology that has large currency in the corporate community. Political philosophers have made ideology a vibrant area of research, with some of the most interesting recent work being done on racial ideology. I do not mean to affirm any particular theory of ideology, but to fix ideas for our illustrative case, I will draw on Tommie Shelby's classic account, supplementing it with some new work on the microfoundations of ideology.[28] Following Shelby, let us suppose that an ideology is a system of belief that distorts our understanding of social reality so as to stabilize and reproduce injustice. Rather than being simply false, ideologies are typically distorting or biased. They involve misleading frames, concepts inadequate for capturing the relevant facts, ways of discounting certain evidence, quick and shallow replies to justified complaints, as well as habits of misusing authoritative sources. Such ideologies inform practices, shape institutional arrangements, and find expression in the public culture through popular media, including the news, entertainment, and academic sources. But ideology also has microfoundations in human cognitive biases that operate in ordinary life and make different groups differentially susceptible to the relevant forms of shoddy thinking.[29] Ideology is not totalizing or inescapable, but it does affect different groups to different degrees in ways that can be explained.

Let us suppose that pro-business ideology fits well the lived experience of business executives and corporate board members and is attractive to them owing to a variety of cognitive biases.[30] One important factor might be the effect of social segregation in communal affiliation: viewing affluent social peers as their in-group, corporate elites are quick to attribute their copious advantages to merit, and the disadvantages of the working-class out-group to personal failures.[31] Furthermore, not wanting to acknowledge the injustice of the broader economic order in which they are so deeply enmeshed, members of the corporate community are quick to cast the system in a positive light where possible.[32] Viewing themselves as answerable to shareholders and customers, they think of themselves as responsible stewards when sidelining the claims of low-wage workers. This way of thinking is reinforced by the theories of business management promoted by paid corporate consultants, who view workers primarily through the lens of productivity and cast success in terms of shareholder value and customer satisfaction.[33] This point of view is echoed, let us suppose, in mainstream business-friendly media, including economically conservative national newspapers and magazines, and in the occasional white paper that crosses their desk from pro-business think tanks and lobbyists.

Let us consider, by contrast, why those who are wronged are often better motivated to pursue voluntary change than those who wrong. Again, let us focus on our illustrative case and ask why low-wage workers might fare better than corporate elites at meeting the voluntariness requirement on being plausible agents of change. It is important to stress again that this is an empirical question that would need to be addressed seriously by an analysis of the reproduction of the injustice in question.

First, low-wage workers are personally affected by the injustice and suffer the harms that result from being wronged. They have experience of their plight and the struggles it entails. Furthermore, they are likely to know many who are similarly situated, including loved ones. The seeds of potential solidarity are contained in this sense of shared harm and the resentment of disrespect. Second, since they suffer the injustice and would be benefited by the radical labor reforms that ameliorate it, they have much to gain from upsetting the status quo. Furthermore, these material benefits are just, and low-wage workers can more easily see how these justice benefits could change the lives of others who share their situation. So material incentives point in the opposite direction from those of the corporate elites. They do not come into competition with considerations of justice but rather operate in synergy with them.

Third, although not unsusceptible, low-wage workers are certainly *less* susceptible to pro-business ideology. Most do not think of the corporate elite as their in-group or their fellow low-wage workers as their out-group. They are thus not led to the same degree to attribute their material disadvantage to personal failures, and the successes of the corporate elites to personal merit. This allows them to view the rules that govern authority in the workplace more skeptically. They also do not come into contact with the same ideological armature. They are not aware of the latest managerial theories of business consultants, whom they view with suspicion to the extent they are aware of their activity at all; they do not read business magazines; and white papers from pro-business think tanks and lobbying groups never pass their (nonexistent) desks. While they may still absorb pro-business ideology from, say, cable television and talk radio, they have less contact with, and are less susceptible to, pro-business ideology than business elites.

To summarize, relevant factors that often separate defenders and victims of an unjust status quo include who is positioned to know best the indignities and harms of an unjust status quo; who, by contrast, is benefited by the maintenance of the unjust status quo; and who is most susceptible to ideology, stigmatizing ideas, or false political beliefs that rationalize the unjust status quo and discount the legitimacy of challenges to it. To the extent that analogous points hold generally in many cases, they provide some reasons for ex ante expecting those who are wronged by an injustice to be good candidates for inclusion within a potential agent of change in solidarity with a variety of other actors, and those who are actively wronging to be worse candidates on epistemic and motivational grounds.

It is important to stress that there are also normative reasons, so far unexplored by us, for including those who are wronged in the potential agent of change. These normative reasons flow from the immanent role of justice, suggesting that justice is often at stake in the inclusion of the wronged in the agent of change.

Consider that as the bearers of the claims that are unfulfilled, those suffering injustice are the source of the authorization to resist injustice on which agents of change may act in pursuing various strategies of resistance. Because they are claim holders, there is often a degree of authority with which those who are wronged are vested in deciding how to resist injustice. For example, sometimes those suffering injustice may be permitted to make certain decisions that others cannot make for them, especially when certain strategies of resistance come with costs for the oppressed, as when only the workers at a firm may decide to risk their own jobs by going on strike in protest over labor conditions. In other cases, things that would be right for bystanders to do with the approval of those suffering injustice are wrong when done contrary to their wishes. For example, a boycott of a firm over labor conditions can be justified when it is called for by workers or when they view it as a helpful act of solidarity. But it can be misguided when it is not called for by the workers and is contrary to their wishes because it threatens their employment and so worsens the already oppressive load they carry. (This can be true even if the boycott would be effective.)

Systems of oppression typically deny the oppressed recognition by failing to fulfill their valid claims. But the very same unjust structures will often also ignore their standing to press their own claims, disregarding their voice and agency in a variety of ways. We have also seen that there is freedom in the struggle for freedom, equality in the struggle for equality, and mutual recognition in the struggle for mutual recognition. We have seen that by struggling against injustice, an agent of change acknowledges the claims of those suffering injustice, takes them seriously, and so gives the wronged recognition. But how can the struggle against injustice manifest recognition of the equal dignity of the wronged in this way if they are treated as passive victims on whose behalf various actions must be taken without consultation? When they are denied agency and freedom, how can those who are wronged find an anticipation of freedom in struggle if they do not act on their own claims and play a robust role in deliberating about strategies of resistance? Indeed, it seems that to the extent this is not the case, agents of change hazard the manifestation of the very injustice they struggle against in their acts of resistance, slighting the voice and agency of the oppressed and enacting hierarchical and demeaning relations even in the struggle against these very injustices. These considerations speak in favor of the oppressed playing a role in their own emancipation on normative grounds connected to the immanent role of justice in struggle.[34]

In summary, although not much that is concrete can be said in advance of the analysis of a given injustice, we can at least say that plausible potential agents of change will satisfy three features: (1) the changes proposed will be dynamically feasible for them to a sufficient degree; (2) they are, or might realistically come to be, motivated to intentionally and voluntarily pursue such a dynamic route; and (3) they will be normatively appropriate candidates for agents of change. We can also note that these three criteria will often converge on including in the ranks of the agent of change those who suffer the relevant injustice, although we must recognize that there will be different trade-offs in different cases between these criteria. Transitional theory must be sensitive to these trade-offs in its identification of the agent of change.

§4.5: THE UNITY OF THE QUESTIONS OF NONIDEAL THEORY

Granting that the identification of a plausible potential agent of change is a relevant problem to be addressed in transitional theory, how central is it? Can we conduct adequate nonideal theory, identifying and diagnosing injustices and specifying remedies to overcome pressing injustices, without yet identifying dynamic paths forward and answering the question of the agent of change? If so, perhaps we ought to hold this question for a merely "pragmatic" stage, where we ask how the remedies we have identified might come about through the actions of different agents. Theory gives us general knowledge of problems and remedies, and in practice we apply this knowledge by reasoning about possible agents who might realize these proposals. Perhaps this is the way theory as something general relates to practice as something particular: through the implementation of something general (theory) by some agents (in practice).

Contrary to this simple picture, the diagnosis of a problem, the recommendation of a viable remedy, and the identification of an agent of change are tightly connected in transitional theory. Entailments between these issues can run in multiple directions. This means that to identify pressing injustices and normatively permissible remedies well, one must think through the question of the agent of change. It is an unavoidable question for transitional theory and can't be held in reserve for a separate "pragmatic" stage.

Let us start by elaborating the picture to be criticized, where the question of the agent of change enters only at the end, at the lowest, "pragmatic" stage. Let us suppose that first we begin with the provisional identification of an injustice drawing on both the resources of ideal theory and empirical information about the relevant injustice. We next proceed to synthesize social scientific information to diagnose the mechanisms of the reproduction of the injustice, arriving at a deeper understanding of the problem. Let us suppose that on the basis of this understanding, we then formulate morally permissible, effective solutions that would ameliorate or remove the injustice. Having hit on our solution, we are equipped finally to raise the questions about practice by considering what agents might effectuate it through which dynamic pathways.

We have seen that feasibility, motivation, and normative appropriateness are relevant for identifying a plausible potential agent of change. Note that our analysis in the prior steps of theorizing puts us in a good position to gauge such factors. First of all, by identifying the mechanisms through which an unjust status quo is reproduced, we have already identified the obstacles to change. Such an identification has ramifications for our understanding of which agents are best positioned to overcome the obstacles by enacting remedies, given their powers and resources in the situation and the forces that oppose them. Different dynamic routes will be feasible, to different degrees, for different agents. By identifying victims and bystanders, and by specifying some agents but not others in the active reproduction of this injustice, and theorizing the basis of their activity, the analysis will contain relevant information for assessing the motivational requirement. The analysis of the reproduction of the injustice might suggest that certain agents are more likely to be motivated to effectuate the chosen remedies than others. In addition, it may also suggest natural alliances with other agents struggling with the same or similar agents of injustice or affected by different but connected injustices. Similarly, the principles of justice in combination with thought about permissible strategies of resistance help equip us to think about normative appropriateness.

So it is indeed possible to work from above in this way. But a problem emerges when we note that entailments can also run upward from thought about plausible potential agents of change to the specification of remedies. To see why, it will help to work through an example. Let us start with an instructive example from one of our practicalists, Elizabeth Anderson. In *The Imperative of Integration*, she criticizes the "left multiculturism" of Iris Marion Young. Both Anderson and Young take as their problem (among other things) racial inequality as it manifests in urban space. Both see the problem as tied to the phenomenon of residential segregation along racial lines, recent phases of which include white flight and the fracturing of the urban metropolis. These phenomena have allowed wealthier white residents to underfund goods and social services in black neighborhoods, which also face high rates of joblessness, crime, and decaying housing stock.

On Young's view, the real problem lies not with the absence of racially integrated neighborhoods, but rather with the unjust exclusion of majority-black neighborhoods from social goods and economic opportunities. Genuine transformative progress will be made when, for example, majority-black neighborhoods receive adequate levels of funding, social service, and investment to generate jobs.

Young argues in favor of a policy of responding to racial inequality in the context of high levels of de facto racial segregation by "moving resources to the people" rather than making the people move to the resources.[35] After all, blacks have many legitimate reasons for wanting to live in majority-black neighborhoods, and the neighborhoods should be properly served regardless of their racial composition. In this connection, she offers an ideal of "differentiated solidarity" that, while removing barriers to integration, would nonetheless be compatible with the existence of high degrees of racial clustering, perhaps rising to the level of veritable de facto segregation in some cases, while nonetheless practicing a politics of solidarity across neighborhood lines that would serve all neighborhoods in an equitable manner.

Anderson's objection to Young's proposal involves, among other things, what we might think of as a line of argument running from thoughts about who is a plausible agent of change to conclusions about what remedies to pursue.[36] Anderson, as I read her, holds that there is no plausible potential agent of change to effectuate the required transformation that Young envisions. The first point, least explicit in her discussion, is about feasibility. In order to properly tackle the problems of disadvantaged urban spaces directly, ambitious egalitarian alliances across racial lines would be necessary. This would involve breaking down the class-exclusionary modes of the funding of social services that have allowed the affluent to hoard opportunities through residential segregation from the poor (of whatever race), and such an effort is sure to meet stiff resistance. Given the racial composition of the United States and the current conditions of inequality, African Americans do not possess the numbers or political resources to accomplish this alone. So Anderson thinks the potential agent of change will have to be multiracial.

However, we saw that identifying a plausible potential agent of change involves considerations not just of feasibility but also of motivation. Anderson sees this as the crux of the problem.

Together, residential segregation, racial inequality, and common cognitive biases produce in whites a set of racially stigmatizing representations of blacks.[37] These stigmatizing representations feed a politics of resentment, undermine political cooperation, and stymie democratic coalition building across racial lines that would be required to address this kind of systematic change. Thus, there is reason to believe that whites, including working-class whites, will not be willing to participate in such a multiracial agent of change. Other arguments that Anderson emphasizes more tacitly presuppose this line of argument. For example, she argues that social capital is the crucial factor in finding employment, and that since most good employment is in white firms and neighborhoods, segregation cuts blacks off from the employment opportunities needed to ameliorate their disadvantage.[38] But this presupposes that no major investment in jobs within majority-black neighborhoods is possible, so that blacks must have white acquaintances to find jobs. But, of course, if black-white coalitions on class lines could be forged in support of radical policies, then it might be possible to pursue policies that brought jobs directly into poor communities of whatever color, or allowed the residents of such neighborhoods easier information about and access to jobs in other, more affluent neighborhoods. However, owing to the racially stigmatizing narratives that circulate among whites and the politics of resentment they feed, her considered view would presumably be that such cross-racial organizing is unrealistic.

Anderson argues that this process could be disrupted if residential segregation could be dismantled, since this would undermine the operation of the cognitive biases that form the basis of these demeaning racial ideas that undermine interracial coalition building.[39] So we should focus first on dismantling residential segregation, rather than attempting to move resources to residentially segregated neighborhoods. Racial integration would enable broader egalitarian political transformation by altering the political environment so as to enable democratic cooperation across race lines, essentially opening up dynamic routes to greater change. In other words, Anderson argues that racial integration is a precondition of the politics of solidarity that Young envisions. In this sense, Young's remedy of differentiated solidarity is a political nonstarter.

This naturally raises the question of who the agent of change is that Anderson thinks might bring about the substantial policy reorientation required to dismantle residential segregation. Although she could be more explicit, her answer appears to be that hope lies with an African American–led social movement that renews the aspiration for integration that (she believes) was central to the civil of rights movement of the 1960s. This is why her extended discussion of the epistemology of social movements occupies center stage in her crowning chapter on democratic theory.[40] In keeping with her Deweyan epistemological conception of democracy as the collective exercise of our practical intelligence to solve social problems, she views social movements as engaged in democratic acts of teaching and learning, under conditions where the epistemological functions of ordinary democratic politics have been disabled by political pathologies. Through targeted disruption of business as usual, collective agents with certain special properties are capable of breaking through the clubby and exclusionary routines that insulate us epistemically and morally from the legitimate claims of others. If such a social movement aimed at racial integration, then targeted gains could be won that would help to undermine the psychological underpinnings of a politics of white resentment, allowing for further egalitarian transformations down the road.

In short, Anderson argues from views about the plausible potential agent to views about what remedies to pursue.[41] Her diagnosis of the problem of racial inequality in the United States has implications for identifying the potential, plausible agents of change, and she uses these implications to support one set of remedies (policies fostering integration) over another set of remedies (policies that directly address inequality). Whatever we think about the merit of Anderson's arguments, they demonstrate vividly that in nonideal theory the problem of the agent of change is tightly connected with the other core tasks of diagnosing a problem and proposing a set of remedies. To diagnose a problem is already to identify various political actors harmed or benefited by, or otherwise implicated in, the perpetuation of an injustice and to specify structural obstacles to the formation of political agents capable of addressing the problem. Views about the plausible potential agent of change can have consequences for what remedies should be pursued to overcome the problem identified. On one understanding of the problem, certain remedies will be political nonstarters owing to facts about feasibility and motivation. Entailments thus run in multiple directions, and these questions must be thought through together.

Given the multiple directions of entailment, one can come at the problem from multiple directions. In some cases, having made a diagnosis, we may work from above, first specifying remedies and only reconsidering our policy recommendations when we find at the end that there is no plausible agent of change. In other cases, having made a diagnosis, we may work upward from the plausible agents of change this diagnosis suggests to a specification of promising remedies. The point is not to mandate one direction of argument or the other, but only to emphasize that the question of the agent is *entangled* with the question of what changes to recommend whatever direction one argues, so that one must think through both together.

Transitional theory thus does not relate to practice by first theorizing a problem and solutions, and then in a "pragmatic" second step casting about for some agent who might act on these proposals in the given circumstances. Since transitional theory aims at action, the conception of the political subject that acts on this theory is internal to the theory. Since transitional theory deals with entrenched injustice that is reproduced as an unjust status quo, and since agency figures in this reproduction in complicated ways, the question of the agent of change is a special problem for nonideal theory. It is not solved merely by having a democratic theory or a doctrine of public reason for a just society, since a just society is not marred in its public discourse and political system by the entrenched practical cleavages produced by doing and suffering injustice. The question of the agent of change is thus an unavoidable and fraught question at the heart of transitional theory.

§4.6: HOW SITUATIONAL IS NONIDEAL THEORY?

We are now in a position to address the first set of questions, about the generality of theory and the particularity of action in a shifting landscape.[42] The philosopher who has done the most to frame the question of the shifting and context-sensitive nature of the problem of the agent of change is Gerald Gaus. He has argued that the sort of feasibility questions involved in the identification of the agent of change and the specification of transformative paths are too variable to serve as the object of theory. It is on this basis that he rejects the dynamic perspective, and so the concept of an end, replacing it with an elaborate formal treatment of these issues.

In setting up his objection, Gaus refers to something he calls "the Orientation Condition." The Orientation Condition tells us that we must be able to make judgments about our proximity to the ideal so that we can orient our practice. His thought is that if nonideal theory does not orient us by allowing such proximity judgments, licensing a change because it brings us closer to the ideal, then Sen is right and a purely comparative approach to justice will suffice, and we will simply be able to compare which situation is more just and move there. Here is what Gaus says about why dynamic feasibility cannot be "the space" in which nonideal theory orients us to the ideal:

I think it is quite clear that, while recent work in political theory has focused on feasibility as central to the "ideal / nonideal debate," it is not an appropriate metric by which to satisfy the Orientation Condition. Notice that feasibility is indexed to agents, time spans, and contexts. Thus outcome O may be feasible for Alf at time t_1 in circumstances C_1, but not at time t_2, but might be again feasible at t_3, though now the circumstances have changed. Perhaps it was feasible for Betty only at t_2 in circumstances C_2. For a theory of the ideal to specify a plausible feasibility space to orient our quest for justice, it would have to specify not only the agent (for example, feasibility could be defined in terms of the US Congress, the American people, Western society), but a time period. Suppose then a theory specifies Z as "any time within the next decade" and X = "US Congress and president." So only things that are feasible throughout the entire decade for the American Congress and president are in the feasibility space. But again, even this claim must be indexed to time.[43]

For these reasons, Gaus recommends an approach that is not centered on feasibility. Gaus also rejects feasibility for the additional reason that it fails to satisfy various formal desiderata that allow for modeling a space.[44] For example, Gaus imposes a constraint on "proximity" such that for any two points i and j, the distance between i and j is the same as the distance between j and i. Dynamic feasibility does not work this way, since it may be very easy to move from point i to j but impossible to go directly from j to i. So j will be very close to i, but i will be very far from j. (Transitivity is another such property that often fails to hold with dynamic feasibility.)

Instead of feasibility, Gaus asks us to consider proximity to the ideal in terms of structural resemblance to what he calls its "justice-relevant features," such as institutional arrangements and policies. First, we are to consider the institutions and policies that would ideally realize the principles of justice in a society characterized by strict compliance. Then we are to construct a space of societies that structurally resemble the just society to greater or lesser extents by strictly complying with some of the institutions and policies that characterize the ideal. Of course, the degree of justice can vary independently from how closely the institutions resemble the ideal, since sometimes removing a single crucial feature can diverge from ideal arrangements and introduce great injustice, and thus a less proximate alternative might be more just. While Gaus admits that the feasibility of moving to at least some of these options plays a background role of giving the investigation relevance, it is not included in the representation of the space, which instead tracks only (1) the justice score of the strict compliance with the institutions and (2) the resemblance score, where the metric is institutional resemblance to the ideal.

We have seen enough to know that Gaus's preferred approach is highly problematic. First of all, our discussion in §3.3 already showed that the purely comparative method is to be rejected and that there is an essential role for the ideal in allowing us to make the noncomparative judgments that are the basis of a significant portion of our thought about justice. Furthermore, we have seen that in addition to a dynamic orientation to an end, other modes of immanent guidance apply that also depend on noncomparative judgments about justice, including understanding values, theorizing modes of resistance, and showing the intrinsic significance of justice in struggle. In short, there are grounds to reject comparativism even if we are unable to satisfy Gaus's orientation condition.

Gaus's space also uses strict compliance (about institutional and policy principles) to map the space of possibilities. In other words, his view employs the compliance conception, combining it with Sen's comparativist presuppositions. To evaluate this aspect of his proposal, we must explore the compliance conception, which I will turn to in Chapter 5.

But, setting aside his positive view for now, let us consider Gaus's objections to using thoughts about feasibility to structure our theoretical orientation to the ideal by starting with his complaint about the formal properties of feasibility. He is certainly right about "distance" when it is conceived as movement toward an end. Indeed, it would be shocking if the dynamic feasibility relations represented by the teleological conception displayed symmetry or transitivity, since practical reasoning usually does not possess either of these features. When we choose to go one way in pursuit of an end, we necessarily foreclose other routes, and it is often impossible to return to a situation that corresponds to the original point of choice. At that point, we have committed, and the ship has sailed, so to speak. Similar remarks apply about transitivity, as he rightly observes. But this is a case where I am happy to say: so much the worse for Gaus's formalism. His theoretical strictures are at odds with the structure of practical reasoning about justice.

What is more serious for our inquiry are the concerns he raises about the context-dependence of feasibility. Gaus makes a point I have emphasized in this chapter—namely, that the availability of routes of change will depend on which agent we specify. He seems to view this as a dizzying and disorienting feature that ruins the possibility of any stable general theory. I have, however, been arguing that the identification of agency is inextricably bound up with the other core tasks of nonideal theory. Arriving at a stance about this is indispensable for political orientation in the face of injustice. But let us ask: How variable is this feature? In particular, is it too variable for us to theorize about it in nonideal theory, as Gaus seems to think?

Nothing a priori can be said here: it all depends on our analysis of the cases. But it is important to note that nonideal theory is usually concerned with abiding injustices that function as an unjust status quo reproduced stably across significant periods of time. While modes of social reproduction do evolve, transforming along various trajectories, they usually have enough stability to characterize them in illuminating ways.[45] For example, we can characterize in stable ways the contributions of the agency of different actors to the problems, specify who is affected in what way—who is harmed and benefited—and characterize the way the problem is taken up or not taken up in our political system. Some problems may evolve too quickly for us to understand them before they have already transformed, but many structural problems are not like this.

Since transitional theory concerns the response to injustice, it is no surprise that transitional theory must change to keep pace with developments in the evolution of injustice. As a phenomenon changes, the theory of the phenomenon must change along with it. But this hardly seems like a reason to give up on theory. Philosophers are helped tremendously by the fact that injustice, in virtue of status as a practical problem, draws the attention of a wide range of theorists, including historians, political scientists, sociologists, and economists. Furthermore, since it is a practical problem, political actors oppose injustice, develop their own analyses, and experiment with strategies of resistance and institutional changes. By drawing on these resources, philosophy can engage productively with present realities and changing circumstances.

§4.7: THE SUBJECT OF THEORY AND PRACTICE

If the agent of change is a necessary question for political philosophy, so, too, is the relationship of the philosopher to the agent of change. According to the teleological conception, the theory of justice is an exercise of practical reason. Ideal theory articulates the end of a just society toward which practice is oriented, and nonideal theory deploys this end both dynamically and immanently in the analysis of injustice and proposals about how to overcome it. As an exercise of practical reason, nonideal theory issues in practical proposals intended as a contribution to deliberation that ultimately issues in action. Furthermore, we have just seen that in nonideal theory the identification of the practical subject of such deliberation is an indispensable topic. As a matter of theory, we must come to view proposed changes as standing in a special relationship to a determinate agent who is or might come to be positioned to intentionally and voluntarily bring them about. This presupposes some conception of the proper relationship of the activity of the philosopher to the agent in question. I have allowed myself to follow linguistic usage of philosophers such as Miller and Rawls who speak of such philosophy as "addressed" to agents. I must now explain what this means.[46]

Speaking about who is "addressed by" or "the audience of" some bit of theory is, on the face of it, a mysterious way of talking that requires philosophical elucidation. Would it be flat-footed to observe that Rawls's lectures on political philosophy were literally addressed to the Harvard students who were in the most obvious sense the audience of those lectures? When his lectures were later published for a broader readership, wasn't his "audience" in the most literal sense the readership of this book? What can it mean to say that some other group (for example, "citizens in general") is the "practical addressee" of these works, to use Miller's phrase? Of course, we are interested in this question not as it figures in Rawls's and Miller's problematic discussion, but in relation to the agent of change as the "practical addressee" of transitional theorizing.

To answer this question, let's start with the appropriate attitude of the theorist of injustice to the injustice so theorized. What our analysis thus far suggests is that the political philosopher is not a neutral knower who stands above the political fray offering expert guidance to an unspecified or universal subject. This picture is at odds with the very idea of transitional theory, which is nonneutral in two ways that often overlap, but can be conceptually separated. As we have seen, injustice already divides people into those who are wronged and those who wrong. In practically opposing injustice, the nonideal theorist takes up the side of the wronged. In the asymmetric relation of doing and suffering injustice, their practical effort is on behalf of the one suffering.

In addition, the account will specify the way in which the injustice is reproduced in part through the organized practical activity of those who perpetrate the injustice, or benefit from it, or hold some other kind of stake in the issue. The theory will also specify an agent of change who is or might come to be in a position to effectuate a change that would in some way address the injustice in the face of the organized defense of the status quo. So the second sense in which transitional theory is written from a nonneutral perspective is that it issues in proposals for deliberation for an agent of change who is or will come to be in struggle against other agents. In the meaning of the term connected with justice, solidarity is the attitude of those who join others in a shared struggle against injustice. Since nonideal theory is practical activity that is intended to join in such struggle, its work is the work of solidarity. Again, this characterization flows from our account of the practical role of transitional theory. As mentioned, these two senses will usually coincide at least in part, because the agent of change usually includes those who are wronged on grounds of motivation and normative appropriateness.

A plausible agent of change is one for whom intentionally bringing about change is feasible and who, realistically, might come to do so willingly. The crucial point is that in virtue of being identified as the agent of change by transitional theory, this agent stands in a special practical relation to the theory that other agents do not. Transitional theory picks out this agent as the one to act intentionally, and so knowingly, to bring about the changes specified. For this to be possible, the agent must come to know about the change as a possible course of action and see it as choiceworthy in the struggle against injustice. Transitional theory thus presupposes the possibility of communication between the philosopher and the agent of change with whom they stand in solidarity. For if transitional theory is to be practical, then its recommendations must be made available to the agent of change it identifies for the purposes of that agent's deliberation and action.

The agent of change is "the practical addressee" of transitional theory because transitional theory picks out the agent as the one to act on the basis of this theory. To say that the agent of change is the practical addressee of the theory is to say that the agent, uniquely among all possible theory consumers, stands in a relation of proposed practical uptake to the theory. Whomever the theorist is literally speaking to, the agent of change stands in a special, practical communicative relation to the theory.

We are now at last in a position to answer our second question, about the potential gap between the nonideal theorist and the subject of practical reasoning. Our question was how transitional theory can be for the sake of action if the one who theorizes, the philosopher, is different from the one who acts, the agent of change. This gap between theorist and agent is to be bridged by deliberative communication offered in solidarity from the theorist to the practical subject as a potential contribution to the practical subject's reasoning in the struggle against injustice.

In this communicative relation, it is of vital importance that the agent of change consists of individuals who possess an engaged sense of justice (§2.4) and so are already political thinkers and actors. For theory raises to systematic self-consciousness piecemeal and fragmentary knowledge that already operates in practice. Members of potential agents of change are already political knowers before they ever come to theory. In addition, contestation about injustice is always underway in some form, and it is likely this struggle that made the injustice salient, putting it on the agenda for theorists as a practical problem in the first place. Some among the potential agent of change are thus likely already involved in contestation around the issue that the nonideal theorist addresses. As engaged in struggle, they often possess much practical knowledge, of necessity having become theorists to some extent, engaging in the identification and diagnosis of injustice, formulating utopian hopes, making judgments about the severity of different wrongs and what forms of resistance are justified, and reasoning about possible remedies. They are also likely to be attuned to the practical landscape of shifting opportunity structures that flies below the general radar of theory.

Additionally, as we have seen, plausible agents of change usually include those who suffer injustice for epistemic, motivational, and normative reasons. Such individuals have experience with the relevant injustice, knowing through their own experience the harm it produces, and are often less susceptible to ideologies that downplay the extent of the harm and distort our understanding of the injustice. They possess a great deal of knowledge through their experience and position in the system, and they are perhaps less susceptible than others to certain ideological deformations. As a result, the nonideal theorist does not typically stand to the agent of change as one who knows and seeks to educate those who are ignorant. Knowledge does not flow primarily in one direction, and so the case of communicating knowledge is not pedagogical, from a teacher to a student, but usually rather dialogical, where each brings to the table different epistemic and practical resources.

In this relation of sharing, it is all too easy for the theorist to reproduce aspects of epistemic injustice, manifesting injustice in the struggle against injustice in an epistemic guise. For example, the philosopher can discount the views, insights, and contributions of marginalized and oppressed members of the agent of change, especially when the philosopher operates from a position of privilege.

To the extent that philosophers think of themselves as superior to the members of the agents of change, they may reenact hierarchical, subordinating, and demeaning relations in their attempt to share their knowledge and practical proposals. Due caution and a dose of humility are necessary here, as well as an understanding of the potential distorting effects that occupying a privileged position can produce on one's perceptions of, and interactions with, the less privileged.

A bitter irony—and maybe also an aspect of injustice—lies in the fact that the academic nature of political philosophy itself serves as an obstacle to philosophers allying themselves with agents of change. By dividing intellectual labor from practical activity and allocating it to specialists in academic and sometimes elite institutions of higher learning, academia divides the philosopher from many agents of change, especially where such agents suffer from serious injustice and oppression that have precluded access to the benefits of higher learning. Of course, the structure of the academy makes it difficult in a different way to pursue what is conceived as an unrewarded "extracurricular" activity. Thus, the very conditions of work that support nonideal theorizing can also function as obstacles to its practical role.

Another pitfall of such communication arises from the posture of uncritical moralism into which political philosophers sometimes sadly fall. Although critical thinking about injustice is essential to transitional theory, it is usually not helpful to think of the political philosopher as calling the political community to righteousness, or as exhorting the wicked, since, as we have seen, the agent of change is often neither citizens in general nor agents of injustice in particular. Furthermore, as we have seen, when the agent of change includes the oppressed and changes that would ameliorate injustice come with high costs to those who are already burdened, it will sometimes be the case that proposals made in nonideal theory will be permissible but not required courses of action for the agent of change. It thus cannot be said in general that the political philosopher relates to change by specifying what some agent must do from the perspective of justice. Instead of either neutral technocratic expertise or moralizing about justice, I would suggest, nonideal theory should in general be viewed as issuing in actionable proposals for further deliberation to be shared with the agent of change who will consider them in the first person (plural) in their practical reasoning.

Nothing general can be said about the form in which such proposals for deliberation are best shared. Depending on the nature of the injustice and the agent of change, different forms of intellectual sharing are feasible. In some cases, the nonideal theorist is part of the agent of change and may participate in the deliberation as part of the practical subject of the deliberation. This will be the case when the agent of change includes philosophers among its ranks, in official or unofficial capacities. In other cases, the agent of change might draw on the work of political philosophers by inviting them to speak or by reading their materials. In other cases, a political philosopher makes work available to agents of change indirectly by releasing it into a public sphere from which the relevant agents may draw in a variety of capacities. There is also teaching through formal institutions, including universities, colleges, high schools, and prisons, where the sharing of knowledge and collective reasoning takes place. It all depends on the nature of the agent of change and the background institutions that exist for the dissemination of knowledge and collective deliberation.

Desire to have one's work considered by an agent of change is not something extrinsic to transitional theory. It is not as though the political philosopher also happens to have a side interest in such things—a side interest that is understandable but by no means necessary—arising from the same bent of character that got her interested in "pressing and urgent" matters to begin with. Such an aspiration rather arises directly from the self-understanding of transitional theory as practical intellectual work in opposition to existing injustice. Philosophy about the pressing and urgent matters is practically engaged philosophy, philosophy addressed to a practical subject in its struggle to remedy injustice. For transitional theory to become the praxis at which it aims, it must be shared with the agents who might act on it. The desire to engage in politics, in the broad sense, with one's political philosophy, is not something that dirties or cheapens philosophy. It does not lead away from philosophy into some different arena. It is rather the realization of the purpose intrinsic to the theory of justice. It is only when theory is taken up in practice that the aims of theory have been achieved. The theory of justice in an unjust society is actualized—and so exists in the fullest sense—in and through the struggle with injustice by agents of change. Theory is complete only when it reaches all the way to action.

Against Strict Compliance

§5.1: PUTTING STRICT COMPLIANCE IN ITS PLACE?

If Chapters 2–4 defended the teleological conception of the theory of justice, what about the compliance conception, the rival identified in Chapter 1? Supposing we accept the teleological conception, how, then, do considerations about compliance come into the division of the theory of justice? As we have seen, Rawls justifies the idealization of strict compliance on the grounds that the principles of justice characterize what it is for citizens to view and treat one another as free equals and to order their institutions accordingly. But, Rawls argues, under strict compliance, citizens so view and treat one another, living up to their commitments. By contrast, to the extent that they fail to comply, they fail to adopt this viewpoint and fail to live up to it in their shared practical life. They thus fail to embody the principles of justice. So if we want to identify the principles of justice by using a procedure of construction like his original position, we should consider what principles representatives would choose on the assumption that individuals and institutions strictly comply with the principles of justice.

The same practical critics who reject the priority of ideal theory have also found this use of idealization objectionable and urge us to reject the project of ideal theory on this ground as well.[1] All these authors think that the principles of justice should take account of the propensity and actuality of the disposition to commit injustice. In Chapter 2, I worked to defuse some of the worries of these very same critics in order to defend the division of the theory of justice along the lines of the teleological conception, whereas in this chapter, I join their cause by arguing that strict compliance is an inappropriate blanket assumption even on a constitutivist account of the principles of justice. Of course, this common cause is limited, since I issue this criticism with a view to defending the teleological conception, including the priority of ideal theory when it is understood in the terms proposed in Chapters 2–4, which, as we have seen, the practicalists view themselves as rejecting. This failure to distinguish the strict compliance conception from the teleological conception is one area where the critics have inherited Rawls's own confusions.[2]

§5.2: THE APPEAL OF STRICT COMPLIANCE

The genuine appeal of strict compliance derives from a powerful and basic distinction in practical philosophy.[3] This is the contrast between internal and external principles or norms. This contrast will be central to the argument to follow. As a first pass, we could say that a principle for Xs is internal if it serves as a standard or measure for Xs that holds in virtue of their being Xs. The idea is that given the kind of thing that X is, there are standards that specify a proper or nondefective X. The standards in question will be part of the account of what it is to be an X insofar as being an X already contains a measure for being a proper or nondefective X. An external principle, by contrast, is one that applies to Xs in virtue of something other than being X. It is a standard to which something is subject that has its source outside the nature of that thing. An account of Xs will not refer to this standard, for it does not serve as a measure that applies to being a proper X.

Let us take a pair of cases to illustrate this distinction, beginning with one from the domain of what Philippa Foot calls "natural goodness." For example, human vision provides information about the color of the objects in a human being's environment. This is one of the things that human vision does qua human vision. A human visual system that does not provide the relevant information about color—say, through the inability to distinguish red from green—is a visual system that is not fully operating as a human visual system, failing to perform one of human vision's functions. By the same token, good vision is vision that, among other things, provides the relevant color information. To describe the principles of the operation of human vision is already to describe good human vision, for good vision is precisely vision that possesses the qualities that a human visual system possesses qua human visual system.

An external norm by contrast is one that applies to things of a given kind not on the basis of what they are, but using some external standard or metric. For example, I might judge a visual system that cannot distinguish red from green good on the grounds that it will allow me to pass off counterfeit money more easily. (Perhaps my high-end inkjet printer leaves a reddish sheen here and there on otherwise flawless counterfeits.) Here my judgment makes reference not to a standard internal to the operation of vision, but rather to the needs of my scheme. When I judge the visual system to be good, I use as my measure of goodness not the operations characteristic of vision but rather the necessities for carrying off my plan. There is thus an external standard that is brought to bear on human visual systems, a standard that arises not from the features of the things to which it applies, but rather from a source that is distinct.

Rawls remarks, in the context of his famous critique of utilitarianism as ignoring the separateness of persons, that "the correct regulative principles for anything depend on the nature of that thing."[4] When he says this, he is apparently thinking of internal norms. For external norms do not, in the first instance, depend on the nature of the things to which they apply, since they apply to those things not in virtue of what those things are, but in virtue of something else. Similarly, when Rousseau begins his discourse on inequality with an epigraph drawn from Aristotle's *Politics*, "We should consider what is natural not in things which are depraved but in those which are rightly ordered according to nature," the form of depravity of which he speaks is clearly failure to fulfill internal norms.[5] For someone who perceives the difference between red and green clearly is wrongly ordered according to the dictates of my scam, but would be an excellent candidate for the study of the operation of the human visual system as a part of "rightly ordered" human anatomy.

A constitutivist defense of principles of justice is a defense of these principles as internal rather than external principles. This is what it means to say that the principles are constitutive of some form of community: they are internal measures that specify what it is for a community of that sort to live up to the standards that apply by virtue of being such a community. The best argument for strict compliance as an assumption in a constructivist program like Rawls's appeals to this constitutivist idea. Wherever we have an internal principle governing an X, that principle will describe what it is for an X to be as it belongs to Xs to be qua Xs. To the extent that an X departs from this, the X fails to embody the relevant principle.

On a constitutivist account of the principles of justice like Rawls's, we treat the principles of justice as specifying the proper relationship between free and equal citizens. By specifying this proper relation, they articulate an ideal of a community of individuals who stand to one another in such proper relationships. For this reason, we must treat deviations from this ideal as we would treat color blindness in account of the functioning of the human organism, as a privation or defect that diverges from citizens' relation as free equals in one society. On this view, injustice is, at bottom, a defect in the relationship of free equals. To the extent that they wrong one another, either through their conduct or through their institutions, citizens depart from the ideal articulated by the principles of justice and so fail to relate to one another as free equals.

When accounting for the principles of justice, we must begin with what it is for individuals to get things right, for them to live up to the ideals of free and equal membership, treating one another accordingly and realizing these relationships through their shared institutions. The principles of justice describe what it is for citizens to interact in this way. The argument for the idealization of strict compliance thus hinges on the claim that the issues raised by being wronged are irrelevant to characterizing the relation of free equals, and so to the principles of justice that articulate this relation. But are they really?

§5.3: THE CASE AGAINST STRICT COMPLIANCE

As long as we're working with anatomical analogies, here's another one to introduce the doubt I intend to foster. An understanding of the health of the human organism might plausibly be said to depend on an understanding of its sound anatomy and biological functioning.[6] If we were willing to speak about "the principles of health" for an organic system, we might say that these principles describe the general functioning of a body insofar as it is healthy. Now imagine a philosopher who tries to infer from this that any mention of illness is out of place in an account of health. Sickness, she reasons, is precisely a departure from health. To the extent that the body is sick, it fails to evince the character of healthy functioning that the principles are intended to capture. So when we describe the principles of health, we must prescind from discussion of the phenomena connected with illness.

We might point out in reply that part of being healthy is having a well-functioning immune system. One's immune system functions well if it has effective ways of protecting from illness, and when illness occurs, of responding to it in such a way as to return one to health. The immune system is a crucial part of human anatomy. Given the ubiquity of pathogens in the environment of a terrestrial organism, the health of terrestrial beings depends on the defense of the body from illness. The immune system is an ordinary part of human anatomy that would be covered in any treatise on human anatomy; in this way, it resembles color vision rather than color blindness. Furthermore, its breakdown is just as fatal to the organism as heart failure or cerebral hemorrhaging. But—and here is the crucial point—to represent the sound operation of the immune system, one must represent the body as both under threat from and succumbing to pathogens. For the healthy immune system functions both to prevent illness and combat it when it arises. In other words, to represent a central aspect of human health, one must depart from assumptions about strict compliance with health. Part of the health of a healthy body is how it responds to sickness.

This suggests an unacknowledged limitation of the constitutivist argument we have sketched. When we provide a constitutivist account of the principles in some subject that govern the prophylaxis against, and rectification of, failures of standard operation, then it will be appropriate to appeal to such deviations in our constitutivist account of the relevant principles. In other words, to say what the ideal is for the subject, we will have to mention such deviations. And when this aspect of the subject is an essential part of its ordinary operation, as the immune system is in the anatomy of human beings, then deviation from the norm, both as looming threats and as realized possibilities, will enter into accounts of the proper functioning of the subject in question.

This analogy suggests a corresponding diagnosis of error in the Rawlsian argument for strict compliance, and correspondingly simple constitutivist explanation of how justice might involve the response to injustice. If the free and equal citizens of a political community stand under temptation to wrong one another, then an account of their sound relations must mention justifiable ways of forestalling such injustice and rectifying it once it arises. But, of course, the whole topic of "the justifiable response to injustice" only shows up if one considers the propensity to injustice in one's account of justice. If we are trying to arrive at the principles of justice specifying the relationship of free equals, we will have to depart from the idealization of strict compliance to capture the relevant aspect of this relationship. This suggests that the assumption of strict compliance might be out of place even in the account of some central dimensions of the relationship of free and equal citizens. If justice describes the norms appropriate to relations of free equals vis-à-vis their shared institutions, then part of the norms will govern handling injustices when they arise. Part of the justice of a just society is how it responds to injustice.

Analogizing the polity to a body, and justice to health, has been put to dubious uses in the history of political thought. Sinister resonances aside, I also wouldn't want to rest the weight of my argument on an analogy. So I will offer a direct argument against strict compliance on constitutivist grounds.

There are special reasons for thinking that justice, of all things, must take account of violations of our duties of justice. These special reasons flow from marks of the concept of justice we had occasion to register in §1.2. As I argued there, drawing on recent writings about second-personal duties in general, justice is an essentially relational phenomenon. Justice involves claims that we can justifiably make on one another, often (although not always) to order our shared institutions. This relational character is dramatized in the primal scene of Rawlsian theory, where a person occupying one representative position calls on another occupying a different representative position to justify the inequality between them. Furthermore, claims about justice have an immediate practical upshot. Those to whom we owe duties of justice typically have standing to hold us to their fulfillment, and so it is to them that we owe accounting for our conduct.[7] Indeed, a common theme of justice is that the wronged need not patiently await the dawning of scruples in their wrongdoers; they are authorized to take an active stance of opposition to the failure to fulfill the obligations. Such righteous opposition takes varied forms in diverse contexts, but justified resistance is central to duties of justice. This also explains the unusual relation that many have (rightly) thought holds between duties of justice and the possibility of justified coercion. Finally, it grounds the internal connection many thinkers have asserted between rights and enforcement.

But, of course, all these topics—of resistance to wrongdoing, of compelling people to fulfill their obligations, and of enforcing rights—make essential reference to wrongdoing, potential or actual. There is thus a special concern that justice involves for responses to injustice that is internal to our understanding of its relational and demanding character and that sets it apart from the other branches of morality.[8] This suggests that a full characterization of relations of justice will require reference to the possibility of wrongdoing and justifiable responses to it. One will not have accounted for essential features of the rights we possess, and the duties of justice we are under, until the response to injustice they license has been brought into view. In short, free and equal citizens will have many claims on one another to order their shared institutions so as to be able to respond to injustice in principled ways that can be justified to all the relevant parties. Thus, to characterize the relationship of free and equal citizens, one must address the response to wrongdoing. Such a response is neither "accidental" to the operation of justice nor a departure from it, but rather part of its core account. It is part of what makes justice what it is.

For illustrative purposes, let us focus on a particular right: the right against assault. It should be uncontroversial that this right authorizes one to put others under a duty to desist from physically harming one's person, a duty that will normally be in effect, absent waiving the right (as we might in a case of elective cosmetic surgery or a boxing match). We will have described this dimension of the right if we simply specify the forms of conduct that are required and forbidden by it. To do so is, of course, to describe modes of conduct that strictly comply with the principles of justice. It is to say how people should comport themselves with respect to physically harming one another so as not to wrong one another.

But let us now ask whether we have exhausted the content of the right against assault in specifying what it would be to fulfill the duties correlative to this right. The intuitive answer would seem to be no. To stop here would omit many essential dimensions of this right—dimensions that differentiate the correlative duties in crucial ways from other moral duties. Start with the way in which the right against assault licenses the individual whose right it is to resist forms of assault on her person. One distinctive dimension of the right against assault is that it licenses defensive action intended to disrupt the violations of the duty correlative to this right, up to and including action that harms the assailant, at least in cases where other recourse (such as flight) is unavailable. To say that the right against assault authorizes defensive action in cases of assault is to say that the right against assault is, among other things, a right of self-defense. When I defend myself from assault, the right to which I appeal for authorization is the right against assault.

This explains why when I lose the right against assault, I also lose the authorization to defend myself from assault. For example, suppose I assault someone else, and that person acts defensively in ways that will foreseeably harm my person. I do not thereby acquire the right to defend myself against my victim's defensive actions. When I assault someone, I forfeit the protection against being physically harmed insofar as such physical harm is necessary in order to deter my wrongful action. The content of my right is altered by my wrongful action so that it no longer covers the necessary defensive actions of my victim. Since I no longer have the right against the victim's necessary harming actions, I can longer appeal to this right to authorize my self-defense. So the right against assault also involves an authorization to act in self-defense when that right is violated.

But let us turn to the more explicitly political manifestations of this right. The right against assault is a political right. For example, it is one of the liberties protected by Rawls's first principle and a core right protected by theories opposed to Rawls's. What does this mean? Presumably, that the right against assault is the ground of claims a citizen has on their fellow citizens to order their shared institutions in certain ways. For example, our right against being assaulted is the ground of our claims on the state to protect us against assault. This includes the claim on our political institutions to provide incentives to deter those who might otherwise be inclined to assault us. It also includes our claim to have assaults against our person investigated once they have occurred and to have some form of justice prevail.[9] Thus, one of the ways that I can be wronged by my political institutions is when assaults against my person are not taken seriously and afforded adequate and equal protection by the law. In short, the right against assault is one of the rights that justify our claims to equal protection by the law. It also justifies claims of restitution of the sort that are codified in either regimes of private law or processes of restorative justice.[10]

To say that the right against assault is a political right, on a constitutivist view like Rawls's, is to say that it is an aspect of the relations of free and equal citizens. But it is also to say that it is a ground of claims that citizens have on their fellow citizens to structure their shared institutions in ways like the ones we have just canvassed, ways that protect individuals against violations of this right and rectify them once they have occurred, to the extent that this is possible. If this is correct, then the right to self-defense, and equal protection against assault, is itself part of the relation of free equals. To specify the right against assault, one must discuss this. And insofar as the relations of free and equal citizens involve this right, this is part of what one must talk about in specifying the appropriate norms governing that relation.

But the assumption of strict compliance puts all of this out of bounds, setting it aside as irrelevant to the specification of the relationship between free and equal citizens. Meditate for just a moment on how strange this assertion is. It amounts to insisting that, strictly speaking, the right against assault is only a claim to a pattern of behavior that involves not being assaulted. It is not a right to defend oneself against assault, or to be protected by the apparatus of government against assault, or to have incentives put in place that will forestall assault, or to have assaults investigated or to rectification after the fact. It says only how well-meaning people will treat one another when nothing goes wrong. This is a strange conception of the content of our political right against being assaulted. Yet it is entailed by the view that strict compliance is the correct assumption for the purposes of specifying the relationship of free equals and so, too, the content of justice.

This point generalizes, since the authorization to hinder violations of the duties of justice is part of the content of the relevant duties and part of what sets them apart from other moral duties. Strict compliance takes consideration of essential aspects of justice off the table and thereby prevents us from theorizing crucial dimensions of the justice of a just society. Given the demanding and relational nature of justice, constitutivists should not employ the blanket idealization of strict compliance in articulating and defending principles of justice. It assimilates claims of justice to those of beneficence and friendship and so fails to capture their character as justice. A more discriminating approach is required.

§5.4: JUSTICE WITH IMPERFECTION

But perhaps we are moving too fast. For we just distinguished what we might think of as different "moments" in an unfolding series of claims of justice, starting with the behavior required from other

individuals and then moving to claims to enforcement and protection of various kinds. This is an ordered sequence in that we cannot
comprehend enforcement until we know what we are enforcing. It
is tempting to infer that the later moments of enforcement are dependent on a fully intelligible "first moment" of claims that must
have been violated before the "prophylactic" or "corrective" principles can even kick in. It is thus tempting to think that this first
moment is the primary one—the most fundamental or basic sort of
justice, justice in the first and proper sense. It is this fully intelligible, self-standing first moment that explains the later moments
that are, after all, "unfolded" from it.

Something close to this line of thought is elegantly expressed by
David Estlund, whose positive view we will engage at length in
Chapter 6. At the risk of getting ahead of ourselves a little, here is
how Estlund makes the point:

> Justice, sometimes, is a way in which things can be right
> even though things have gone wrong. It is just, and in
> that way right, for the thief to compensate the victim, or
> maybe even to be punished. . . . This aspect of justice,
> that it can be a virtue in a context of vice, is sufficiently
> striking that, at least in the case of social justice, it is
> sometimes thought to be of its essence. I think this is a
> mistake, and that recognizing the mistake leads us to the
> unfamiliar idea of justice for morally flawless people. In
> turn, we will see that this initially frivolous-sounding
> topic exposes something important about the structure of
> moral normativity more generally, namely, the primacy
> of non-concessive standards—standards of right that are
> not occasioned by wrong.[11]

Estlund supports the primacy of what he calls "non-concessive"
standards by arguing that the requirements that arise from "concessive" standards do not apply ("evaporate") in contexts where

the nonconcessive standards are met, while the opposite does not hold. Furthermore, it is not only that the concessive standards seem to hold in all and only those cases where the nonconcessive standards are not met, but also that they hold *in virtue of* the failure of the nonconcessive standards. It is *because* (legitimate) property claims have been crossed that the owner of the stolen goods has a claim on the thief to restitution. There is thus a one-way relation of explanatory dependence that shows that the bottom strata of nonconcessive standards is what he calls, in a provocative phrase, "prime justice."[12]

Furthermore, Estlund argues that once we depart from this fundamental nonconcessive level, there is no principled place to stop. He encourages us to ask where we are to set the level of noncompliance for the purposes of specifying the principles of justice. There is a principled distinction between compliance (full stop) and noncompliance, but surely there is not a principled distinction between different levels of noncompliance. Thus, if we wish to develop an account of the principles of justice, we will have no principled background of assumption about compliance unless we choose the first point of full compliance. Anything else is arbitrary.

The problem with the idea that nonconcessive justice is fundamental is that you cannot understand the sort of claims in which justice consists, even in the allegedly primary nonconcessive moment, without bringing in the response to wrongdoing. The community of free equals is a community of individuals who have the standing to place one another under stringent requirements in their external actions and shared institutions and to hold one another to their fulfillment. The claims the members of this community place on one another are pregnant with the necessitation that flows from their enforcement. This is, in part, what sets them apart from other claims of morality, including the claims of kindness and generosity, and those of friendship. To view the relevant claims without understanding them as containing an implicit authorization to resist wrongdoing is to view them as something less than and different from claims of justice. For in that case, they are not issued as valid claims that individuals have the standing to hold one another to fulfill.

Nor is it clear that I can view you as a free equal in the relevant sense, without understanding your claims as the source of valid enforcement. To be a free equal is to have a standing that necessitates others to respect one's rights and claims. To restrict ourselves to considering the fulfillment of duties by scrupulous and well-meaning individuals is to elide the difference between what behavior is morally right and what behavior I can hold another to as a matter of justice. To view another as a free equal is not only to view them as someone whom I must, as a matter of morality, treat decently. For this might be true of someone who is my unfree inferior with no authority to complain or resist if I treat them shabbily, or in a community, like Joel Feinberg's imaginary "Nowheresville," where none had the conception of themselves or the others as free equals.[13] To view someone as a free equal is also to view the person as someone both who compels me to better behavior as my equal and to whom I am accountable for my wrongdoing.

Supposing this is right, what about Estlund's challenge about how much noncompliance to assume? This is an important question, and it leads deeper into our present topic. To identify a principle of justice is to say what valid claims we have on one another. To say what justice requires is to say how things stand when our claims on one another have been fulfilled. But given the kind of claims to which justice gives rise, to specify them requires developing the various rights of resistance, enforcement, and rectification to which these claims give rise. One way to express this view is to say that these things come as a package or, perhaps better, as unfolding moments in a single account. To theorize a dimension of justice adequately, one must think these moments through to completion.

This is not to say, of course, that we cannot draw distinctions between the moments, as I plainly did in discussing the right against assault. In the specification of the relevant claims, we can sometimes distinguish the treatment required by the right (that is, not assaulting one another; the first moment) and the various aspects of prophylaxis, resistance, rectification, and enforcement that arise from this requirement in light of the possibility of violations (later moments). Furthermore, Estlund is right that in virtue of the fact that the treatment required by the right fails to be forthcoming, or threatens to fail to be forthcoming, enforcement is justified as an authorization that flows from the original claim. Even when one can distinguish a first nonconcessive moment, as was the case with assault, it is the sequence of moments that specify right relations between free equals. The very same claim against assault gives rise to the duty not to assault, and also to the various further claims of deterrence (in light of possible future assault) and resistance (in light of actual present assault), as well as reparation (in light of past assault). To think through a principle is to unfold the consequences of the valid claims that it articulates through these further moments of development. Such further authorizations are part of the essence of justice, explaining as they do the normative force of the original claim.

When we develop a set of claims from a first moment to later moments, there are three possible relations that modes of prophylaxis, enforcement, and rectification can stand in to the original claims. (I will refer to them all as "modes of enforcement" henceforth as shorthand.) A mode of enforcement might be required as such by the original claim. In that case, the mode of enforcement will be necessary. The failure to recognize as legitimate or embody the mode of enforcement will then be a failure to honor the original claim. By contrast, a mode of enforcement might be incompatible with an underlying claim. In that case, the mode of enforcement will be forbidden absent special exemptions (more on this shortly).

To embody this mode of enforcement will be to fail to uphold the original claims that it is intended to uphold (or other equally important claims). A third possibility is that a mode of enforcement might stand in a contingent relation to a set of claims. For example, it might be required in order to uphold the original claim under some empirically specifiable circumstances, as well as incompatible with the underlying claim (or other claims), and so forbidden under other empirically specifiable circumstances.[14] To think through a set of claims, like the right against assault, it is necessary to see the deontic space of enforcement they limn. This is one way that principles of justice pave the way for concrete institutional thinking: by preparing a space of permissions and requirements to enforce that can be schematized by various empirical facts to arrive at institutional proposals.

As an example of this unfolding of a deontic space of enforcement from an original claim, let us take rights of democratic participation. Democratic theory is a tremendously difficult aspect of the theory of justice, so we can do no more here than touch on a few salient points. Democratic theory must be developed in tandem with a view about the authority of the political community to legislate. When we articulate and defend principles of justice ascribing rights of democratic participation to citizens, we will do so, first of all, in the context of a view about the rule of law. To articulate rights of democratic participation is, among other things, to hold a view about how enforceable laws should be legislated.

Whether a mode of enforcement having to do with democratic theory is a matter of basic right or a matter of context-dependent institutional principle will depend on our substantive theory of justice. For example, some defend a process of judicial review of legislation by a body responsible for safeguarding our fundamental rights as necessary for the rule of law and, indeed, for the claims of democratic participation to be satisfied.[15] Something like judicial review is, on this view, part of the constitutive framework of enforcement, prophylaxis, and rectification necessary for democratic decision-making to have legitimacy. Others argue that judicial review is compatible with rights of democratic participation in some context but not others, being a form of prophylaxis against, and rectification of, injustice that justice allows when it is necessary or likely to be efficacious under determinate sociological and historical conditions. An institution with the shape of judicial review is not per se incompatible with the rights of democratic participation and the rule of law, but nor is it entailed by them, except under certain special conditions. Still others argue that judicial review traduces on the rights of democratic participation and is incompatible with the aspect of justice pertaining to democratic equality.[16] Judicial review might still be justified under some circumstances, but the circumstances will be such that democratic justice is out of reach for the moment and, from the point of view of justice, not having a process of judicial review will be worse than having one.

On the first view, our articulation of rights of democratic participation and the rule of law will unfold a mode of enforcement corresponding to judicial review as one necessary constituent of any set of just institutions. On the second view, our articulation of rights of democratic participation and the rule of law will develop judicial review as one permissible element of prophylaxis to be employed in a set of just institutions when certain empirical conditions are met. On the third view, our articulation of rights of democratic participation will exclude judicial review as incompatible with democratic equality between free and equal citizens. Institutions of judicial review will thus be incompatible with the justice of a just society.

The basic point is that we cannot have a democratic theory—understood as a fragment of ideal theory dealing with principles of democratic participation—without answering questions such as these. One cannot understand rights of democratic participation without understanding what elements of enforcement flow (or do not flow) from these rights, either as permissions under certain empirical conditions or as necessary constituents of a democratic society. The principles of justice, including the principles of democratic theory, must and do reach questions like this.

With this in mind, let us now return to Estlund's question about the assumed level of compliance. In one way, the fact that we can make distinctions between different necessary moments in the unfolding of claims into a deontic space of enforcement should lead us to reject Estlund's question about the assumed level of compliance as ill formed. There is not only one role for compliance in the specification of the principles. The profound truth in the constitutivist argument for strict compliance is that there are many such roles. For if we want to say what the pattern of behavior required by well-meaning people is when it comes to assault, we will precisely be asking how people who comply with (part of) the relevant principle behave. When we think about the modes of enforcement that arise in later moments of the articulation of this dimension of justice, we will now be thinking about noncompliance and the claims to enforcement to which (the possibility of) such noncompliance gives rise. Furthermore, these modes of justification may themselves vary with certain facts about noncompliance, with certain modes of enforcement being justified under some conditions and levels of noncompliance, and others being justified under different levels. Thus, there may be no one level of compliance relevant to our thinking this issue through here.

But, of course, to think of a mode of enforcement is to think of a set of further claims in relation to these modes. It follows that in this later moment, where we are considering the response to noncompliance, we are once again thinking of compliance, in this case with respect to the unfolding permissions, requirements, and injunctions involved in these further developments of justice that arise in light of possible or actual noncompliance. How far this process need go in our reflection is a substantive question about justice.

The problem is not that strict compliance is an inappropriate assumption for the specification of principles, but rather that if we view strict compliance as one totalizing assumption, rather than a series of idealizations at different points, in relation (sometimes) to noncompliance, then we cut off the first moment of a claim of justice from its further development and thereby lose a part of its character as a claim of justice. Rawls's monolithic plateau of a uniform strict compliance is better thought of as a differentiated landscape, with separate idealizing assumptions necessary for thinking through different moments in the unfolding of our claims, sometimes in response to noncompliance.

However, there is a sense in which Estlund's question about the nonarbitrary level of compliance is well formed, and I have an answer to it. I stressed in §3.4 that there was need to work with a partition between justice and injustice and so a need to discuss justice simpliciter. Furthermore, I asserted that the concept of justice simpliciter is, ultimately, the concept of a just society treated by realistic utopian theory. I also advanced a nonarbitrary basis for distinguishing realistic utopian theory from transitional theory in the teleological conception of the theory of justice. While a just society may include various modes of enforcement, and so its status may be compatible with a range of noncompliance that these modes operate on, there will be kinds, degrees, and extents of noncompliance that are flatly incompatible with the idea of a just society. This level of noncompliance will place us in transitional rather than realistic utopian theory, and such noncompliance will be something to be overcome in the pursuit of the end of a just society.

To provide an account of justice simpliciter is to locate this dividing line. While one cannot concretely specify the dividing line absent a substantive theory of justice, one can say in advance that the nonarbitrary level of noncompliance will be incompatible with the idea of a just society understood as an end for practice. It will be at exactly that point where our theory withdraws the claim that the society in question is just. To be on the far side of that dividing line is to be in a space where we must reason about transition to a just society. To be on the near side of that line is to be in a space where we reason about the stability and reproduction of an already just society. This is a principled distinction. The work of the theory of justice is to make it concrete.

§5.5: RECONCILIATION

In a certain sense, this chapter is a Rawlsian project of reconciliation.[17] A project of reconciliation, as Rawls understands it, seeks to quiet our rage against some aspect of our social world that seems to put justice beyond reach. We might characterize the rage in question as righteous indignation, combined with a perhaps inchoate hopelessness about overcoming what we indistinctly perceive is a deeply abiding feature of our social world. We are able to reconcile ourselves to this aspect of our social world, Rawls thinks, when we do two things. First, when we show that the relevant aspect is necessarily bound up with great goods of justice, so that to rage against this aspect of our shared life is to rage against justice itself. Second, when we show how a robust ideal of a just society can be conceived so that it is compatible with this aspect of our social world. The first part of the reconciliations shows us that this aspect of our social world is to be affirmed as necessary on grounds of justice, and the second that our practical despair is not warranted, at least once we properly understand justice. We are then able to affirm the feature of our social world on grounds of justice without giving up our practical hope for a just society.

Thus, Rawls famously argues that the "fact of reasonable pluralism," against which we are prone to rage, arises from the existence of free institutions under modern conditions of pluralism. According to Rawls, to rage against the fact of reasonable pluralism is to rage against freedom itself, at least under modern conditions. Rawls's late *Political Liberalism* is dedicated to showing that such reasonable pluralism is also compatible with a robust ideal of a just society, once we see that it is possible to conceive justice along politically liberal lines. In this way, Rawls tries to reconcile us to reasonable pluralism by showing that it is tied up with great goods of justice (freedom) and that the appearance that it puts realistic utopia out of reach is an illusion.

One way to see this chapter is as an attempt to reconcile us to the concessive aspects of our social world, regimes of prophylaxis, rectification, and enforcement that are responsive to the tendency to commit injustice. I have argued that such elements are, generally speaking, constitutive of the status of free equals who hold one another to the fulfillment of their duties. Indeed, I have sought to reconcile us to them by arguing that they are bound up with the very idea of justice as a stringent necessity that has its source in another. They are to be affirmed as good on the same grounds that we affirm justice to be good. To rage against them is to rage against justice itself and so against the right relations of free equals to one another.

Furthermore, I have argued that this aspect of our social world is not incompatible with the development of a theory of justice, including fundamental principles of justice. Part of the justice of a just society is how it responds to injustice. For these principles specify what institutions will have to be like in order to satisfy our valid claims on one another, including institutions of enforcement. A robust justice is thus compatible with the propensity to injustice. However, there is a sense in which merely stating this point in the abstract is only a formal reconciliation; true reconciliation would come only with a theory of justice that showed such elements to be compatible with a developed conception of a just society understood as a realistic utopia. I have tried to present us with general conceptual tools that allow us to understand how this could be possible in the abstract. But only when we see this possibility actualized in a developed theory of justice will we be able to comprehend justice as compatible with modes of enforcement *in concreto*.

Hume once described justice as "the cautious, jealous virtue."[18] I do not agree with him in substance or expression: the justice of realistic utopia, on the views about justice that I hold, is neither cautious nor jealous. But I recognize something close to true in his characteristically polished turn of phrase. Perhaps we would better capture what is right in it if we likened justice to a "pied beauty" for which the poet Gerard Manley Hopkins praises God in this famous poem.[19]

Pied Beauty

Glory be to God for dappled things—
    For skies of couple-colour as a brinded cow;
     For rose-moles all in stipple upon trout that swim;
Fresh-firecoal chestnut-falls; finches' wings;
    Landscape plotted and pieced—fold, fallow, and plough;
     And áll trádes, their gear and tackle and trim.

All things counter, original, spare, strange;
    Whatever is fickle, freckled (who knows how?)
     With swift, slow; sweet, sour; adazzle, dim;
He fathers-forth whose beauty is past change:
       Praise him.[20]

I have argued that into the fabric of justice something counter is woven. A claim of justice must be understood in connection with the authorization to resist its violation. To see justice adazzle with righteousness, you must understand the contrast between light and shadow. You can only understand the power—strange and spare— of its illumination if you see it as the power to drive away and hold at bay the dim shadows. The community of free equals is thus a "dappled thing" in which the aspects of justice, and the enforcement of that justice against injustice, are inseparable.

Other images from this poem are apt as well. To the monolithic, windswept plateau of Rawlsian strict compliance I have counter-posed a landscape plotted and pieced, the plowed fields of compliance alternating with fallows and folds of prophylaxis, enforcement, and rectification. There is as much variegation in justice as in the "rose-moles all in stipple upon trout that swim." We should affirm this as good and as compatible with our hope for a just world.

Were I a believer in God, I would say: praise him for this.

Against the Antipracticalists

§6.1: THE ANTIPRACTICALISTS

As we saw in Chapter 2, the teleological conception of the theory of justice faces criticism from two directions. It is subject to criticism from the practical critics. I have found much common ground with them, affirming as valid their critique of the genetic interpretation of the priority of ideal theory and rejecting for my own reasons the compliance conception. Above all, I have elaborated the same master thought that moves them: that political philosophy is, and must be, practical and that in an unjust society it must aid agents of change in their confrontation with injustice. However, I have also defended the teleological conception from their criticisms by identifying a practical explanatory priority of ideal theory and by showing that one can reject strict compliance theory while embracing the teleological conception.

But as we have seen, the teleological conception is subject to criticism from the opposite direction as well. For it is subject to criticism from the antipracticalists such as G. A. Cohen and Adam Swift. I engaged with Cohen's view in Chapters 2–4, arguing that it is a bad fit with the practical character of our thought about justice. Indeed, what Cohen and Swift say about justice is sufficiently unattractive that I suspect it to be motivated by the conviction that the alternative is confused. My response has been to develop the teleological conception, showing that it is coherent. But a full treatment obviously requires an extended dialogue with the antipractical critique, and a positive reply to their best arguments, along with the affirmation of what is sound in their views.

In this chapter, I pursue this aim through dialogue with the work of David Estlund. In a series of essays and a monograph, *Utopophobia*, David Estlund has developed a critique of "practicalism" in political philosophy in what I take to be especially systematic and careful form.[1] I believe that Estlund has given the most judicious and plausible expression of this antipractical tendency in contemporary political philosophy. As with the practical critics, I have many points of agreement with Estlund. Most importantly, my defense of the teleological conception turns on an affirmation of the centrality of a utopian aspiration to political philosophy the defense of which is Estlund's core concern. There is a profound truth in the uncompromising approach that Estlund champions. But the very point of my agreement with the practical critics is the point of my disagreement with Estlund. For I will argue that his view abandons the practical character of political philosophy in ways that are, although nuanced, ultimately unnecessary.

§6.2: SO WHAT IF THE THEORY IS HOPELESS?

In several places, Estlund remarks that ambitious theories of justice are often subject to skepticism on the grounds of a sneering cynicism about the moral dispositions of human beings. Although nothing in his arguments turns on the substantive political content of justice, Estlund remarks that egalitarian or socialist positions are often subject to this sort of skepticism.[2] In orienting the reader to his proposed reply, Estlund notes that questions at philosophy talks tend to take one of two forms: "Oh yeah?" and "So what?"[3] Estlund tells us that socialists have tended to reply to the challenge of the sneering cynics with "Oh yeah?" They argue that the views they champion do not require unrealistic degrees of moral rectitude and self-sacrificing attitudes and that, once the motivational distortions of the incentives induced by capitalism are removed, the institutions are not infeasible in light of our moral dispositions.

By contrast, Estlund wishes to respond with "So what?" Suppose that the sneering cynic is right and we know that what some theory of justice requires will never happen because people will never do what is required of them to make the relevant institutions work. This problem lies not with the theory of justice in question, but with us. The theory of justice might perfectly well be true, even if we are not good enough to ever realize its principles. Thus, when the cynic objects (as he thinks), "But that will never work, given how people will act!" Estlund gives us the following reply in defense of our ambitious theory of justice: "I never said it would. That doesn't mean the theory isn't true."[4]

While requirements of justice may be shaped by, and respond to, many aspects of the human condition, they do not bend to accommodate people's morally reprehensible motives and unjust dispositions. To argue that in light of these unseemly features we should revise the principles of justice downward to something with a better chance of being met is to bring considerations of realism into the theory of justice in the wrong way. In essence, it is to drag justice down into the muck of human failure. While we can, of course, ask how justice requires us to act given that we will not meet various requirements, we should recognize that such concessions to human badness do not amount to full justice. In an evocative phrase, Estlund calls this view that the principles of justice are uncompromising in the face of human badness "Justice Unbent."[5]

Justice unbent is related to the availability of the "So what?" reply to the cynic. For if such a reply could rightly be given to the cynic on behalf of some theory of justice, then the theory could maintain an uncompromising stance on the nature of justice. Since justice is not concessive to our moral recalcitrance, it might very well be hopeless, practically speaking, without that speaking against the truth of the theory. Rather than contest the cynic's challenge, the theorist of justice could rightly shrug it off. Justice does not bend to the kinds of considerations that the cynic adduces.

In trying to vindicate this reply to the cynic, Estlund seeks to demonstrate the intelligibility and legitimacy of what he calls "hopeless nonconcessive theory."[6] Hopeless nonconcessive theory involves the following three elements: (1) the specification of principles of justice; (2) the identification of institutions that, when coupled with appropriate individual behaviors, are both necessary and sufficient to realize these principles; and (3) the assertion that these justice-realizing institutions should not serve as a "practical goal" for the sake of which we act. It thus tells us what justice requires, both in the abstract (as principle) and in concreto (as institution-cum-behavior). But it does not set this as an end for practice, for it identifies institutions that are, we are to suppose, almost certainly going to fail to realize principles of justice, owing to the fact that people will almost certainly fail to do what is required of them to make the institutions work.

Speaking generally, ends that are almost certainly bound to fail are, eo ipso, bad practical proposals. True, on occasion, we might be justified in pursuing hopeless ends—for example, where doing so risks no great hazard and falling short might still achieve something good. It is also true, as Estlund himself points out, that we often don't know what's possible, and so we underestimate the degree to which our social world can be changed. But Estlund asks us to suppose that is not the case here and, instead, that tilting at mills hazards disaster and that better results can be pursued more effectively by permanently giving up on winning justice. He wants to defend the claim that supposing the cynic is right, hopeless nonconcessive theory is nonetheless perfectly legitimate, and furthermore, if this turns out to be the plight we are in, it is the only kind of theory that can provide us with the ultimate truth about the nature of justice.

Estlund says in a candid moment, "It is hard to resist the sense that a hopeful theory is a better kind of theory. Still, I think this is an important mistake. There is no defect in a hopeless normative theory, and so none that hopeful theories avoid to their advantage."[7] One has the nagging sense, Estlund admits, that there must be something wrong with a theory of justice on which justice is a lost cause. But he argues that we should work hard to resist this sense. To be sure, it would be nice if justice was not hopeless for the likes of us; there is something terrible in the thought that justice is a lost cause. But we should not allow this to affect our evaluation of the truth or plausibility of a theory of justice. For hopelessness is no defect in a theory of justice, and if hopelessness is not a defect, then hopefulness is not a virtue.

§6.3: HOPELESS BUT NONETHELESS PRACTICAL

Now, Estlund is willing to grant that it is a requirement even on hopeless nonconcessive theory that it respect the thought that we are only required to do what we are able to do.[8] Perhaps the requirements that the principles of justice lay on us should mention only institutions that it is possible for human beings to bring into existence and maintain. This is one of many ways that his view differs from that of Cohen's even more uncompromising view. This might seem in tension with the idea that we can be virtually certain that individuals will fail to do what is required of them to make the institutions work. But Estlund argues that this is a mistake, for this almost certain failure need be explained not by the inability of individuals to do what is required of them, but by their unwillingness to do so.

In order for us to see the relevant distinction, Estlund asks us to focus on an individual case.[9] Let us suppose that a system of garbage pickup and recycling is part of a rational collective response to a problem about dealing with refuse. Suppose further that the rules are no more difficult to follow than those followed regularly by homeowners in any number of present US cities. Now, suppose that there is an individual, Bill, who does not do his bit by sorting and putting out his garbage; instead, he always dumps it by the side of the road. Let us suppose the reason for this behavior is Bill's selfishness and ensuing lack of public-spiritedness—a flaw that shows up in a whole range of his other attitudes and actions. The reason Bill does not and will not follow the garbage policy, despite perhaps recognizing it as a rational policy that would solve a genuine collective problem, is because he is too selfish to spend the modest time and energy required.

If his selfish attitude were to change, let us suppose, the policy would be very easy to fulfill, since there are no obstacles outside the small sacrifice of time and energy that the policy requires. He has mastered all the rudimentary skills necessary. He deploys them all the time in his ordinary life—for example, when he sorts his prized baseball card collection into different piles, changing the arrangement of his display of prize cards and carefully packing up the rest.[10] Bill is perfectly capable of sorting his trash, but it is virtually guaranteed that he will not do it. We may even suppose that it is more likely that any given person will be struck by lightning than that Bill will do what is required of him to contribute to solving the refuse problem.

We can draw several morals from this case. The likelihood that someone will fulfill his duty is different from the ability to fulfill it. As Bill so vividly shows, someone might be able to do his duty, but not exercise that ability owing to a character flaw. A moment's reflection also shows that the fact that Bill is virtually guaranteed not to sort his garbage does not somehow exempt him from the duty to do so. This is true if Bill is shameless about his dereliction, openly choosing not to sort his garbage. But it is no less true if he is weak willed and, although wishing to be a good recycler, just can't bring himself to sort his trash. Furthermore, it no more exempts Bill from his duty when we add that a general tendency that manifests itself throughout his practical life explains why he is almost certainly not going to sort his trash.

Our knowledge of Bill's general disposition can give us excellent insight into his virtually guaranteed failure to sort his garbage. It makes any plan of ours on which we depend on Bill to voluntarily sort his garbage a flawed plan. If we ask where the problem lies, here it seems right to say that the problem lies with Bill, not with our view about what requirements Bill is under (along with the rest of us).

Thus far, this is about Bill, who differs from so many other Americans in his unwillingness to follow basic garbage policy. If the problem with the garbage policy is only Bill and a handful of people like him, this isn't yet very hopeless. It can be handled by institutions that establish proper incentives and rectify injustices when they arise. If we write Bill a ticket that forces him to sell his Derek Jeter rookie card, can he sort his trash now? He should be able to if selfishness is his problem. And even if Bill doesn't sort his trash, perhaps efficient street cleaners can pick up after the few dumpers like him, and people (or machines) can be employed to sort what garbage remains unsorted in their slovenly piles. Thus, it is easy to maintain a belief in the sanity of the garbage policy and thus easy to maintain our judgment that Bill is under the relevant duty despite his predictable failure to comply. He is, after all, the lousy exception rather than the rule to a policy that otherwise is potentially an effective response to the refuse problem.

For the policy to be hopeless, it can't just be about Bill. Of course, the sneering cynics never make a claim about Bill. They indict humanity with their unflattering generalizations. The tendencies in question are supposed to be general tendencies that condition the possibilities for our collective action, putting off the agenda ambitious egalitarian responses to the problems of our political life. In order for Estlund to defend the possibility of hopeless aspirational theory, he needs to scale up the conclusion about Bill. He has to show how it could be true both that some institutions are required by justice and that there is no hope in their succeeding, given our general tendencies as human beings.

Estlund scales the case of Bill up, reasoning as follows.[11] We make a judgment about Bill alone. Suppose all humans are in a line and we make a judgment about each one taken seriatim. In each case, we will have no more or less reason to make the judgment in the case before us than we had in Bill's case. In each case, the problem lies not with our view about the requirement they are under to institute the solution, but with the individual in question and his selfish tendency. So we ought to make the same judgment in each case— namely, that people are under the duty to sort their trash and are blameworthy for (predictably) failing to fulfill this duty. But when we make this series of judgments, the product of our judging in the aggregate will be the following resolutely hopelessly combination of views: (1) a collective problem we face requires us to institute and comply with a policy of individuals sorting their own trash; (2) we can be virtually certain that no one will do this, and by this very fact, we can infer this is not a good "policy proposal" in the ordinary sense of that term; so (3) we ought not to try to institute it as a policy.

This is not yet explicitly about justice. But let us add that solving the refuse problem in an effective and fair way is a requirement of justice, and the only policy response sufficient to do this involves individuals sorting their own garbage. Perhaps a similar problem besets more elaborate and far-reaching questions of justice, like those that govern the role of the economy, and the contributions of the individual. If people are typically like Bill, why not? Selfishness and a lack of public-spiritedness is a general disposition that would presumably affect behavior across the board. But if so, on the one hand, justice demands that we build and comply with certain institutions, but on the other hand, the institutions might be hopeless as a practical proposal owing to people's general rottenness. The theory can state true requirements, even if it does not propose that we attempt to meet the requirements. The right thing to say will be that the fault lies with us rather than the theory. The problem isn't the theory of justice; it's the long line of the Bills of the world, a line in which you and I might very well be standing.

If the combination of views is as intelligible in the collective political case as it is in the individual case, then it would appear that hopeless nonconcessive theory is intelligible. In that case, Estlund has made available the reply "So what?" to the defender of ambitious left theories of justice. However, even if this vindication of the neglected reply to the cynic is successful, it raises a natural worry. For it might seem that the reply, as Estlund has developed it, amounts to a pyrrhic victory. The cynic was pressing the challenge that the ambitious theory of justice isn't realistic as a ground for rejecting it. But this reply seems to grant the cynic everything they thought they were asking for in order to hold on to the truth about justice, now understood in such a way that it bears no relationship to political action. The connection to political action thus severed, it is natural for the puzzled cynic to reply, "Fine. But isn't this an argument that we ought not care about the truth about justice that your ambitious theory supposedly uncovers?" The response "So what?" thus raises in a startling way the question of the significance and value of ambitious political theorizing.

Now, one way we might reply to the cynic about the value of a hopeless nonconcessive theory of justice is to point out that, although hopeless, it might still play various practical roles.[12] Even when we are cut off by a precipice from a dynamic approach to the telos of a just society, the telos might still guide our practical thought through what I called its immanent dimension. For example, it might vindicate and systematize judgments about the severity of various sorts of injustice. It might also help us think about ways in which we could partially or approximately realize justice, compatible with the insuperable obstacles we face. Even if grievous injustice will remain forever and ever, with no hope of ever overcoming it, still we might do better or worse in coping with it. Knowing about the end of a just society might help us to handle our practical failure in productive ways. And there might be substantial justice to realize in the struggle against injustice itself, even if it takes the form of disaster mitigation. So one answer to the cynic is that hopeless theory might very well still have some practical value.

But Estlund is interested in pursuing a different answer as well, one that calls into question the presuppositions of this worry about pyrrhic victories and practical value in more thoroughgoing fashion. Estlund criticizes what he calls a "deep kind of practicalism" about value prevalent in political theory.[13] Practicalists, as Estlund understands them, hold that the value of the theory of justice is practical. For the sake of argument, he wishes to grant that hopeless nonconcessive theory has no practical value. Since he believes that hopeless nonconcessive theory is an intelligible sort of political theory that might lack practical value, he views practicalism as a denial of the value of such a theory. His picture is that there are two sorts of theories of justice—"hopeful" and "hopeless"—and each could equally well be true. The practicalist says that only one of those two has value (on our current supposition) and that the other is valueless. Practicalism is thus a form of skepticism about the value of an otherwise fine and legitimate theory. Estlund wishes to undermine such skepticism by showing that hopeless theories may have value of some other kind.

Estlund begins by arguing that some intellectual work has nonpractical value. His plausible example is pure mathematics, mathematics with no practical application.[14] Here the work in question is pursued out of intellectual curiosity, rather than a sense of any utility the work might have. Perhaps a hopeless theory of justice might have this kind of nonpractical value. The problem is that this is not an easy proposition to defend.

First, not just any body of truths has value in the way that pure mathematics has value. The phone book, for example, is a systematically ordered body of truths, with no value apart from its usefulness in contacting people.[15] Furthermore, unlike pure mathematics, the theory of justice is about requirements on action. Presumably it is this (along with the sense—so hard to shake!—that something is wrong with a theory of justice that is not actionable) that accounts for the attraction of practicalism in the theory of justice. What we need in order to show that the victory against the cynic is not pyrrhic is some way of saying what the nonpractical value of a hopeless theory of justice is.

Estlund does this by tying hopeless theory to the virtue of justice, understood as a part of individual ethics.[16] The kind of understanding that a hopeless nonconcessive theory would provide of justice, supposing that it is the true theory, is necessary to achieve the individual virtue of justice. Estlund's thought is that the virtue of justice involves not only acting justly, but also being properly affected by justice and injustice. The just person is someone who rejoices in justice and laments the existence of injustice. If we are separated from the peaks of justice forever by human rottenness, then the just person is someone who will grieve at this fact and who will never be straightforwardly happy with whatever forms of injustice we have to settle for.[17] The just person will recognize this hopeless situation as something to sorrow over. Perhaps they will even feel shame at the badness of humanity, for they too are human.[18] But for the just person to have this proper reaction, they will need to know about justice. For it is only by knowing what justice is, and how far we are—and will forever be—from justice, that enables the just person to react in the appropriate ways to this unhappy situation. Even if we can't do any better, we can at least be straight with ourselves about it, and the virtuous person will be one who looks at this the right way. So, paradoxically, the hopeless theory of justice comes here to have value not for politics and political action, but for individual morality as the grounds for moral honesty, righteous lamentation, and justified shame.

§6.4: HOPELESSNESS AND THE CLAIMS OF JUSTICE

Estlund's defense notwithstanding, it is natural to think that there is *some* kind of tension in the combination of views that hopeless nonconcessive theory puts forward. For it claims that we ought to do what the principles of justice require. It also identifies some institutions as necessary for realizing these principles, and so insists with the necessity of justice that we ought to build and comply with the institutions that are necessary. But, nevertheless, it says that we ought not to build the institutions—given that they are almost certain to fail. It thus seems to put forward and simultaneously retract some practical proposals. Estlund captures this apparent dynamic nicely when describing the kind of necessity to build the institutions that we are to imagine the principles of justice single out. He describes the requirement to build these institutions as an "institutional principle" to distinguish it from a proposal for action. He writes, "An institutional principle describes institutional arrangements as part of a broader prescription or proposal, even if the described arrangement is not itself proposed or prescribed."[19] Institutional principles describe institutional arrangements that are part of a broader prescription or proposal that justice requires. But because we know that they will never be complied with if instituted, they belong to the class of hopeless proposals and fruitless prescriptions. They are valid prescriptions that are nevertheless not to be prescribed.

Estlund's way of understanding the problem is through the idea of a contradiction between deontic statements.[20] What makes for the seeming instability, on his view, is the combination of nonconcessive-ness and hopelessness. Since hopeless nonconcessive theory is non-concessive, it tells us that we ought to realize the principles of justice (do A) and so do what is necessary to bring about A—namely, the combination of B and C (build the institutions and comply with them). But it also tells us that we ought not to do B (build the institutions), since there is no real hope we will do C (comply with them) so as to do A (realize the principles). It thus presupposes that we can be required to perform an action (A) and, in light of this fact, be required to perform the combination of actions (B and C) necessary to bring this about, without being required (or even permitted) to perform one element of this combination (B). It thus seems to presuppose the intel-ligibility of a variety of puzzling deontic claims of a general sort, most troublingly the intelligibility of the necessity to perform actions that are incompatible—that is, both A and B and ~B.

This issue is, for better or worse, entangled with the debate about the positions called "actualism" and "possibilism" in deontic logic, stimulated recently by the seminal papers of Frank Jackson and Robert Pargetter.[21] The actualists hold that what you ought to do depends on what will actually happen if you do it, so, for example, if we will actually fail to comply with the institutions if we build them, then we ought not to build them since doing so will be worse than not. The possibilists, by contrast, think that we should reach conclusions about what we ought to do based on what it would be possible for us to do. So if we ought to build and comply, then we ought to build the institutions since it will be possible for us to also comply with them (even if we won't). This literature is discussed with great care and precision by Estlund. What he needs to main-tain is both that trying to bring about the relevant institutions would be a bad idea and that justice requires us to bring them about and comply with them. Estlund canvasses several ways, com-patible with both actualist and nonactualist positions, that he can maintain a version of these two claims. He seems to think that if he can vindicate the bare possibility of holding that combination of views, then he has defended the possibility of a legitimate hopeless nonconcessive theory.

But he needs something significantly more than that. In Estlund's view, to say that a theory of justice is hopeless is not to deem it defective. It follows from this that we have no reason to try to revise a theory if it is hopeless. By the same token, it does not count in favor of a theory that it is not hopeless. In other words, Estlund needs it to be the case not just that it is logically possible to hold the combination of attitudes coherently, but that holding that combination of views is a satisfactory outcome for a theory of justice as such. Hopelessness provides no reason to reconsider the theory, no reason to revise it, no theoretical reason to look for alternatives, and not even a reason to favor another theory that is otherwise as well motivated but hopeful. Only defects in a theory can do that, and hopelessness is not a defect.

Reconciling this thought with the concept of justice is hard, even if affirming it does not involve confusions in deontic logic. It is worth noting that the literature Estlund refers to discusses deontic claims in general and not claims of justice in particular, much less the theory of justice. But as we have seen, claims of justice have special features that set them apart from other deontic claims. It is those special features of justice to which I would like to appeal in making my case that a hopeless theory of justice is defective as a theory of justice.

As we have seen, if duties of justice are violated, we do not merely act wrongly, but we wrong another. Those who are wronged have standing to demand or insist that those who wrong them stop. As I have suggested, this standing partly explains why coercion and enforcement of various kinds is permissible with duties of justice, unlike other moral duties. But in Estlund's view, when we reflect on what justice requires, we are leaving it an open question whether we should, on balance (taking account of our Billish tendencies), do anything to satisfy the claims of justice we identify.[22] If settling what justice requires leaves it an open question whether we are to act to satisfy these requirements, then those to whom we owe such duties cannot have the relevant deontic powers. For they cannot be in a position, we might think, in virtue of possessing the claims they do, to insist or demand that we act to respect their claims. Estlund might say that we ought to institute certain institutions that treat some fairly, wronging them if we don't, yet it will still be an open question whether we should ever act so as to institute them. How, then, can we affirm the stringency of justice and the authorization of those who are wronged to hold people to the fulfillment of duties of justice?

Estlund has a ready reply: that hopeless nonconcessive theory is not a bad fit with the concept of justice, even granting its stringency. For, as I mentioned in introducing it, this stringency comes with an exception for cases where reforming unjust institutions would lead to greater injustice than leaving them in place, at least where countervailing dynamic considerations do not speak for making the change as a step on the way to greater justice in the future. Aren't cases where we hazard disaster if we push forward precisely covered by this exemption? Perhaps the authorization for the wronged to pursue change does not apply in cases like this, given the threat of worsening the situation. In that case, hopeless nonconcessive theory would not seem to be a bad fit with the concept of justice, once we understood the stringency of justice as qualified in plausible ways.

This brings us to a difficult issue that I have not confronted thus far, about how to understand the exemption and what role it plays in the theory of justice. For hopeless nonconcessive theories of justice to be adequate as theories of justice, it must be possible for the exemption to be permanent, putting off the agenda forever the pursuit of justice. This leads us to the next question. How, under such a permanent exception, are we then to understand the second-personal duties of justice? While Estlund seems at least open to the idea that injustice always involves someone having a grievance, he argues that hopelessness often leads to situations where no one has a duty to rectify the situation producing the grievance.[23] On the face of it, this is strange, since in hopeless nonconcessive theories we are envisioning situations where people will fail to act out of bad and blameworthy dispositions. How could the Bills of the world (taken as individuals) get out of their duties to others? Hasn't Estlund argued to the contrary that Billishness doesn't get us off the hook?

The case he asks us to consider is that of two doctors, Slice and Patch.[24] They are both surgeons. Slice is an expert in cutting, and Patch is an expert in stitching wounds. A patient needs surgery now if he is to live. Justice requires, first of all, that he receive it. Justice also requires that if he doesn't receive it, the patient not be made to die a death more painful than he would without the surgery. Now this surgery will only be successful if each surgeon deploys his special expertise in jointly performing the operation. Here are the possible outcomes of their actions: (1) If Slice and Patch do not operate, the patient will die. (2) If the patient is cut by Slice and stitched by Patch, he will live and recover. (3) If the patient is cut by Slice but not stitched by Patch, or vice versa, he will die a more painful death than he would without surgery. Furthermore, suppose that meeting the requirements of justice is hopeless because Slice and Patch are cads who are each going to go golfing instead of performing surgery no matter what the other does. Now, let us consider the respective duties of these unscrupulous surgeons.

Since Patch is going golfing no matter what Slice does, it seems that Slice should not cut the patient, since Patch will not stitch and so the incisions will only result in outcome 3, a terribly painful death that justice requires each to avoid when a less painful death is possible. But since Slice isn't going to cut no matter what Patch does, it seems that Patch should not stitch the patient either, since stitching without an incision will only result in outcome 3, a terribly painful death. It thus seems that neither Patch nor Slice is under a duty to operate on the patient. This is puzzling, since we also think that the patient is wronged by their decision not to operate. It seems that the patient has a grievance although no one is under a duty to do what would be required to do right by the patient.

Estlund explores many possible ways to resolve this puzzle by assigning the relevant duty to some agent; he argues that they all fail.[25] For example, he argues that various ways of trying to trace the duty to Patch and Slice as individuals fail. He also argues that attempts to lay the duty on the pair of them as a single agent fails, since they are not yet performing surgery and so are not a group agent in any relevant sense who might be under the relevant duty, and even if they did do the surgery together, he doubts that they would constitute a group agent. There is no way out, he thinks. If true, this is troubling, because the problem is not an isolated one arising only in artificial cases. Estlund rightly points out that this structure holds generally in conditions of hopelessness. For if a principle is (currently) hopeless, then in most cases, the bad dispositions of other agents alter what each agent ought to do. It will usually be the case in conditions of hopelessness that *no* agent is under a duty to do what justice requires. Yet those who are wronged will still have their grievances. Estlund posits a "plural requirement," a requirement of justice that is not a requirement on agents, that can render this grievance intelligible without a corresponding duty on an agent.[26] But the point is that in cases of hopelessness, there is not a stringent, directed duty that some agents are under to rectify the injustices done to others. When we qualify the stringency of justice in ways that are compatible with hopeless nonconcessive theories, Estlund suggests, we qualify the second-personal form of injustice as well and lose our grip on the corresponding duties, as well as the authorizations to hold others to account. Estlund's plural requirement is what remains when all of this has slipped away.

§6.6: THE EXEMPTION AND SECOND-PERSONAL DUTIES OF JUSTICE

Let us turn to Rawls's exception. It is worth pointing out that Rawls does not seem to accept Estlund's understanding of it. Rawls's discussion occurs in the context of his famous analogy between the truth of "systems of thought" and the justice of institutions. A natural reading of his discussion would identify the "systems of thought" in question with the natural and social sciences in which theoretical reason issues. About these, Rawls argues that we are sometimes justified in sticking with a scientific theory, even when there are clearly problems with this theory, and so the theory in its current form is false. What justifies us in continuing to operate with it, despite its falsity, is that we currently lack a better alternative theory, a theory that is or might be true. Although we are justified in temporarily persisting with the false scientific theory in our scientific practice, the theory is nonetheless a failure as a scientific theory, since truth is "the first virtue of systems of thought."

Qua scientists, the proper stance to take to this failure can only be to try to overcome it by coming up with a better theory, a theory that is better insofar as it is true. The exception tells us we can temporarily operate with a theory that we know is a failure as a theory only under the circumstances where we have not yet hit on a better theory but are trying to do so. The scientist qua scientist may not give up the quest for truth, but must treat the exemption as a temporary condition that could one day be overcome through the exercise of theoretical reason. This is, we might say, a presupposition of operating qua scientist.

Now, in this passage, Rawls is analogizing institutions to "systems of thought" and justice to truth. He has not yet introduced in the text the idea of "the theory of justice." But insofar as the quest for just institutions is being likened to the quest for truth, the natural reading of the exemption would treat it in parallel fashion. We can persist in upholding unjust institutions for the moment only because better institutions are not yet available and the changes we can make at present will only further deteriorate the situation. Any exemption for unjust institutions must be temporary as we search for a way toward justice. We cannot put off reforms ad kalendas Graecas, as Kant says when making essentially just this point.[27] Any exemption must be conceived as temporary in form even if we do not at present know precisely how to overcome the problem that triggers it.

To bring us back to the theory of justice, this suggests that when qua theorists of justice we find ourselves saddled with a theory that triggers the exception in ways we do not yet know how to overcome, we are justified in acquiescing temporarily, but only as we search for a way toward justice. Furthermore, the analogy suggests that we view the situation qua theorists as one in which our theory is failing in whatever the practical correlate is to falsity in science. That is, it suggests that we treat the hopeless nonconcessive theory as having a problem qua theory precisely insofar as it is hopeless, and that if we must affirm it for the moment, we do so only in the consciousness of it as a failure in light of its hopelessness, while we search for a theory that does not have the problem of hopelessness. That is, the parallel reading would suggest that any theory that triggers a permanent version of the exemption is defective as a theory of justice. Qua theorists we have reason to expect, hope, and strive for a theory that is better precisely because it is not hopeless.

Are Rawls's instincts good here? To answer this question, we need to finally explain what is behind the hard-to-shake sense that a hopeless nonconcessive theory is an inadequate resting place for our reflections on justice. The teleological conception provides us with a ready answer. The theory of justice itself is the work of the sense of justice. It is oriented to the end of a just society as an end of political hope and action. The political philosopher qua theorist is also oriented to this end as something to bring into existence through our collective action. This is not something they "personally happen to care about," but something that is internal to the role of the political philosopher. They wish to understand justice not to contemplate it—even for noble purposes of moral honesty or righteous lamentation—but to see it done. The theory of justice tries to articulate this structure of orientation to an end for the sake of political action, bringing this practical structure to self-consciousness and reflective knowledge.

To succeed, the theory of justice must specify an end that is capable of playing both the immanent role and the dynamic role in practice. It must annunciate an end and bring the reasoning about that end all the way back to action, connecting it with practice through an agent of change. Although the end of a just society specified by hopeless nonconcessive theories may play the immanent role to some extent, it cannot, in virtue of its hopelessness, play the dynamic role. These two roles are not arbitrary projections of the theorists onto the subject matter of justice; rather, they arise from the practical character of the sense of justice. In failing to articulate this structure, hopeless nonconcessive theories fail to connect our thinking about justice to practice. This is a failure of them as theories of justice, for our thought about justice is practical. It is this failure rather than a puzzle about deontic logic that explains the seeming inadequacy of hopeless nonconcessive theories of justice.

What, then, are we to say about Patch and Slice? On whom do the second-personal duties that we cannot yet satisfy under conditions of hopelessness fall? I will address the case of these unscrupulous doctors and then turn to the political questions that lie behind it.

Focus first on a case where only Patch is a cad. Let us suppose he will go golfing no matter what Slice does, but Slice is desperate to save the patient. As the patient lies dying in Slice's arms, who wrongs the patient? The answer is intuitively clear: it is Patch. But how? After all, neither Patch nor Slice performed the actions necessary to save his life, so why single out Patch in particular? The explanation is that Slice was unable to cut only because Patch refused to stitch. It is not the case that had Patch been willing to operate, Slice would not have done his bit. Although Slice was willing to operate, Patch refused nonetheless. Thus, Patch's wrongful omission explains Slice's rightful choice not to cut, but not vice versa. We can bring this out if we imagine someone racing onto the scene and yelling, "Why aren't you two operating? What's the holdup?" Slice will be able truthfully to say, "It's Patch. He won't agree to stitch. So I can't cut." Patch will not be able to offer the same reply as he coolly pulls on his golfing gloves; it would be nothing short of grotesque bad faith for him to represent things in this way. Thus, when the patient dies, his death is on the head of Patch rather than Slice. Slice did not violate his duty, while Patch did. We trace responsibility for the death asymmetrically in this case, sourcing it to the bad actor. In Kant's language, we impute the deed to Patch rather than Slice owing to Patch's willful omission to do what justice requires.[28]

But if this is right, let us return to the symmetrical case. In this case, Estlund has set up the case so that both Patch and Slice will omit to operate no matter what the other does. Each coolly pulls on the white gloves, so to speak, while the patient lies dying. So in neither case does the wrongful choice of the other explain the omission to perform the operation; what explains the omission is rather the intention of each to golf come what may. That means that each of the pair is in the position of Patch in the asymmetrical case. So, by parity of reasoning, the wrongful death is rightly imputed in this case to both for exactly the same reason it was imputed to Patch in the asymmetric case. Intuitively speaking, this is the right verdict. It is clear who wronged the patient: both Patch and Slice, who each chose to go golfing rather than perform an operation we are assuming justice required in some manner.

Now, it is also true that another aspect of this problem divides me from Estlund's approach. I would be happy to say that Patch and Slice, were they to have performed the surgery, would have acted together in doing so. And in every case where people act together, I would be happy to describe the set of individuals as a collective agent. I have elaborated my "Anscombian account" of collective action that vindicates these assertions elsewhere.[29] Here are the essentials of my view. What is required for acting together is this: I and you act together if we can each explain our individual actions by what we are doing together, where the relevant form of explanation is capable of being transposed into a purposive idiom ("in order to," "for the sake of"). I am acting together with you if I can explain why I'm doing action A by saying truly that "I'm doing A because we're doing C," and you can likewise truly say, "I'm doing B because we're doing C," and where we could each gloss those explanations by saying that "I'm doing A (or B) in order to (for the sake of doing) C." In cases where that holds, the actions of multiple individual agents can be explained by the actions of plural agents. This is, on my view, acting together. And talk of a collective agent here is warranted because a plural subject is essential to the forms of explanation in question.

Does the operation fit this account? Well, in the case where the two doctors go ahead with the surgery, Slice can say, "I'm cutting because we're performing an operation on the patient" as well as "I'm cutting in order to perform an operation on the patient." Likewise, Patch can say, "I'm stitching because we're operating on the patient" as well as "I'm stitching for the sake of operating on the patient." The surgery is something they do together, and the pair constitutes a plural subject in relation to this action.

Estlund calls this "easy agency" because it rejects the demanding conditions imposed by, for example, Philip Pettit and Christian List, who hold that something is a group agent only under elaborate special conditions that allow for the rational aggregation of preferences. They believe that for there to be a group agent, the group must form something like a democracy of a special kind that has a decision procedure that relates the "preferences" of each to the "preferences" of the others so as to determine their collective intentions. I don't begrudge them their exalted conception of "group agency," although I do not think it explains the primitive phenomenon of acting together, which must be explained before we can ever hope to explain the higher, more complex, lofty cases. In my own treatment I try to dissolve worries about "a group mind," arguing that it need not be attributed to collective agents except as a unity of explanation that has a certain form. Since Pettit and List motivate their demanding conception of group agency by appeal to the idea that only the relevant lofty sort of preference-aggregating agent can realize the relevant mental states, I would reject their view as a general account of collective agency. In short, as Estlund and I have argued that social choice theory is a faulty guide to the basic idea of justice that requires a noncomparative concept of just and unjust, I would argue that it is not a good guide to the metaphysics of collective action.

In the case of Patch and Slice, I am happy to say that they wrong the patient by omitting to assist each other in surgery, which is a case of acting together if anything is. So I'm also happy to say that their injustice takes the form of refusing to "form a collective agent." This is quite important, since overcoming injustice usually involves acting together with others in various social collectivities. The form of wronging by bystanders and others who could act to overcome the injustice can usually be rightly described as a failure to act together with others and so to form collective agents of diverse kinds, from loose collectivities engaged in a boycott or protest, to more organized social movements, all the way up to disciplined organizations with set structures of decision-making, like trade unions or political parties.

In sum, in cases of injustice, one must trace the source of injustice to the actions and omissions of agents. This is not especially hard to do in cases of hopelessness, where the blame lies squarely with the Bills of the world. As we saw in Chapter 4, such tracing is important to diagnose the obstacles that confront us, to identify possible agents of change who might oppose this injustice, and to attribute the responsibility for wrongdoing to agents against whom other agents have claims. The attribution of responsibility thus often takes the form of specifying collective modes of action, and so injustice often takes the form of the failure to act together with others.[30] We need not qualify the second-personal form of justice in the way Estlund envisions.

Where does this leave Estlund's argument? Remember—Estlund represented the situation as one where there are two sorts of theories, hopeless and hopeful, either of which might be unimpeachable. He represented practicalism as skepticism about the value of one of those kinds of theory. But if hopelessness is a flaw in a theory of justice, then hopeless and hopeful theories are not two theories on a par. We are now in a position to see that practicalism is not skepticism about an otherwise valid and successful kind of theory. Hopeless theories fail as theories of justice. It follows that practical value is a value all theories of justice have insofar as they are successful as theories of justice. To the extent they lack it, they fail as theories. There is no need to find another kind of value for successful theories of justice.

§6.7: HOW TO REASON WITH THE CYNIC

How, then, are we to handle the charge of the sneering cynic? Perhaps as we reason we find ourselves saddled with the combination of views characteristic of hopeless nonconcessive theory. This is certainly possible, as Estlund rightly insists with great skill and patience. However, for the reasons we have just sketched, this situation is a problem for theory. In these circumstances, the end of a just society is severed from action permanently. Theory is failing to develop the concept of justice into a structure adequate for practice. The combination of views we have, while perhaps not a problem of deontic logic, does not accord with the practical structure of the theory of justice.

Let us focus on the cynic's charge that motivates Estlund's approach in his earlier papers. Suppose that we have a set of principles, as well as some thought about what would be required for their possible institutional realization. Suppose that a cynic provides a credible argument, bolstered by impressive empirical evidence, that the institutions in question would not in fact realize the relevant principles, owing to how people are likely to act (Billishly) under the institutions and the incentive structures they establish. According to our argument, at this point, far from shrugging our shoulders, we are under some pressure to arrive at a view more adequate to the idea of justice. There are many possibilities to explore.

The first point to make is that perfect realization is not in question, since on the view I have defended in Chapter 5, we must allow that the response to injustice will be part of a just society, and so we are allowing deviations from perfect justice in our idea of a practical good. Ours is a conception of justice that includes and copes with imperfection. What is in question is a realization of the principles sufficient for us to judge that the society in question is a just one, handling the limited injustice that arises under its arrangements in sane, effective, and fair ways. So we must imagine that the cynic provides compelling evidence that the institutions necessary for sufficiently realizing the principles will in fact fail to do so owing to human badness and that they will thus not embody the underlying values to a sufficient degree. Let us imagine that the injustice under them will be so grievous, given the likely failure of individuals to comply with the institutions, that we ought not to even try to bring them about.

Now, at this point, we have the option to say, "Oh yeah?" and to undermine the cynic's arguments by showing that this person is wrong. Remember the cynic needs a solid empirical case that the relevant institutional proposals are almost certainly bound to fail; such cases are not so easy to come by and are often open to credible contestation once produced. But we are supposing that we are not able to so contest their argument.

The next option is to revise our institutional specification of the principles. Perhaps we were wrong that these institutions were necessary in order to realize the principles to a sufficient degree. Perhaps other institutional specifications would suffice to realize them, and perhaps these other institutions are sufficiently different so that they are not subject to the cynic's arguments. If so, it was our failure of institutional imagination that produced the problem, and the issue is resolved. Knowledge of institutional possibilities is hard to come by; it often requires much democratic experimentation, as well as spontaneously arising possibilities that are often impossible to anticipate. Estlund himself recognizes this when he emphasizes how little we know about what is impossible usually—part of this condition of uncertainty is a lack of knowledge of the space of institutional possibility. But let us follow Estlund and assume that this route has been closed. We *know* that institutionalizing it this way won't work, and we know that it cannot be institutionalized in any other way. The only possible institutional realization of the principles is hopeless given our Billish dispositions.

We have a series of further options to explore in trying to arrive at a more adequate practical knowledge. The first option is to revise our principles of justice. But our hopeless principles have not come out of the air; rather, they have been defended by reference to our general convictions about justice. Perhaps another principle can be supported by those very same convictions. If this other principle is not hopeless, and so can be institutionalized, then we are out of the woods. Such principles, after all, play a mediating role between different levels of generality of our thought. If this other principle will mediate the levels of our thought, while also unifying and explaining our lower-level judgments without giving rise to our practical difficulty, then so much the better. But perhaps we cannot see how to do this. Our arguments for the hopeless principle from our general convictions is airtight.

In that case, the next option is to consider whether some of those general convictions underlying the principles might be mistaken. If we can see where we went wrong in making them, understanding what true thoughts we were confusing them with, or what made them falsely appealing, we will be in a position to revise our general convictions. With a different set of convictions, perhaps we can revise the principle they support, and perhaps this revised principle will not be hopeless. But let us suppose that we cannot do this either. As far as we can tell, the general convictions are right, and they support only a principle that is hopeless.

If there is no escape from the relentless challenge of the cynic, we are in a terrible situation both as agents and as theorists of justice. The best we can do is to persist in a state of uncertainty and practical failure, testing this way and that way to try to bring our thought about justice into a shape that is adequate to the idea of justice, while engaging in damage control and trying to avoid practical despair.

That my view leaves our practical thought in an unsatisfactory shape in the circumstances that Estlund asks us to envision might seem a problem. Yet it seems to me that something like the opposite is true, for the terrible circumstances Estlund asks us to imagine could be seen as spelling failure for our practical thought about justice. About this state, John Rawls remarks, echoing Kant, "If a reasonably just Society of Peoples whose members subordinate their power to reasonable aims is not possible, and human beings are largely amoral, if not incurably cynical and self-centered, one might ask, with Kant, whether it is worthwhile for human beings to live on the earth."[31] I follow the spirit but not the letter of this statement. I do not think we should ever ask what Rawls would have us ask under this dark hypothetical—namely, whether it might not be better for the human race to perish. We should never leave it an open question whether the annihilation of the human race is something for which to wish. But Rawls's remark—following Kant—contains a profound truth insofar as it registers the depth of the horror in the thought that there is no hope that humans will live justly with one another. "So what?" is not a pose the theorist who has taken in the depth of the problem can strike. Under these circumstances, our practical thought fails to accord with the idea of justice as developed into self-conscious theory. The goose of our theory of justice is cooked along with our practical hopes for a just future for humankind. Consolations will be false.

It is very important to say that the hypothetical situation as described is one that I believe has never been realized. This is actually the most important point. For the same reason that the theory of justice has the structure of the teleological conception, the proper attitude in approaching the task is one of practical hope. As in any inquiry, we assume in setting out as inquirers that there will be some way to arrive at an adequate understanding, and we take our task to be to rise collectively to the occasion. We thus attempt to meet challenges as theoretical and practical obstacles to be overcome. Furthermore, in this case, that hope is a practical one bolstered by the necessity of justice flowing from the claims of our fellow human beings. To conclude that justice is impossible is to conclude that we must acquiesce in wronging, or being wronged by, one another. The stakes are much higher, insofar as this is a necessary moral end rather than a discretionary end of technical or theoretical inquiry. What is required for us to give up our practical hope in a just world is remarkable. Until we know that it is impossible, we are justified in assuming that there is a way forward yet to be found.[32] I have followed Estlund's cynic to the end of the line, emphasizing how many stops there are to disembark the cynic's train. Who among us can claim that they know what is required?

Not the most well-informed IR theorist if they are honest, much less my cynical barber.

In light of these reflections, must I deny "justice unbent"? I do not think so, at least given the interpretation of that idea compatible with the arguments of Chapter 4. Justice unbent seems to me a crucial insight of Estlund's that helps us to see what the proper role of realism is in the theory of justice. The truth of justice unbent has to do with how we understand the justification of principles. But our bare knowledge that the institutions necessary to realize a principle are hopeless owing to human badness is not sufficient by itself to discredit the principle. For whatever arguments spoke in favor of the principle still speak in favor of the principle. It is supported from above by being grounded in general judgments on which it depends, and it receives confirmation in the unification, explanation, and understanding it provides of lower-level judgments. The bare fact that the principle cannot be successfully institutionalized owing to human badness is not sufficient to dislodge it. Instead, this bare fact prevents the principle from successfully playing the role that a principle plays in the developed theory of justice, of specifying an end to be pursued in our action, and triggers our practical and theoretical search for viable alternatives.

Coming to understand that a principle is hopeless gives us very strong reason to look for another way forward, deploying any of the many routes I mentioned previously. It might seem as though I must deny justice unbent. After all, if a principle cannot be realized owing to human badness, this makes a theory of justice defective on my view. Doesn't this defectiveness give us a reason to reject the principle, lowering the horizons of justice by conceding to human badness? I don't think so, for while the hopelessness of principles does put pressure on us as theorists and agents, it does not license accommodating human badness by lowering the horizon of justice. None of the ways I canvassed in reply to the cynic involved deploying a modus tollens to simply dismiss a principle and put in its place a principle that was easier to satisfy.[33] We have strong reason to revise a hopeless principle, but not by dishonestly lowering our horizons. Estlund is right to buck at this idea and to scent in it a grotesque perversion of the idea of justice. What a successful theory of justice does is provide a set of unbent principles that are practical. We are not guaranteed to succeed, but we must try, and if we fail, then our theories fail with us.

Political Philosophy as
Practical Reasoning

*T*he argument of the preceding chapters has been complicated and dense. It is time to present an overview of the teleological conception of the theory of justice I have defended. With this overview in hand, I will turn to consider the senses in which political philosophy is practical on the teleological conception. I will then consider some pressing objections to this conception of political philosophy that may have been troubling the reader. Like the ouroboros, this book on method ends by circling back to reflect on how methodologically to understand the claims about method it has advanced.

§7.1: THE TELEOLOGICAL CONCEPTION: IDEAL THEORY

The theory of justice can be looked at genetically or structurally. Genetically, we consider how political philosophy works with prephilosophical materials to construct a philosophical understanding of justice. Structurally, we consider the idea of a complete theory of justice toward which political philosophy drives. Both perspectives are crucial to understanding the way the teleological conception relates theory and practice. I will start with the structural one, turning to the genetic one later.

According to the teleological conception, in unjust societies, the theory of justice can be divided into two parts: realistic utopian theory and transitional theory. These two parts are differentiated by the practical roles they play. Realistic utopian theory articulates the idea of a just society as an end for our political hope and action. Transitional theory discusses how to respond to injustice in the present in principled ways so as to move us toward the end of a just society.

The primary task of realistic utopian theory is to articulate and defend principles of justice that specify our valid claims on one another vis-à-vis our shared institutions and practices. These principles constitute a unitary end for two reasons. The first is that the requirements of justice are stringent: when institutions fail to satisfy them, we must reform or replace the institutions unless doing so will introduce a greater injustice. For this reason, we must pursue the satisfaction of all the principles taken together, for it is only when institutions satisfy all the principles that we manifest in our shared life the end set for practice by the idea of justice. The second reason is that principles of justice interact with one another, since what would otherwise be a valid claim can give way when another principle of justice takes precedence in a given context. That someone would have a claim under one principle absent countervailing considerations is not sufficient to show they in fact have a claim. We need to know how this prima facie claim interacts with the claims associated with other principles. For this reason, ideal theory not only specifies a set of principles but also specifies the provenance and role of each principle, including relations of ordering, dependence, and mutual limitation between the principles of justice, which must be fitted together so as to be possible to pursue as a single end.

Furthermore, since justice is enforceable and gives rise to claims to enforcement, in specifying these principles, realistic utopian theory must also specify a deontic space of just enforcement. For any given principle, some modes of enforcement are mandatory, some are permissible, and some are impermissible. Furthermore, the deontic status of a mode of enforcement can be affected by different scenarios of noncompliance, in that a mode of enforcement that is mandatory under one scenario, where it is needed to uphold claims, may well be impermissible in another scenario where it is excessive. Realistic utopian theory considers all and only those scenarios of noncompliance that are compatible with the existence of a just society, understood as one where justice is secured in part through the enforcement of our claims on one another.

The principles of justice, once related to one another and elaborated into a deontic space of enforcement, also call for institutionalization. A just society can be realized only through a set of shared institutions that render determinate claims and empower actors. Furthermore, institutional proposals concretize the end of ideal theory, allowing it to play a greater role in practical reasoning. However, we need to bear in mind that institutional specifications at a distance will usually be tentative and exploratory, since the question of which of these is to be pursued may well be indeterminate until one is close enough to the end to view the dynamic landscape of shifting opportunity structures. Insofar as institutional proposals depend on the adequate performance of the relevant institutions under different empirical scenarios, it is also often impossible to obtain the necessary information to select institutions without democratic experimentation under realistic conditions. So although they have a place in realistic utopian theory, we should not overestimate the role of concrete institutional proposals, especially where current institutions are far from just.

To put this all together, on the teleological conception of the theory of justice, realistic utopian theory consists of (1) the articulation and defense of a set of principles of justice; (2) the specification of the relation of the principles to one another, so as to constitute a unitary end, including discussion of their provenance and role, relative priority, weighting, and mutual limitation; and (3) the elaboration of this set of mutually limiting principles into a deontic space of enforcement under a range of empirical scenarios compatible with justice. Here we look for forms of enforcement that are mandatory or permissible under a range of scenarios; rule out those that are impermissible; and, where possible, (4) institutional proposals that might realize this enforceable set of principles, keeping in mind the limitations on our institutional knowledge far in advance of realization.

Together, 1–4 draw a crucial dividing line between utopian and transitional justice. In specifying the end of a just society, realistic utopian theory simultaneously draws the theoretically crucial dividing line between justice reproduction (ideal theory) and justice production (nonideal theory). This same dividing line demarcates justice simpliciter from the many degrees and kinds of injustice.

§7.2: THE TELEOLOGICAL CONCEPTION: NONIDEAL THEORY

According to the teleological conception, nonideal theory is transitional theory. It is the theory of the principled transition from injustice to justice. As a theory of transition, one crucial task of nonideal theory is the identification and weighting of injustice. Nonideal theory must say what institutions and practice are unjust and why they are unjust. This involves saying whose legitimate claims they fail to fulfill and who is under the corresponding duties to alter the institutions and practices. It must also weigh the grievousness of the relevant injustices.

For these purposes, transition theory draws on two things: (1) an empirical account of the functioning and reproduction of the relevant unjust status quo and (2) realistic utopian theory. Transitional theory draws on social science to develop an empirical theory of the reproduction of the relevant unjust status quo. Such empirical theories inform the identification and weighing of the injustice in question, since how a putatively unjust status quo functions and is reproduced is relevant to the assessment of its injustice and severity. Injustice is the failure to fulfill legitimate claims, which are, in the first instance, specified by the principles of justice articulated in realistic utopian theory.[1] Realistic utopian theory also informs our judgment of the grievousness of the relevant injustice by specifying the cutoff line in relation to which severity can be judged against the baseline of justice simpliciter, and by ordering principles within a certain range.[2] But transitional theory has much independent work to do in specifying the severity of injustice that departs from justice simpliciter along multiple dimensions.

Having identified and weighted injustices, transitional theory reasons about the appropriate response to them. Realistic utopian theory plays a dynamic role in reasoning about the appropriate response to injustice. Dynamically speaking, justice is something to be pursued by agents working outward from the present through dynamic pathways of change that ameliorate or overcome injustice. The identification of such pathways toward justice is the heart of transitional theory's dynamism.

One aspect of the identification of dynamic pathways is the specification of proposed remedies that would ameliorate or remove an injustice if introduced. Such practical proposals draw on the empirical diagnosis of the injustice, since we must have reason to believe that instituting these changes would effectively disrupt the reproduction of injustice or diminish its extent. Questions arise for nonideal theory here insofar as such changes can pertain to different dimensions of justice (multiple principles) and also affect different groups, leading simultaneously to a greater fulfillment of the claims of one group and the lesser fulfillment of the claims of another group. The questions of when such trade-offs are permissible and when they result in a greater justice on the whole are normative questions at the heart of nonideal theory.

Such remedies are effectuated by agents of change who employ strategies of resistance to injustice. The identification of plausible agents of change is another aspect of dynamic reasoning in transitional theory. In identifying plausible agents of change, transitional theory looks for three things. The first is capacity: the agent must have or be able to acquire the capacity to overcome obstacles and effectuate the proposed change. The second is motivation: the agent either is or might become sufficiently motivated to bring about the relevant changes. To arrive at views about motivation, analysis of reproduction is once again crucial, including the role of ideology, unconscious bias, and self-interest in undermining willingness to address legitimate grievances, as well theories about other obstacles to political cooperation and coalition building. The third is normative appropriateness: the agent must be normatively appropriate, keeping in mind the special relationship of those wronged to the struggle against injustice.[3] Transitional theory also reasons about the strategies of resistance that these agents of change may employ in order to effectuate the remedies that will ameliorate or remove injustice. Many crucial questions arise here, including how grievousness injustice must be to justify more contentious resistance, how the riskiness and likely costs of such engagement enter into the equation, and who is permitted to employ what modes of resistance under what conditions.

These three aspects—proposing remedies, identifying agents, and specifying strategies of resistance—are entangled since certain pathways to change will be open to some agents and closed to others. Whether a pathway is a promising route to address an injustice will depend both on how effective the remedy is at addressing the injustice and on whether there is a plausible agent to traverse it. Furthermore, different agents of change may be able to employ different strategies of resistance to bring about the change, given how they are placed in the system and given their different normative permissions. These issues must be thought through together.

This brings us to the immanent role of the end of a just society in transitional theory. Transitional theory must also take account of the intrinsic significance of the struggle against injustice, including the claims of the oppressed understood not merely as stepping-stones to a brighter future but as subjects worthy of just treatment now. Among other things, it must address the ways in which there is justice in the struggle for justice (for example, how mutual recognition and right relations are prefigured in the solidarity of struggle). Transitional theory must also address the relation between the immanent and dynamic dimensions, articulating in clear ways the trade-offs involved in various courses that may need to balance doing greater justice now against diminished prospects for future transformation.

This brings us to the final topic in transitional theory: the relationship between the philosopher and agents of change. Having identified plausible agents of change and the dynamic pathways to them to ameliorate or overcome injustice, this piece of transitional theory stands in a special relation to the agents of change so identified. I have said that the philosopher reasons in solidarity with the agent of change: they reason with a view to making a contribution to the activity of the agent so identified. This presupposes the possibility of communication and the sharing of knowledge between the theorist and the agent of change. Another normative field in nonideal theory concerns the proper relationship between theorists and agents, bearing in mind that agents of change are already political thinkers and that learning happens in both directions. The ethics of communication in struggle are an essential part of transitional theory.

In sum, transitional theory considers dynamic pathways from injustice to justice. In doing so, it serves to mediate between realistic utopian theory and political action by drawing on empirical theories about the reproduction of the status quo. In opposing injustice, nonideal theory works on behalf of those who are wronged, and it stands in solidarity with agents of change. The core tasks of transitional theory include (1) identifying injustices, (2) weighting their severity, (3) identifying effective and permissible remedies, (4) identifying normatively appropriate agents who might plausibly come to be willing and able to effectuate these remedies, (5) explaining the justification and limits of the strategies of resistance they might employ, (6) exploring the dimensions of justice that are realized in and through their struggle, (7) theorizing the trade-offs between immanent and dynamic justice, and (8) providing a theory of the relationship of theory to practice, understood as a principled exchange between the agent of change and the political philosopher.

§7.3: IN WHAT SENSE IS POLITICAL PHILOSOPHY PRACTICAL?

Let us now summarize the senses in which political philosophy is practical according to the teleological conception. Returning to the genetic perspective we set aside, one sense in which political philosophy is practical is its starting point in our practically engaged sense of justice. The materials with which it works are judgments about justice and injustice that we make in the course of our ordinary political and interpersonal lives and that we take as reasons to act and be properly affected. Given the stringency of justice, many of these foci of practical attention are perceived injustices, which are salient because they call out for redress and change so that we might fulfill the claims people have on us to order our shared institutions and practices. Furthermore, these injustices are almost always already sites of contestation. They are usually brought to our attention and made salient through the political activity of agents attempting to address them. The injustices and the effort to overcome them raise for us practical questions about how as agents we are to relate to this struggle. The materials with which political philosophy works, and which it attempts to understand by raising to self-consciousness and theory, are practical.

When we look at the structure of the theory of justice toward which philosophy drives on the teleological conception, further practical dimensions emerge. The theory of justice is organized by practical concepts, and it can be divided into parts that correspond to differing practical roles. Ideal theory identifies the principles of justice, which are practical principles that unify and explain our lower-level practical judgments, uniting our thought about justice and injustice and mediating between lower- and higher-level judgments. Furthermore, these principles together constitute a conception of a just society, an end to be pursued in practice. This structure of orientation to an end is not something the philosopher imposes from outside on the subject matter of political philosophy but is rather a structuring concept that orders the theory of justice. Furthermore, we have seen that the proper default attitude of the philosopher to the achievability of this necessary moral end is not detached open-mindedness, much less cynicism, but practical hope, an attitude of trust that some way forward is possible, in the absence of conclusive evidence that it is not.

Further practical dimensions of the theory of justice can be found in the way transitional theory mediates between the end of a just society and political action in the present. Transitional theory considers the pressing injustices that confront us with the goal of fashioning principled responses that if acted on will advance the cause of justice. Furthermore, it brings reasoning about justice all the way back to agents of change and the specification of dynamic pathways they may pursue to overcome obstacles, including the activity of other agents who oppose change. The proposals are actionable intelligence, things to be done for the sake of justice. The topic of how theorists relate to agents of change when sharing such actionable intelligence is itself an important part of nonideal theory. The question of how theory can become practice in opposition to injustice is not something extraneous we add on to satisfy our (perhaps legitimate) personal purposes, but rather a central topic in transitional theory that arises from the orientation of that theory to action.

Political philosophy on the teleological conception is profoundly practical: in its starting points in our engaged practical thought about justice, in the concepts that organize it, in the division of the theory into ideal and nonideal components, in the aim or purpose internal to those parts, in the practical attitude of the theorist to justice, and in the relationship of theorists qua theorists to the agent of change and to struggle. The theory of justice is organized throughout by practical concepts and can be said nonmetaphorically to aim at action and change in straightforward and intelligible ways. These are the many senses in which the theory of justice is practical on the teleological conception.

Is political philosophy, then, practical reasoning? I am sympathetic to an understanding of practical reasoning capacious enough to include the philosophical reasoning contributing to the theory of justice. But the arguments of this book do not depend on such a capacious understanding. If some should hold a narrower view of practical reasoning, we need not disagree. When I say that political philosophy is practical on the teleological conception, I mean neither more nor less than what I have already said. If someone thinks that it is a stretch to call the making of conceptual distinctions, or the development of empirical theories of injustice, practical reasoning, this presents no obstacle to affirming what I have said. Similarly, if one thinks that practical reasoning strictly so called is only means-end reasoning, or if one thinks that the subject of practical reasoning must be identical with the agent who acts, we need not disagree, provided that one affirms the connections between the theory of justice and practice that I have identified. Similarly, while

I think it would be natural and illuminating to connect the teleological conception to more systematic views about the philosophy of action, I have not made the philosophy of action the centerpiece of my argument. I have gestured in this direction where locally relevant—for example, in my exchange with David Estlund. In the main, although taking inspiration from certain strands in the philosophy of action, my annunciated arguments are compatible with a range of views about action.

§7.4: OBJECTIONS

A host of objections could be raised to the substance of this view about the nature of political philosophy and its method, which I would like to address as an occasion for thinking about how best to understand claims about the nature of political philosophy.

Let's start with a simple question. Where are we to find an example of a theory of justice that comes close to doing all the things the teleological conception says a theory of justice must do? If by "a theory of justice" we mean a single work—say, a book—of philosophy, then the answer is obviously "nowhere." Even the most systematic and ambitious works of political philosophy, like John Rawls's *A Theory of Justice*, don't come close to addressing the full range of topics that have a role in the theory of justice. This is partly due to problems in Rawls's approach to nonideal theory, but it is mainly due to the fact that Rawls was only one person. Doesn't the teleological conception set the bar impossibly high for political philosophy? Indeed, isn't this a conception of a theory of justice fit for angels or gods rather than human beings?

But this objection misunderstands the nature of the theory of justice, as a system into which all our cognition about justice could be fitted, were it raised to reason and self-consciousness. It is the structure of an entire discipline, a field of thought that reaches down to ordinary political practice and out to other fields that engage with pressing injustice. It is not something that could ever be contained within a single book. In fact, the objection has things backward: far from being nowhere, the theory of justice is everywhere. The contributions to it are legion. First, agents of change who are engaged in struggle have, of necessity, become theorists of justice to some extent, so a good bit of the theory of justice arises organically from, and is embedded in, practice. Among professional philosophers, every book on fundamental questions about the principles of justice, from Martha Nussbaum's *Frontiers of Justice* to Philip Pettit's *Republicanism* or Thomas Christiano's *The Constitution of Equality*, can be viewed as work in ideal theory. Philosophical books on race, labor, feminism, and queer theory, as well as on more concrete issues, such as immigration and international labor standards, can all be seen as contributions to nonideal theory. Although each takes its own point of view, tackling only a subset of problems and issues, all can be viewed as attempted contributions to the greater tapestry. The theory of justice, like justice itself, is a collective task.

But let us try turning this objection around, asking not if the conception of the theory of justice is too broad, but whether it is too narrow. In particular, does the theory rule out by fiat work that does not fit neatly into the structure articulated? What does the teleological conception say about the views of the practicalists and antipracticalists I have criticized, whose understanding of what they are doing departs from the views about method defended here? When they fail to recognize the structure of the theory of justice I have sketched, and so depart from the methods I defend, must I say that they are not only wrong but not even doing political philosophy? The worry here is that my strictures unfairly rule the views of others out of court. This would be awkward, amounting to churlish and indefensible gatekeeping.

In fact, it would be worse than awkward: it would be incoherent. For how could I criticize the practicalists or antipracticalists for failing to do political philosophy well if they are not even doing political philosophy? I must bring them under the concept that supplies the relevant norms if I am to criticize them in light of these norms. This is a general point that we can tie to our discussion in §5.2 of internal norms. Remember that an internal norm is a standard that applies to an X in virtue of being an X. When internal norms apply, to say what it is to be an X, we must say what it is to be a proper or nondefective X. This presupposes that something can be an X while also failing to exhibit some of the features proper to an X. For example, to say I have poor human vision is to say that my visual system doesn't do some of the things that human vision does.

Similarly, here I have said that a relation to practice is internal to political philosophy, structuring the theoretical enterprise in a variety of ways. Someone's political philosophy can fall short when it fails to exhibit this structure or is incompatible with it. When that happens, the philosopher in question is doing political philosophy all right, but in ways that can be criticized for failing to live up to standards that are internal to the enterprise. They advance claims about justice, we might say, that fail to live up to the idea of justice. The antipracticalists are clearly doing political philosophy and make many very valuable contributions, such as Estlund's profound defense of justice unbent and his critique of Sen's comparativism. But they do so in a defective way that I have tried to criticize by developing a conception of political philosophy that contains internal standards linking theory to practice.

We can see from this that the point of advancing a theory of the nature of political philosophy is not to draw a boundary line, ruling some work in and other work out of political philosophy. The point is not gatekeeping but rather critique. I have tried to provide an account of a method that articulates internal norms to which the theory of justice is accountable as a basis for a critical intervention in a field that is in a moment of transition and creative ferment.

Those who disagree with me should not feel that I somehow write them out of the conversation. To the contrary, I hope that my work fosters dialogue with them.

But can the antipracticalists perhaps evade the critique by granting me the term "political philosophy" and saying that they do not care if what they are doing can be criticized as failing to live up to standards internal to political philosophy? Perhaps they can perform an activity that is just like political philosophy but lacks the relevant norms. But our arguments have proceeded from the idea of justice. I have emphasized that justice constitutes a unitary end, and so this structure is not one we impose on justice from outside. Justice is a unitary end because of the stringent second-personal practical character of justice, and the way our thinking about justice occurs at multiple levels in such a way as to be gathered together in principles. To treat this as something we could evade by simply shifting or redefining our activity is to represent the end of a just society as something personal that we bring to the table and might simply disavow by abandoning the relevant purposes. This is exactly the picture I have been resisting throughout.

Instead of worrying that the teleological conception rules out the work of the antipracticalists, one might worry that it rules out reflection on institutions that one cannot affect. It takes off the menu of topics for theory the justice and injustice of things that we cannot change. Now, since we live in one mutually influencing interconnected world, it is hard to think of a contemporary society we could not affect at least through communication with an agent of change. One possibility to consider might be a contemporary society or institution that it is normatively inappropriate for the theorist to intervene in, given their identity and position, even through a respective communicative exchange with plausible agents of change. In other words, one might think, on the basis of views about the normatively appropriate agent of change and the ethics of communication, that as a theorist one should just stay out of it politically. In that case, the theory of justice would be cut off from practice. What then?

First, I would point out that to formulate this possibility, we must advert to various aspects of the teleological conception, including views about the appropriate agent of change and the relation of theory to practice. Indeed, the practical conception of political philosophy helps us to understand how this is at least a conceptual possibility. For this reason, it is hard to view this as an objection to the teleological conception. It seems rather to elaborate one possible outcome of reasoning on the teleological conception. But what does the conception say about this peculiar outcome?

The teleological conception identifies a problem here. We are supposed to imagine that theorists are engaged in theorizing that, because of their identity and position, cannot play the practical role at which it aims. To what agent are they making their proposals for change, given their own views on the inappropriateness of sharing such proposals? If the theorist thinks that what they are doing is inappropriate to even share respectfully with a potential agent of change, then this does raise in an almost comical way the question of why they are the ones doing the theorizing. The theorizing is, in this sense, frustrated from doing what such theories do, since it is impermissible to address the remedies proposed in transitional theory to an agent of change. While this doesn't as such call into question the truth of their reflections, it does suggest that something is going pretty seriously wrong with their theorizing. The solution to their conundrum is relatively simple, however: let others who are normatively appropriate theorists theorize instead. This seems to me like the right result, and the teleological conception explains both the problem and the solution well.

Perhaps we are worried that the teleological conception will rule out reflection on some society that is not normatively inappropriate to change but rather physically or metaphysically beyond change through our action. Science fiction provides fanciful cases. More prosaic (and useful) ones come from our reflection on the past, since we cannot affect past societies and institutions, although we do sometimes assess their injustice.[4] Now this case is harder, and we are less prepared by our preceding reflection to address it. Dealing with it properly would require an explanation of how history is related to the theory of justice and so political philosophy. In what sense are theories of justice historically situated, and how do they relate to the evaluation of the past? Are the principles of justice historically contextual? Here is a huge, important topic that this book has not addressed. But we can make a few points in a tentative spirit about the objection, keeping in mind that a fuller treatment is required.

First of all, reflection on the justice of past institutions can have many practical purposes in the present. For example, Marx discusses feudalism, along with ancient slaveholding societies, as a way of bringing out certain continuities with the present. He argues that capitalism, for all its historical distinctiveness, shares with older modes of production the feature of being exploitative. His point is to see the continuities of the injustice of the present with the injustice of the past. Someone might also inquire into the injustice of the past as a way of commenting on what is good about present conditions from the point of view of justice. Or someone might use historical discontinuity to do the opposite, investigating the past as a different way of criticizing the present, by showing that the past did some things better, with respect to justice, than we do. This might be useful not only for bringing injustice to light, but also in showing that the injustice of the present is not eternal and inevitable but arose under determinate conditions and so might pass away in the future through our practical efforts. The teleological conception can welcome all these normative reflections on past institutions as ancillary but important contributions to the theory of justice, aiming as they do at informing our thought about action in the present.

But suppose we wished to investigate the justice of past institutions without any of these practical interests in the present. What does the teleological conception say about this endeavor? Many questions could be raised, such as what role the principles of justice are playing in this enterprise. If they are simply carried over from the theory of justice and applied to the past, then the teleological conception would probably say that the investigation is an application of political philosophy proper to history. If the principles of justice are somehow drawn from the past, then we would need to hear a lot more about how this works to know exactly what to say about their relation to the present's principles of justice. But, again, this backward-looking enterprise, entirely cut off from practical interests in the present, will be an ancillary activity that is political philosophy only in an attenuated sense. Since the activity doesn't aim to reflect on justice with relevance to the present, and doesn't even draw on such reflection, it is probably not in the same business as political philosophy, although this is not necessarily a criticism.

§7.5: THE PRACTICALITY OF THIS VERY BOOK

Let us pose one final question. Is this very book political philosophy on the teleological conception? Given that on the teleological conception political philosophy is the theory of justice, and the theory of justice has two parts, we might further ask whether this book is part of realistic utopian theory or transitional theory. It seems to belong to neither, since it neither identifies principles of justice nor proposes action to overcome injustice. If this very book is ruled out by its own conception of method, this would be a reductio ad absurdum. I am hoist with my own petard.

It is true that in laying out a framework, I have found it unavoidable to work with some very high-level considered judgments about justice that are part of the material of both ideal and nonideal theory. But setting aside this kernel, I agree that this book is not in the main a book of political philosophy. It is a book about what it is to do political philosophy that does not advance any very substantive claims about justice. By reflecting on the method of the discipline, it advances claims about the structure of the theory of justice that do not belong to the substance of either part of this structured theory. But nothing about the teleological conception suggests that there is anything wrong with writing a book about political philosophy in this sense.

To the contrary, this book makes a contribution to the theory of justice conceived along the lines of the teleological conception. A sense of the form of the theory of justice is helpful for the work of both ideal and nonideal theory. For example, realistic utopian theory is hampered when modes of enforcement are mistakenly thought to belong, as such, to transitional theory or when realistic utopian theory is thought to bear no essential relation to practice, as some antipracticalists think. In this way, by providing methodological correction, I try to help ideal theory serve its practical role of articulating an end for practice while staying true to the utopian impulse that has animated political philosophy from its inception.

Similarly, nonideal theory is hampered when it is divorced from ideal theory out of a mistaken sense that ideal theory is irrelevant, or even opposed, to nonideal theory, as some practicalists think. As I have argued, this has deleterious consequences for practice, insofar as ideal theory plays a dynamic and immanent role in nonideal theory. What one gets is not an autonomous nonideal theory, but rather a nonideal theory that assumes half-digested and unarticulated views about justice as its basis. Worse problems still arise when nonideal theory is done in the absence of serious thought about agency and change, since this suppresses most of the topics with which nonideal theory needs to engage. My critique of the appeal to the overinclusive "we," for example, is a corrective intended to foster a real engagement of nonideal theory with practice. Indeed, my reflection on the form of the theory of justice shows us how the relation of theory to practice is an essential question for theory rather than a pragmatic afterthought. An understanding of method wards off confusions like these that put up obstacles to the practical work of the theory of justice.

This book contributes to the theory of justice, when conceived along the lines of the teleological conception. Its contribution consists in making explicit and defending the form of the theory of justice. Although it does not say in what principles justice consists, or what an end for practice may be, or how agents of change are to pursue this end in their struggle with injustice, this book does remove obstacles to theory's doing these things. Indeed, by contributing to the practical role of the theory of justice, thought about its form is itself practical in an extended but intelligible sense.

Although bad theory is not injustice, I think we could nonetheless by analogy speak of the practical addressee of this book in the special political-philosophical sense we analyzed in connection with the agent of change. This book could be viewed as sharing proposals about the activity of political philosophy—proposals that are addressed to other theorists of justice. These proposals are intended to clarify the practical self-understanding of theorists of justice so that their theorizing might become properly practical. Indeed, this book is a product of meditation on ongoing, excellent, practically engaged work in political philosophy. My intention has been to provide an explicit framework that might bring this work together and, by making its practical form explicit, remove obstacles to its progress. In political philosophy, even reflection on form is for the sake of action.

NOTES

Introduction

1   In the week before completing this manuscript, I was happy to discover a new contribution to this disciplinary conversation by Simon Hope that pursues some of the themes of this book, drawing on a few of the same sources. I was delighted to find that it fills a lacuna in my argument, since he criticizes the realists, whereas my engagement is with the authors I call "practicalists" (nonideal theorists) and "antipracticalists" (utopians). Simon Hope, "Political Philosophy as Practical Philosophy: A Response to 'Political Realism,'" *Journal of Political Philosophy* 28 (4): 455–475 (2020).

2   See, for example, G. A. Cohen, *Rescuing Justice and Equality* (Cambridge: Harvard University Press 2008); Elizabeth Anderson, *The Imperative of Integration* (Princeton: Princeton University Press 2010); Amartya Sen, *The Idea of Justice* (Cambridge: Harvard University Press 2011); and Gerald Gaus, *The Tyranny of the Ideal: Justice in a Diverse Society* (Princeton: Princeton University Press 2016).

3   For a small sampling from a vast literature, see Charles Mills, "'Ideal Theory' as Ideology," *Hypatia* 20 (3): 165–184 (2005); Amartya Sen, "What Do We Want from a Theory of Justice?" *Journal of Philosophy* 103 (5): 215–238 (2006); Colin Farrelly, "Justice in Ideal Theory: A Refutation," *Political Studies* 55: 844–864 (2007); Raymond Geuss, *Philosophy and Real Politics* (Princeton: Princeton University Press 2008); and David Wiens, "Prescribing Institutions without Ideal Theory," *Journal of Political Philosophy* 20 (1): 45–70 (2015).

4   See Andrew Mason, "Just Constraints," *British Journal of Political Science* 34 (2): 251–268 (2004); Cohen, *Rescuing Justice and Equality*; and David Estlund, *Utopophobia* (Princeton: Princeton University Press 2020), 140–146.

5   Gerald Gaus also emphasizes the long history of such debates. See Gaus, *Tyranny of the Ideal*, 2–3.

6   See Aristotle, *Nicomachean Ethics*, trans. Roger Crisp (Cambridge: Cambridge University Press 2000), 1139a ff. I discuss Aristotle further in Chapter 2, where a set of citations to relevant secondary literature can be found.

7   Aristotle, *Nicomachean Ethics*, 1141b–1142a.

8   Aristotle, *Nicomachean Ethics*, 1094ab.

9   Aristotle, *Politics*, trans. C. D. C. Reeve (Indianapolis: Hackett Publishing Company 1998), 1275ab, 1323a–1326b.

10 Immanuel Kant, "The Metaphysics of Morals" in *Practical Philosophy*, trans. Mary J. Gregor (Cambridge: Cambridge University Press 1996), 6:214.

11 Kant, "The Metaphysics of Morals," 6:313; Immanuel Kant, "On the Common Saying: That May Be Correct in Theory, but It Is of No Use in Practice" in *Practical Philosophy*, trans. Mary J. Gregor (Cambridge: Cambridge University Press 1996), 8:297.

12 Kant's discussion of the "moral politician" who brings the principles of right to bear on reform in pursuit of the idea of a republic is relevant here. See Immanuel Kant, "Towards Perpetual Peace" in *Practical Philosophy*, trans. Mary J. Gregor (Cambridge: Cambridge University Press 1996), Ak 8:372.

13 See Kant, "Towards Perpetual Peace," Ak 8:347–8:349.

14 John Rawls, *The Law of Peoples* (Cambridge: Harvard University Press 1997).

15 Karl Marx, "Theses on Feuerbach" in *The Marx-Engels Reader*, ed. Richard Tuck (New York: W. W. Norton & Company 1978), 145. On my reading, Marx is calling for a genuinely practical philosophy and castigating philosophers for treating what are real problems to be solved through action as intellectual puzzles to be solved in thought. But it is possible to read this remark as calling instead for an alternative to philosophy. The most careful development of this reading is Daniel Brudney, *Marx's Attempt to Leave Philosophy* (Cambridge: Harvard University Press 1998).

16 Karl Marx, "Estranged Labor" in *Economic and Philosophical Manuscripts of 1844* (Amherst: Prometheus Books 1988), 69–84. For a late statement limning the practical good to be pursued, see Karl Marx, "Critique of the Gotha Program" in *The Marx-Engels Reader*, ed. Richard Tuck (New York: W. W. Norton & Company 1978), 525–542.

17 In order to bring Marx into proper dialogue with the themes of this book, one would need to resolve the interpretative dispute about Marx on justice. A useful overview of the debate on Marx on justice is Norman Geras, "The Controversy about Marx and Justice" in *Marxist Theory*, ed. A. Callinicos (Oxford: Oxford University Press 1989). While I would affirm much of what Geras says, I am skeptical of his treatment of justice as an ahistorical doctrine of natural rights. Thanks to Pablo Gilabert for useful advice on Marx scholarship around these questions.

18 Gerald Gaus makes a similar point about the long history of theorizing about these topics in *The Tyranny of the Ideal*, 2–3.

19 Arthur Ripstein, *Force and Freedom: Kant's Legal and Political Philosophy* (Cambridge: Harvard University Press 2009).

1. Two Conceptions of the Theory of Justice

1 For bemused (and slightly exasperated) commentary on this state of affairs, see Gaus, *The Tyranny of the Ideal*, 1–2. Especially helpfully taxonomic contributions include Laura Valentini, "Ideal vs. Non-ideal Theory: A Conceptual Map" in *Philosophy Compass* 7 (9): 654–664 (2012); Zofia Stemplowska and Adam Swift, "Rawls on Ideal and Nonideal Theory" in *A Companion to Rawls*, ed. Jon Mandle and David A. Reidy (Hoboken: Wiley 2014); and Pablo Gilabert, "Comparative Assessments of Justice, Political Feasibility, and Ideal Theory," *Ethical Theory and Moral Practice*, 15: 39–56 (2012). My contribution to this effort, on which this chapter is based, can be found in "Strict Compliance, Realistic Utopia, and Constructivism," *Philosophy and Phenomenological Research* 97 (2): 433–454 (2018).

2 I draw here most heavily on the methodological remarks from the early portions of *A Theory of Justice*. But I do not restrict myself only to Rawls's brief comments on the concept of justice, drawing on the surrounding material and a broader interpretation of core elements of his approach to fill out the approach. Especially relevant is John Rawls, *A*

Theory of Justice: Revised Edition (Cambridge: Harvard University Press 1971), 3–15.

3   My discussion here draws on, and is generally congenial to, the treatment of justice in Pablo Gilabert, "Justice and Beneficence" in *Critical Review of International Social and Political Philosophy* 19 (5): 508–533 (2016).

4   For a recent discussion of relational normativity, including justice, see Stephen Darwall, *The Second-Person Standpoint* (Cambridge: Harvard University Press 2009).

5   For a discussion that emphasizes the second-personal nature of justice, and connects this with the directedness of duties of justice, see Michael Thompson, "What Is It to Wrong Someone?" in *Reason and Value: Themes from the Moral Philosophy of Joseph Raz*, ed. R. J. Wallace, Samuel Scheffler, and Michael Smith (Oxford: Clarendon Press 2004), 333–384; R. J. Wallace, "Reasons, Relations, and Commands: Reflections on Darwall," *Ethics* 118 (1): 24–36 (2007); and Stephen Darwall, "Bipolar Obligation" in *Morality, Authority, and Law* (Oxford: Oxford University Press 2013).

6   Indeed, correlativity is probably too weak a concept here. Wesley Hohfeld famously claimed that the correlated pair of duty and claim are in fact a relation that can be looked at from two sides: your claim as a patient *is* my duty as an agent. There is an insight here, although the relationship has an importantly asymmetric structure: since claims (or entitlements) are the grounds of duties of justice and not vice versa. See Wesley Hohfeld, "Some Fundamental Legal Conceptions as Applied in Judicial Reasoning," *Yale Law Journal* 23 (1): 16–59 (1913); Martha Nussbaum, *The Frontiers of Justice*, 275 ff; and Joel Feinberg, "The Nature and Value of Rights," *The Journal of Value Inquiry* 4:243–260 (1971).

7   My understanding of generosity has been shaped by the discussions in Cicero and Kant of the difference between justice and beneficence. See Marcus Tully Cicero, *On Duties*, trans. E. M. Atkins (Cambridge: Cambridge University Press 1991), 1–25; and Kant, "The Metaphysics of Morals," 6:376–6:396.

8   It is crucial that we not conflate the idea of a duty not correlative to a claim with the idea of supererogatory acts. An act is supererogatory if we are not under a duty to do it but it would nevertheless be morally good to do it. A supererogatory act is, intuitively speaking, one that is more than morality requires of us. On my view, we can be under moral

duties to perform acts without those acts being correlative with the claims of others. These acts, being morally required, are not supererogatory. Some acts of generosity or kindness, for example, that are not correlative with a claim are required on my view, while others are supererogatory (more than is required). I thus reject the view of Matthew Kramer, which he traces (questionably, in my view) to Wesley Hohfeld, that all duties are correlative with claims. On my view, Kramer wrongly assimilates the whole of morality to justice. See Matthew Kramer, "Rights without Trimming" in *A Debate over Rights: Philosophical Enquiries*, ed. Matthew Kramer, N. E. Simmonds, and Hillel Steiner (Oxford: Oxford University Press 1998), 7–112.

9   See Elizabeth Anderson, "What's the Point of Equality?" *Ethics* 109 (2): 287–337 (1999); and Samuel Scheffler, "What Is Egalitarianism?" *Philosophy and Public Affairs* 31 (1): 5–39 (2003).

10 Elizabeth Anderson, "The Fundamental Disagreement between Luck Egalitarians and Relational Egalitarians," *Canadian Journal of Philosophy*, supplementary volume 36, 1–23 at page 3 (2010).

11 See, for example, Philip Pettit, *Republicanism: A Theory of Freedom and Government* (Oxford: Oxford University Press 1999).

12 See Sheffler, "What Is Egalitarianism," 8–12; and Anderson, "The Fundamental Disagreement between Luck Egalitarians and Relational Egalitarians," 6–17.

13 See Rawls, *A Theory of Justice*, 5, 115–117.

14 Robert Nozick rightly draws attention to the dialogical, or second-personal, form of Rawls's reasoning. See *Anarchy, State, and Utopia* (New York: Basic Books 1974), 189–204. For some relevant passages where the less advantaged and the more advantaged address claims on one another in light of their inequality, see Rawls, *A Theory of Justice*, 87–90; and John Rawls, *Justice as Fairness: A Restatement* (Cambridge: Harvard University Press 2001), 122–126.

15 See Rawls, *A Theory of Justice*, 8–9.

16 See, for example, Cohen, *Rescuing Justice and Equality*, 7, 89–91.

17 Gaus, *The Tyranny of the Ideal*, 25–26.

18 Cohen thus denies the previous mark as well. On his view, there can be an injustice, even where no one has a legitimate claim on others to order their actions or institutions differently. In Chapter 6, I respond to some arguments by David Estlund that we must recognize injustices where claims are not coupled with duties.

19 This is the master thought of Kant's approach to justice (right) in the *Doctrine of Right*. It is expressed in his famous argument in §D about hindering a hindrance to freedom. I discuss this argument, situating it in the broader context of his relational view of right, in "Kant on Strict Right." Kant's insights will receive greater prominence in Chapter 5. See Ben Laurence, "Kant on Strict Right," *Philosopher's Imprint* 18 (4): 1–22 (2018).

20 The assertion of a connection between rights and coercion, and the contrast with other moral duties such as charity, plays a large role in authors as different as Nozick, *Anarchy, State, and Utopia*; Thomas Pogge, *World Poverty and Human Rights* (Molden: Polity Press 2008); and Arthur Ripstein, "Authority and Coercion," *Philosophy and Public Affairs* 32 (1): 2–35 (2004).

21 The connection of rights and enforceability is a rare common theme in the otherwise sharply diverging contributions to Matthew Kramer, N. E. Simmonds, and Hillel Steiner, *A Debate over Rights: Philosophical Enquiries* (Oxford: Oxford University Press 1998).

22 Rawls, *A Theory of Justice*, 7–8. See also 351 and 453–454.

23 Rawls, *A Theory of Justice*, 453–454.

24 Rawls, *A Theory of Justice*, 7–8, 351.

25 Rawls, *Justice as Fairness*, 8–9.

26 For another reference to "the numerous simplifications of justice as fairness," see *A Theory of Justice*, 517.

27 Rawls, *Justice as Fairness*, 9. For another reference to the concept of a well-ordered society as "very idealized," see John Rawls, *Political Liberalism* (New York: Columbia University Press 1993), 35.

28 Onora O'Neill is a critic of ideal theory who quite early distinguished between idealization and abstraction and drew the connection to the philosophy of science. Many later critics build on O'Neill's insights. See Onora O'Neill, "Abstraction, Idealization, and Ideology in Ethics," *Moral Philosophy and Context* 22: 55–69 (1987); Onora O'Neill, *Towards Justice and Virtue* (Cambridge: Cambridge University Press 1996), 38–48; and Simon Hope, "Idealization, Justice, and the Form of Practical Reason," *Social Philosophy and Policy* 33 (1): 372–392.

29 Peter Godfrey-Smith, "Abstractions, Idealizations, and Evolutionary Biology" in *Mapping the Future of Biology: Evolving Concepts and Theories*, ed. A. Barberousse, M. Morange, and T. Pradeu (New York: Springer 2009), 47–56; Martin Jones, "Idealization and Abstraction: A

Framework," *Poznan Studies in the Philosophy of Science and the Humanities* 86 (1): 173–218 (2005); and Michael Weisberg, "Three Kinds of Idealization," *Journal of Philosophy* 104 (12): 639–659 (2007).

30 Strict compliance and the concept of a well-ordered society are far from the only idealizations Rawls employs in the construction of his ideal theory. Notable and controversial further idealizations include his stipulation that society is a closed economy that does not interact with the economies of other societies and that all the citizens enter the community by birth and exit it by death. But these other idealizations are auxiliary assumptions Rawls introduces to bracket questions of international justice while investigating what he takes to be prior questions about domestic political justice. He thus introduces them for specific and discrete theoretical purposes within the broader project of ideal theory. Strict compliance, by contrast, is the idealization that he employs to *define* ideal theory itself and to demarcate it in a principled fashion from nonideal theory. Among his idealizations, it thus occupies a special place. See John Rawls, *Political Liberalism* (Columbia: Columbia University Press 1993), 12; and Rawls, *Justice as Fairness*, 12–14. See also the useful discussion of different kinds of idealization in Ingrid Robeyns, "Ideal Theory in Theory and Practice," *Social Theory and Practice* 34 (3): 341–362 (2008) at 352–360.

31 See John Rawls, "Kantian Constructivism in Moral Theory" in *Collected Papers*, ed. Samuel Freeman (Cambridge: Harvard University Press 2003), 303–358 at 307–315; and Rawls, *Justice as Fairness*, 8–9.

32 Contrast this with the cannonball: the uniform gravitational pull over its arc is not proper to the cannonball. There is no sense in which cannonballs should be like this, and so no sense in which cannonballs that fail to possess this feature are defective or bad as cannonballs. The sense in which it is an idealization is that it is a simplification for the purposes of constructing a simple theory. (We might say that it is "ideal" for the theorizers, not for the cannonball qua cannonball.)

33 It is the fact that the "assumption" of strict compliance is normative in this sense that explains why the principles specified on that assumption also place requirements in circumstances where the assumption does not hold. For a discussion of ideal theory and conditional and unconditional requirements, see Estlund, *Utopophobia*, 120–122.

34 Since the purpose of the original position in Rawls's philosophy is to defend principles of justice by posing a situation of choice, the most

direct way to do this is simply to have the representatives choose principles for free and equal moral persons on the assumption that these persons will publicly affirm and comply with the selected principles. See John Rawls, "Kantian Constructivism" in *John Rawls: Collected Papers*, ed. Samuel Freeman (Cambridge: Harvard University Press 1999), 303–358 at 310–311; Rawls, *Political Liberalism*, 22–28; and Rawls, *A Theory of Justice*, 145.

35 For some representative samples from the later works, see Rawls, *Justice as Fairness*, 4–5; and especially Rawls, *The Law of Peoples*, 11–12, 89–90.

36 Rawls, *A Theory of Justice*, 246.

37 Rawls, *A Theory of Justice*, 219.

38 Rawls, *The Law of Peoples*, 89–90; and Rawls, *Justice as Fairness*, 13.

39 Rawls, *A Theory of Justice*, 245; and Rawls, *The Law of Peoples*, 89.

40 Rawls, *Justice as Fairness*, 4–5; and Rawls, *The Law of Peoples*, 11–12.

41 Rawls, *The Law of Peoples*, 14.

42 Rawls, *Justice as Fairness*, 185.

43 Rawls, *The Law of Peoples*, 11–13.

44 The best discussion of feasibility, which I draw on throughout this book, is Pablo Gilabert, "Justice and Feasibility: A Dynamic Approach" in *Political Utopias: Contemporary Debates*, ed. Michael Webber and Kevin Vallier (Oxford: Oxford University Press 2017), 95–126. This draws on an earlier paper by Pablo Gilbert and Holly Lawford-Smith, "Political Feasibility: A Conceptual Exploration," *Political Studies* 60: 809–825 (2012).

45 For able defenders of the widely accepted requirement of realism, see David Miller, *Justice for Earthlings* (Cambridge: Cambridge University Press 2013); and Joshua Cohen, "Taking People as They Are?" *Philosophy and Public Affairs* 30 (4): 363–386. For some strong dissenting opinions, see Cohen, *Rescuing Justice and Equality*; and Mason, "Just Constraints." For a more nuanced partial dissent, see David Estlund, "Human Nature and the Limits (If Any) of Political Philosophy," *Philosophy and Public Affairs* 39 (3): 207–237 (2011). I discuss Cohen in Chapter 2 and Estlund in Chapter 6.

46 Rawls, *The Law of Peoples*, 7.

47 Rawls, *A Theory of Justice*, 454.

48 Rawls, *The Law of Peoples*, 13.

49 For an illuminating discussion, see Anderson, "The Fundamental Disagreement between Luck Egalitarians and Relations Egalitarians," 18–19.

50 Rawls, *Theory of Justice*, 144, 504. The link between stability and feasibility is also stressed by Erik Olin Wright, *Envisioning Real Utopias*. Note that he calls stability "viability," and he distinguishes this from another dimension of feasibility that he calls, following G. A. Cohen, "accessibility." See Erik Olin Wright, *Envisioning Real Utopias* (London: Verso 2010); and G. A. Cohen, *Why Not Socialism?* (Princeton: Princeton University Press 2009), 56–57.

51 The most sophisticated discussion is to be found in Paul Weithman, *Why Political Liberalism? John Rawls's Political Turn* (Oxford: Oxford University Press 2011), 42–68.

52 Rawls, *A Theory of Justice*, 457–458.

53 Rawls, *Political Liberalism*, xxxvii, 142–43.

54 Rawls, *A Theory of Justice*, 456.

55 Rawls, *A Theory of Justice*, 453–479.

56 Rawls, *A Theory of Justice*, 5.

57 The fullest discussion of publicity is found in Rawls, *Political Liberalism*, 66–71, 77–81. See also *A Theory of Justice*, 133–136.

58 Rawls, *Justice as Fairness*, 184–185.

59 Rawls, *Justice as Fairness*, 4.

60 Rawls, *The Law of Peoples*, 89–90.

61 A. John Simmons, "Ideal and Nonideal Theory," *Philosophy and Public Affairs*, 38 (1): 5–36 at 12 (2010).

62 Rawls, *A Theory of Justice*, 8, 216–217.

63 Pablo Gilabert also refers to the perspective of nonideal theory as "transitional." See Gilabert, "Justice and Feasibility."

64 I take this general metaphor of pathology and its treatment from Anderson, *The Imperative of Integration*, 3–7.

65 Rawls, *The Law of Peoples*, 89–90.

66 Rawls, *A Theory of Justice*, 215–216. For a very similar passage from later in his career, see *Justice as Fairness*, 13.

67 This view is not "teleological" in Rawls's technical sense of that term, since it does not define "the Right" in terms of "the Good." It is only teleological in that the view involves orientation to an end. See Rawls, *A Theory of Justice*, 21–22.

68 Rawls, *A Theory of Justice*, 216–220; and Rawls, *Political Liberalism*, 16–20.

69 See Estlund's illuminating remarks about the difference between people being required to do something and "getting people to do that thing," *Utopophobia*, 125.

70 Here I diverge from Swift and Stemplowska, who interpret Rawls as arguing that strict compliance is realistic and so practically possible. As I read the relevant passages, Rawls argues instead that in a just society the inclination to injustice would be greatly limited and reduced, so that stabilizing forces would suffice to rectify problems of injustice when they arose. But he does not argue that strict compliance is practically possible for a human society. See Swift and Stemplowska, "Ideal and Nonideal Theory," 115.

2. From Practice to Theory

1 Cohen, *Rescuing Justice and Equality*, 268. Similarly, Adam Swift writes, "Why not allow conceptual space for the possibility that even political philosophy (like other kinds of philosophy, such as logic or epistemology) aims primarily at truth—truths about which states of affairs, or which actions in which circumstances, are 'just' . . . But the goal would be rather to know or understand something about justice than to motivate action towards it. We do not evaluate the work of mathematicians or astrophysicists or archaeologists, or even moral philosophers, by considering the extent to which they help us make the world a more just, or in any way better, place (except insofar as knowledge is good in itself). Their aim, we might say, is epistemological, not practical." Adam Swift, "The Value of Philosophy in Nonideal Circumstances," *Social Theory and Practice* 34 (3): 363–387 (2008) at 366.

2 Cohen, *Rescuing Justice and Equality*, 267.

3 Cohen, *Rescuing Justice and Equality*, 306; see also 247. Again, Swift expresses similar sentiments. See Swift, "The Value of Philosophy in Nonideal Circumstances," 366.

4 Cohen, *Rescuing Justice and Equality,* 307.

5 Cohen, *Rescuing Justice and Equality*, 307.

6 Adam Swift writes that the injunction that political philosophy is practical "is more helpfully conceived as a normative claim about what kind of theoretical work is important or valuable than as an attempt to identify the proper purpose of political philosophy." In other words,

the purpose of pursuing justice is a valid purpose of ours (by reference to which we can judge which work is "normatively valuable"), but it does not belong to political philosophy. Swift, "The Value of Philosophy in Nonideal Circumstances," 368.

7   For Cohen's rejection of the feasibility constraint, and so realism, see Cohen, *Rescuing Justice and Equality*, 250–254.

8   Cohen, *Rescuing Justice and Equality*, chapter 6.

9   Rawls, *A Theory of Justice*, 7–8. See as well 351, 453–454.

10 Rawls, *A Theory of Justice*, 7–8.

11 Rawls, *A Theory of Justice*, 216.

12 Rawls, *The Law of Peoples*, 89–90.

13 I do not think fixing on these temporal formulations leads to a charitable construal of Rawls's view. Indeed, many things in his view speak decisively against taking them at face value, including his account of the starting points and process of reflective equilibrium. I take them at face value for the moment only to make clear the force of the critique of the temporal ordering of ideal theory and nonideal theory by Rawls's practical critics.

14 John Simmons seems to assert this when defending the priority claim. See Simmons, "Ideal and Nonideal Theory," 34.

15 Anderson, *Imperative of Integration*, 3.

16 Anderson, *Imperative of Integration*, 3.

17 Sen, *The Idea of Justice*, 104–105, 144–145. This formulation actually grants Sen a concept to which he is not entitled by his own lights— namely, the noncomparative concept of "unjust." On his view, judgments of justice are all to be analyzed as having a comparative form, and all noncomparative judgments are dispensable. I discuss this issue further in Chapter 3.

18 Anderson, *Imperative of Integration*, 3.

19 Mills, "'Ideal Theory' as Ideology," 171–172.

20 Cohen, *Rescuing Justice and Equality*, 291–292.

21 Plato, *Republic*, trans. C. D. C. Reeve (Cambridge: Hackett Publishing 2004), 427ae. Plato appears in this passage to say, among other things, that objections to the practicability of his account of justice are irrelevant to the specification of the form of justice. I say "appears to" because the rhetorical context of the extended discussion of practicability in *Republic* is complex even by the high standards of the Platonic dialogues. Furthermore, I speak here only of the Plato of the *Republic* and

do not consider *The Laws* or *The Statesman*, where Plato further theorizes the relation of theory and practice.

22 We might, in stylized fashion, group together two opposing tendencies of commentators on the *Nicomachean Ethics*. The intellectualists, like C. D. C. Reeve and Terence Irwin, rightly struck by the theoretical ambitions of Aristotle's approach, wrongly assimilate phronesis to scientific knowledge. The anti-intellectualists, like Sarah Broadie and John McDowell, rightly struck by Aristotle's emphatic contrasts between phronesis and sophia, wrongly assimilate phronesis to a kind of nontheoretical perceptual capacity. While the intellectualists miss the sense in which theory is practical, the anti-intellectualists miss the sense in which practice is theoretical. The line of interpretation I find compelling emphasizes the way in which phronesis and so politike draws on a theory (philosophy) that is practical by its very nature. I take this way of dividing the secondary literature and characterizing the alternative from Dhananjay Jagannathan, "Labors of Wisdom" (2017), University of Chicago, PhD dissertation. For intellectualists, see Terence Irwin, "Ethics as an Inexact Science: Aristotle's Ambitions for Moral Theory" in *Moral Particularism*, ed. B. Hooker and M. Little (Oxford: Oxford University Press 2000), 100–129; and C. D. C. Reeve, *The Practices of Reason: Aristotle's Nicomachean Ethics* (Oxford: Oxford University Press 1992); for anti-intellectualists, see Sarah Broadie, *Ethics with Aristotle* (Oxford: Oxford University Press 1991); and John McDowell, "Some Issues in Aristotle's Moral Psychology" in *Mind, Value, and Reality*, ed. John McDowell (Cambridge: Harvard University Press 2001), 23–49. Thanks to Martha Nussbaum for invaluable guidance on the secondary literature.

23 Aristotle, *Nicomachean Ethics*, 1139a–1143b.

24 The best treatment of practical truth is David Charles, "Practical Truth: An Interpretation of Parts of *NE* VI" in *Virtue, Happiness, Knowledge: Themes from the Work of Gail Fine and Terence Irwin*, ed. David O. Brink, Susan Sauvé Meyer, and Christopher Shields (Oxford: Oxford University 2018), 149–168. For another provocative, but ultimately less satisfying, treatment, see G. E. M. Anscombe, "Thought and Action in Aristotle" in *New Essays on Aristotle and Plato*, ed. Remford Bambrough (Philadelphia: Routledge Press 2012), 143–158.

25 Aristotle, *Nicomachean Ethics*, 1139a.

26 Aristotle, *Nicomachean Ethics*, 1112ab. For a good start on thinking about the elevated sense of action, see John McDowell, "The Role of

Eudaimonia in Aristotle's Ethics" in *Mind, Value, and Reality*, 3–22, although in my view McDowell's treatment unnecessarily "Stoicizes" Aristotle on the relation of external goods and praxis. A good antidote to this Stoicization can be found in Martha Nussbaum, *The Fragility of Goodness* (Cambridge: Cambridge University Press 2001).

27 Aristotle, *Nicomachean Ethics*, 1141b. In accepting this identity at face value, I follow the analysis of both Reeve and Jagannathan. Some commentators, such as Jessica Moss, try to downplay this identity by claiming that only a special philosophical ("architectonic") version of phronesis, different from that exercised by the phronimos, is the same state as politike. On a natural construa, *Nicomachean Ethics* 6 would seem to be innocent of this distinction between practical wisdom(s), as Jagannathan convincingly (to my mind) argues. See C. D. C. Reeve, *Aristotle on Practical Wisdom: Nicomachean Ethics VI* (Cambridge: Harvard University Press 2013), 190–192; Dhananjay Jagannathan, *The Labors of Wisdom*, 123–135; and Jessica Moss, *Aristotle on the Apparent Good: Perception, Phantasia, Thought, and Desire* (Oxford: Oxford University Press 2012), 183–185.

28 Aristotle, *Nicomachean Ethics*, 1095.

29 Aristotle, *Nicomachean Ethics*, 1094b.

30 Aristotle, *Nicomachean Ethics*, 1094a–1098a.

31 Aristotle, *Nicomachean Ethics*, 1103b.

32 Aristotle, *Nicomachean Ethics*, 1105b.

33 Aristotle, *Nicomachean Ethics*, 1095ab.

34 The argument of this section is influenced by Rawls's discussion of reflective equilibrium. The interpretation of reflective equilibrium I follow is roughly that presented by T. M. Scanlon. Note that I depart from Scanlon in taking more seriously Rawls's claim that the theory of justice is a theory of our sense of justice, understood as a moral power. I depart from Rawls by emphasizing injustice as a starting point. See T. M. Scanlon, "Rawls on Justification" in *The Cambridge Companion to Rawls*, ed. Samuel Freeman (Cambridge: Cambridge University Press 2002), 139–167; Rawls, *A Theory of Justice*, 40–46; and Rawls, *Justice as Fairness*, 29–32.

35 This formulation is Aristotle's. For an illuminating discussion of being properly affected, see Aryeh Kosman, "Being Properly Affected: Virtues and Feelings in Aristotle's Ethics" in *Essays on Aristotle's Ethics*, ed. A. Rorty (Berkeley: University of California Press 1980).

36 Rawls, *A Theory of Justice*, 46; and Rawls, *Justice as Fairness*, 29.

37 See Rawls, *Justice as Fairness*, 30. Scanlon also emphasizes this feature of considered judgments.

38 My remarks about the marks of the concept of justice in §1.2 were higher-level judgments about justice.

39 The sense of justice is one of the two powers through which Rawls defines the concept of a citizen. It is the power of practical intellect that citizens exercise when they deliberate about the justice and injustice of their institutions and engage in political action.

40 Tommie Shelby, *Dark Ghettos: Injustice, Dissent, and Reform* (Cambridge: Harvard University Press 2016).

41 They can, of course, raise the question of which side one is on in a scholarly controversy about the solution to the relevant intellectual puzzle. But this drawing of sides is not internal to the problem so represented; rather, it comes from the factional arrangement of academia and scholarship through which the relevant discipline is socially organized.

42 It was a major flaw in Rawls's early presentations of reflective equilibrium that he was not yet clear on this point. By the time he wrote "The Independence of Moral Theory," he had won his way to clarity on this topic and remained consistent on it for the rest of his career. I should note that that essay, however, is not without problems of its own. A treatment focused on the evolution of Rawls's own views on reflective equilibrium would need to bring out the many shifting tensions between British empiricist and German idealist strands in his thought. See John Rawls, "The Independence of Moral Theory" in Freeman, *Collected Papers*, 286–302.

43 In Rawls's system, many high-level judgments motivate "ideas of reason" that help us to articulate and defend principles. This includes the citizen as the possessor of two moral powers, the original position, the veil of ignorance, and others. To explore which considered judgments these ideas work up, and how such ideas of reason mediate between considered judgments and principles in his view, would take us too far afield, since our concern does not lie with Rawls's system. Thanks to Pablo Gilabert for raising this point.

44 See Rawls, *A Theory of Justice*, 319, for a discussion of the Difference Principle as extending our judgment into "questions that common sense finds unfamiliar and leaves undecided."

45 Rawls, *A Theory of Justice*, 48.

46 Rawls, *A Theory of Justice*, 48.

47 Rawls, *Justice as Fairness*, 30–31.

48 This does not fit well with Rawls's early—in my view highly unfortunate— representation of the theory of justice as an attempt to understand "one person's" sense of justice, a solipsistic attempt in which the reflections of others serve merely as an occasion to "clear one's own head." Rawls's views shifted on this over the course of his career. What I say here fits better with Rawls's later remarks, made in the context of his methodological rethinking of the theory of justice in light of political liberalism, that considered judgments about justice are drawn from a public culture. See Rawls, *A Theory of Justice*, 44; and John Rawls, *Political Liberalism* (New York: Columbia University Press 2005), 8ff.

49 This is what Rawls called "the priority question," to which his doctrines of lexical priority spoke. See Rawls, *A Theory of Justice*, 36–40.

50 This pressure to think through the relation of principles arises also from the urgent need to theorize pressing injustice. For example, consider what theorists following the pioneering work of Kimberlé Crenshaw term "intersectionality." Theorists of intersectionality rightly encourage us to think about the special claims that arise from the interaction of multiple modes of oppression, encouraging us to theorize, for example, a feminism that is not geared solely to the claims of wealthy white women. Here we find pressure to theorize gender oppression in tandem with class oppression and racial oppression. But since injustice is explained by principles of justice, the very same pressure is also to cospecify the principles of gender, class, and racial justice and explain how they relate to one another. When such multiple aspects of justice are in play, our nonideal theory of oppression cannot be intersectional until our principles of justice are theorized in tandem.

51 See Isaiah Berlin, "Two Concepts of Liberty" in *Liberty*, ed. Henry Hardy (Oxford: Oxford University Press 2002), 166–218 at 212–217; Isaiah Berlin, "Pursuit of the Ideal" in *The Crooked Timber of Humanity: Chapters in the History of Ideas*, ed. Henry Hardy (New York: Knopf 1991), 1–16; Bernard Williams, "Liberalism and Loss" in *The Legacy of Isaiah Berlin*, ed. Ronald Dworkin, Mark Lilla, and Robert B. Silvers (New York: New York Review Books 2001), 91–104.

52 Berlin, for example, calls it an "ancient faith" and a "deep and incurable metaphysical need." Perhaps its "depth" is supposed to explain how, by Berlin's own lights, most philosophers in the tradition succumbed to this

error. This alleged depth is hard to reconcile with the fact that Berlin thinks it conflicts with "obvious commonplaces" and is transparently and obviously false. See Berlin, "Two Concepts of Liberty," 217.

3. From Theory to Practice

1   See Sen, "What Do We Want from a Theory of Justice?"
2   Simmons, "Ideal and Nonideal Theory," 34–36. Ingrid Robeyns also uses the metaphor of a journey to a destination ("paradise island") to characterize the dynamic role of ideal theory. Ingrid Robeyns, "Ideal Theory in Theory and Practice," *Social Theory and Practice* 34 (3): 341–362 (2008) at 344–346.
3   This kind of a change is what Aristotle calls *kinesis*. He contrasts kinesis with another sort of change that he calls *energeia*. My arguments are based on the fact that pursuit of justice is energeia rather than kinesis. This is connected with Aristotle's distinction between praxis and poesis, although the exegetical difficulties here are serious.
4   Sebastian Rödl, *Self-Consciousness* (Cambridge: Harvard University Press 2007), 125–135. He draws on some of the remarks about action and temporality by Michael Thompson, *Life and Action* (Harvard University Press 2008), 120–146. Although I arrived at it independently, a similar connection to Rödl's and Thompson's work is also made in Simon Hope, "Political Philosophy as Practical Philosophy: A Response to 'Political Realism,'" 465–466.
5   Rödl, *Self-Consciousness*, 36–43.
6   For this language, see Gilabert, "Justice and Feasibility: A Dynamic Approach." Burke Hendrix, in several illuminating discussions, refers to this role of the conception of a just society as the "navigational" role. See Burke Hendrix, "What Should Nonideal Theory Hold Constant?" (MS); Burke Hendrix, *Strategies of Justice* (Oxford: Oxford University Press 2019), 32–115.
7   Special thanks to Chiara Cordelli for raising this objection to the teleological conception vividly on several occasions, helping me to feel its force. Thinking through her probing questions helped me to develop the idea of the immanence of justice in struggle.
8   The same point can be made about Robeyns's analogy to the travel to the destination of "paradise island." See Ingrid Robeyns, "Ideal Theory in Theory and Practice."

9 See Gilabert, "Comparative Assessments of Justice, Political Feasibility, and Ideal Theory," 45–46.

10 See Estlund, *Utopophobia*, 249–257; David Estlund, "Just and Juster" in *Oxford Studies in Political Philosophy, Volume 2*, ed. David Sobel, Peter Vallentyne, and Stephen Wall (Oxford: Oxford University Press 2016).

11 For Sen's rejection of "a grand partition," see Sen, "What Do We Want from a Theory of Justice?," 216–218.

12 Estlund, *Utopophobia*, 252–253.

13 Sen, "What Do We Want from a Theory of Justice?," 219–221.

14 Rawls, *A Theory of Justice*, 216; Simmons, "Ideal and Nonideal Theory," 20.

15 This is one of several ways in which Martha Nussbaum's development of the capabilities approach has advantages over that of Sen. For she develops the capabilities in order to specify a threshold that corresponds to an important requirement of justice. The development of this noncomparative partition introduced by the threshold of human dignity allows her to avoid all the problems I have identified here. For some related comparisons between their approaches that also speak in favor of Nussbaum's approach, see Nussbaum, *Women and Human Development*, 11–15.

16 For congenial views that approach the topic of practical reason by thinking about the dynamic role of ends in deliberation, I consulted the following resources: Elizabeth Anscombe, *Intention* (Cambridge: Harvard University Press 2000); Elizabeth Anscombe, "Practical Inference" in *Human Life, Action and Ethics: Essays by G. E. M. Anscombe*, ed. Mary Geach and Luke Gormally (Exeter: Imprint Academic 2005), 109–147; Anselm Mueller, "How Theoretical Is Practical Reason?" in *Intention and Intentionality: Essays in Honour of G. E. M. Anscombe*, ed. Cora Diamond and Jenny Teichman (Ithaca: Cornell University Press 1979), 91–108; Patricio Fernandez, "Practical Reasoning: Where the Action Is," *Ethics* 126 (4): 869–900 (2016); and Will Small, "The Practicality of Practical Inference" (MS).

17 In this and what follows, I draw on the perceptive remarks of Anton Ford, "On What Is in Front of Your Nose," *Philosophical Topics* 44 (1): 141–161 (2016).

18 Burke Hendrix emphasizes this point as well. See Hendrix, "What Should Nonideal Theory Hold Constant?," 7–12.

19 Gilabert, "Justice and Feasibility: A Dynamic Approach," 118–123.

20 Compare Gilabert, "Justice and Feasibility: A Dynamic Approach," 114–116.

21 This is "the problem of the second best," originally formulated in R. G. Lipsey and Kelvin Lancast, "The General Theory of the Second Best," *Review of Economic Studies* 24 (1): 11–32 (1956–1957). Estlund has an excellent, careful discussion. See Estlund, *Utopophobia*, 259–270.

22 See Estlund, *Democratic Authority: A Philosophical Framework* (Princeton: Princeton University Press 2008). See also Elizabeth Anderson's remarks about how "civility" can shut down the expression of legitimate democratic dissent, drawing on the history of the civil rights movement in North Carolina. See Anderson, *The Imperative of Integration*, 98–99.

23 See Estlund, *Utopophobia*, 277–291.

24 For illuminating broader concepts of "democratic action" that show allegiance to democratic values while simultaneously operating in resistance to ordinary democratic politics, see Rawls, *A Theory of Justice*, 335–347; and Anderson, *The Imperative of Integration*, 89–111.

25 Tommie Shelby offers the most sophisticated treatment of topics in nonideal theory of which I am aware that is sensitive to the principled character of proposals for change and has squarely in view what I would call the tension between dynamic and immanent considerations. His work has shaped my whole understanding of this issue. Shelby, *Dark Ghettos*, 96–100.

26 Shelby, *Dark Ghettos*, 99–100.

27 The question of when the oppressed can be made to bear costs in transition is central to Shelby's critique of Elizabeth Anderson and other "new integrationists." Shelby, *Dark Ghettos*, 62–76.

28 Gilabert, "Justice and Feasibility: A Dynamic Approach," 118–120.

4. Agents of Change

1 Here I take seriously and draw on a line of thinking about practical reasoning that sees the conclusion and sometimes the premises of practical reason as actions. Among the works in the philosophy of action that inform my thinking on this subject are Anscombe, *Intention*; Anscombe, "Practical Inference"; Mueller, "How Theoretical Is Practical Reason?";

Thompson, *Life and Action*; Rödl, *Self-Consciousness*; Fernandez, "Practical Reason: Where the Action Is"; Ford, "On What Is in Front of Your Nose"; Eric Wiland, "In the Beginning Was the Doing: The Premises of the Practical Syllogism," *Canadian Journal of Philosophy* 43 (3): 303–321 (2013); and Small, "The Practicality of the Practical Inference."

2   By far the best discussion of these issues is found in the work of Erik Olin Wright. Other great resources on which I draw freely in this chapter include the evolving work of Pablo Gilabert on what he calls *dynamic duties* and *dynamic powers* and Burke Hendrix's probing methodological reflections on nonideal theory. My debts to them will be obvious to anyone who is familiar with their work. See Wright, *Envisioning Real Utopias*, 1–10, 273–307; Gilabert, "Comparative Assessments of Justice, Political Feasibility, and Ideal Theory"; Gilabert, "Justice and Feasibility: A Dynamic Approach"; Burke Hendrix, "Where Should We Expect Social Change in Non-ideal Theory?," *Political Theory* 41 (1): 116–143 (2013); Hendrix, "What Should Nonideal Theory Hold Constant?" (MS); and Burke Hendrix, *Strategies of Justice* (Oxford: Oxford University Press 2019).

3   Anderson, *The Imperative of Integration*, 3–18.

4   I draw inspiration for this example from Elizabeth Anderson, *Private Government* (Princeton: Princeton University Press 2017).

5   John Rawls, *Lectures on the History of Political Philosophy* (Cambridge: Cambridge University Press 2007), 1.

6   David Miller, *Justice for Earthlings* (Cambridge: Cambridge University Press 2013), 34.

7   Rawls, *Lectures on the History of Political Philosophy*, 3–5.

8   Rawls, *Lectures on the History of Political Philosophy*, 10, emphasis in the original. The other roles Rawls mentions include "orientation," "reconciliation," and the fourth and final role, which he calls "probing the limits of practical possibility." He associates this final role with the realistic utopian conception of ideal theory. Despite his view that ideal theory presents the long-range goal, guiding the course of social reform for nonideal theory, he does not describe realistic utopianism as the practical role. The seeds of a better account of the relation of theory and practice lie with this aspect of Rawls's view.

9   I have benefited from Raymond Geuss's discussion of "Who Whom" in *Philosophy and Real Politics* (Princeton: Princeton University Press 2008), 23–30. However, we do not share a conception of political

philosophy, since I treat the question of the agent of change as one that arises in the theory of justice, whereas he views the theory of justice as hopelessly utopian and moralistic.

10 For some illuminating remarks on this point, see Hendrix, *Strategies of Justice*, chapter 1.

11 For essential history, see David Vogel, *Fluctuating Fortunes: The Political Power of Business in America* (New York: Beard Books 1989). For the increasing role of individual firms in lobbying, see Lee Drutman, *The Business of America Is Lobbying* (Oxford: Oxford University Press 2015).

12 For the concept of "business unity issues," see Dan Clawson and Alan Neustadtl, "The Logic of Business Unity: Corporate Contributions to the 1980 Congressional Elections," *American Sociological Review* 51 (6): 797–811 (1986). For controversial claims about how the capacity for business to achieve unity has changed over time, see Mark Mizruchi, *The Fracturing of the American Corporate Elite* (Cambridge: Harvard University Press 2013).

13 Among the relevant literature on this divergence of opinion and the effect of economic elites on the political system, see Martin Gilens and Benjamin I. Page, "Testing Theories of American Politics: Elites, Interest Groups, and Average Citizens," *Perspectives on Politics* 12 (3): 564–581 (2014); Benjamin I. Page, Larry M. Bartels, and Jason Seawright, "Democracy and the Policy Preferences of Wealthy Americans," *Perspectives on Politics* 11 (1): 51–73 (2013); Larry M. Bartels, *Unequal Democracy: The Political Economy of the New Gilded Age*, 2nd ed. (New York: Russell Sage Foundation 2016); and Martin Gilens, *Affluence and Influence: Economic Inequality and Political Power in America* (Princeton: Princeton University Press 2012).

14 Eric Beerbohm, *In Our Name: The Ethics of Democracy* (Princeton: Princeton University Press 2012); and Thomas Nagel, "The Problem of Global Justice," *Philosophy and Public Affairs* 33 (2): 113–147 (2005).

15 The most illuminating philosophical treatment of parties in democratic theory is Lea Ypi and Jonathan White, *The Meaning of Partisanship* (Oxford: Oxford University Press 2016). There is strong evidence that US parties are *very* far from satisfying their elevated conception of the normative role of parties in democracy.

16 When it comes to labor reforms in the United States, one of the two parties, the Republican Party, is the self-avowed party of business. The

other party, the Democratic Party, unlike center-left parties in many other countries, is not and never was a labor party. Since the 1980s, it has been split by a progressive wing and a pro-corporate wing that emerged to compete with the Republican Party for corporate dollars under the influence of the Democratic Leadership Council. For a compelling account of the evolution and splitting of the Democratic Party, see Jacob Hacker and Paul Pierson, *Winner-Take-All Politics: How Washington Made the Rich Richer—and Turned Its Back on the Middle Class* (New York: Simon and Schuster 2010).

17 Here we find another echo in the Marxist tradition that treated the working class as "the universal class." For, in the Marxist analysis, by overthrowing their own oppression, the working class would simultaneously end class society as such and so bring about general human emancipation. This is a great theme in Lukács as well, who is probably the greatest theorist of the agent of change in the socialist tradition. See Marx, "Estranged Labor," 82; and Georg Lukács, "Class Consciousness" in *History and Class Consciousness*, trans. Rodney Livingstone (Cambridge: MIT Press 1968), 46–83 at 82.

18 My account draws on Onora O'Neill's pathbreaking work on "agents of justice." There are several differences from her approach, however: (1) she tends to blur the assignment of duties and the identifications of agents of justice; (2) she is not necessarily concerned with change; and (3) her typology of primary agents of justice (states) who are primary obligation bearers, and secondary agents who fill a role delegated to them by primary agents, is insufficient to capture the forms of agency I focus on. Onora O'Neill, "Agents of Justice," *Metaphilosophy* 32 (1/2): 180–195 (2001).

19 Whatever sense of intentionality we employ will have to be flexible enough to capture more and less coordinated actions of possible shifting coalitions of actors. I have tried to articulate a relevant sense of intention elsewhere at length in Ben Laurence, "An Anscombian Approach to Collective Action" in *Essays on Anscombe's Intention*, ed. Anton Ford, Jennifer Hornsby, and Fred Stoutland (Cambridge: Harvard University Press 2011), 270–295.

20 Admittedly, the requirement of voluntariness, like that of acting intentionally, deserves further investigation. For example, does an agent that intentionally but opportunistically supports a change for reasons other than ameliorating an injustice count as voluntarily pursuing the

change? I would be inclined to say yes, but this and related questions deserve further exploration.

21 The two most relevant (and important) papers are Gilabert and Lawford-Smith, "Political Feasibility: A Conceptual Exploration"; and Gilabert, "Justice and Feasibility: A Dynamic Approach." For helpful further thoughts, see also Holly Lawford-Smith, "Understanding Political Feasibility," *Journal of Political Philosophy* 21 (3): 243–259 (2013); Nicholas Southwood, "The Feasibility Issue," *Philosophy Compass* 13 (8): 12509 (2018); and Mark Jensen, "The Limits of Practical Possibility," *Journal of Political Philosophy* 17 (2): 168–184 (2009).

22 Gilabert and Lawford-Smith, "Political Feasibility: A Conceptual Exploration," 812.

23 Gilabert and Lawford-Smith, "Political Feasibility: A Conceptual Exploration," 812–814.

24 Gilabert, "Justice and Feasibility: A Dynamic Approach," 118–123.

25 For this sort of approach, see Lea Ypi, *Global Justice and Avant-Garde Political Agency* (Oxford: Oxford University Press 2012).

26 Lawford-Smith and Gilabert insist that we separate feasibility from questions of willingness to perform the action. I think they are right to do so. Gilabert and Lawford-Smith, "Political Feasibility: A Conceptual Exploration," 817–818.

27 Thanks to an anonymous reviewer from Harvard University Press who pressed me to reflect more seriously on the question of motivation and who made many helpful suggestions that I incorporated in this discussion.

28 Tommie Shelby, "Ideology, Racism, and Critical Social Theory," *Philosophical Forum* 34 (2): 153–188 (2003).

29 The best general treatment I know of microfoundations is unpublished work by Jaime Edwards, including "'Everything Is as It Seems, and All Is for the Best!': The Origin of Ideological Belief in Cognitive and Motivated Biases" (MS). There is an informative discussion of the microfoundations of racial ideology (she calls it "racial stigmatization") in Anderson, *The Imperative of Integration*, 44–66.

30 The emphasis on ideology as arising from the lived experience of differently positioned groups is a centerpiece of Barbara Fields's masterful discussion of slavery and racial ideology in the United States. Barbara

Jean Fields, "Slavery, Race and Ideology in the United States of America," *New Left Review* 1 (181): 95–118 (1990).

31 This would be a case of "in group favoritism" bias. See S. T. Fiske, "Stereotyping, Prejudice, and Discrimination" in *The Handbook of Social Psychology*, ed. D. T. Gilbert, S. T. Fiske, and G. Lindzey (New York: McGraw-Hill 1998), 357–411. Cited in Anderson, *The Imperative of Integration*, 205.

32 This would be a case of "system justification bias." See Anderson, *The Imperative of Integration*, 46.

33 A fascinating history of the influence of management consultants as conduits of trendy business management theories that sideline the interests of workers can be found in Louis Hyman, *Temp: The Real Story of What Happened to Your Salary, Benefits, and Job* (New York: Penguin Publishing 2018).

34 How we are to understand such an active role and inclusion is a difficult topic deserving extended treatment given that the oppressed do not speak with one voice and often do not have institutions that represent them in a robust way.

35 Iris Marion Young, *Inclusion and Democracy* (Oxford: Oxford University Press 2000), 196–236.

36 It also involves a normative critique of Young's multiculturalist democratic theory. Anderson, *The Imperative of Integration*, 187–189.

37 Anderson, *The Imperative of Integration*, 44–66.

38 Anderson, *The Imperative of Integration*, 33–55.

39 Anderson, *The Imperative of Integration*, 112–134.

40 Anderson, *The Imperative of Integration*, 95–102.

41 Other recent arguments that have this direction of argument include Tommie Shelby's critique of the political proposals of the Black Power movement on the grounds that class divisions in the black community pose a significant challenge to the formation of an all-black agent of change, and Alex Gourevitch and Lucas Stanczyk's argument against basic income as a replacement for the efforts of a flagging labor movement, for Gourevitch and Stanczyk argue that given the organized obstacles that face an ambitious basic income, the only plausible potential agent of change is a mobilized and vastly empowered labor movement. Tommie Shelby, *We Who Are Dark: The Philosophical Foundations of Black Solidarity* (Cambridge: Harvard University Press 2015),

101–135; and Alex Gourevitch and Lucas Stanczyk, "The Basic Income Illusion," *Catalyst* 4 (1): 151–177 (2018).

42 I thank Martha Nussbaum for first raising this question for me in a trenchant form. I have been thinking about it ever since.

43 Gaus, *The Tyranny of the Ideal*, 57.

44 Gaus, *The Tyranny of the Ideal*, 59–61.

45 The need for a theory for the evolution of modes of reproduction of injustices is emphasized by Erik Olin Wright. Wright, *Envisioning Real Utopias*, 297–302.

46 This topic was an abiding preoccupation of philosophers in the Marxist tradition. Indeed, Georg Lukács made this question the central question for Marxism. Chapter 4 could be viewed as an attempt to generalize some of Lukács's concepts to a wider array of nonideal theories outside the context of Marxism. Obviously, I cannot pursue here the connection to Lukács, who is a challenging thinker. See especially Georg Lukács, "What Is Orthodox Marxism?" in Livingstone, *History and Class Consciousness*, 1–26.

5. Against Strict Compliance

1 See for example, Sen, *The Idea of Justice*, 68–69; Mills, "'Ideal Theory' as Ideology," 170; Farrelly, "Justice in Ideal Theory: A Refutation"; and O'Neill, "Abstraction, Idealization, and Ideology in Ethics."

2 In "Strict Compliance, Realistic Utopia, and Constructivism," I explore a way the two conceptions could be combined coherently, and I connect it with some themes in *A Theory of Justice*. We can use the teleological conception to order the theory of justice but treat ideal theory as a multistage affair that begins by identifying principles of justice using strict compliance and then relaxes the idealization to arrive at the idea of a practical good. While I reject this position for the reasons that follow, that it is possible shows that the teleological conception is flexible enough to accommodate the other conception in a subordinate role.

3 For discussion of this distinction, see Thompson, *Life and Action*, 73–82; Philippa Foot, *Natural Goodness* (Oxford: Oxford University Press 2001), 25–37; Rödl, *Self-Consciousness*, 18–21; and Douglas Lavin, "Forms of Rational Agency," *Royal Institute of Philosophy Supplement* 80: 171–193 (2017).

4   Rawls, *A Theory of Justice*, 25.

5   Jean-Jacques Rousseau, *The Major Political Writings of Jean-Jacques Rousseau*, ed. John T. Scott (Chicago: University of Chicago Press 2012), 39.

6   I was helped in thinking through this analogy by Thompson's *Life and Action*, 25–84. Note that my argument raises complications for Thompson's "simple-minded principle of inference" discussed at 80 ff.

7   This is the master thought of Kant's approach to justice (right) in the *Doctrine of Right*. It is expressed in his famous argument in §D about hindering a hindrance to freedom. See Immanuel Kant, *Practical Philosophy: The Cambridge Edition of the Works of Kant* (Cambridge: Cambridge University Press 1996), 6:231; and Ben Laurence, "Kant on Strict Right," *Philosopher's Imprint* 18 (4): 1–22 (2018).

8   My thinking here has been shaped by Arthur Ripstein, "Authority and Coercion," as well as the entire line of argument of his *Force and Freedom* (Cambridge: Harvard University Press 2009).

9   I am not assuming that this "having justice prevail" must take the form of punishment, much less incarceration. It could, for example, include positive forms of community involvement in the mode of restorative justice. These are substantive questions about justice.

10   For a recent account of private law that puts the upholding of rights center stage, and is generally compatible with my analysis, see Arthur Ripstein, *Private Wrongs* (Cambridge: Harvard University Press 2016).

11   Estlund, "Prime Justice" in Webber and Vallier, *Political Utopias*, 35–57 at 35.

12   Prime justice actually involves even more than the idea of all requirements of justice being met—it also involves the idea of all claims of morality being met. The points I make here will also speak against the more ambitious notion with which Estlund works.

13   Feinberg, "The Nature and Value of Rights."

14   There are more complicated forms of contingency. For example, a mode of enforcement might under some empirical conditions be permissible without being required.

15   This is how I understand Ronald Dworkin's view in, for example, *Taking Rights Seriously* (New York: Gerald Duckworth & Co. 1977).

16   This is how I understand certain strands of Jeremy Waldron's argument in, for example, "The Core of the Case against Judicial Review," *Yale Law Review* 115 (6): 1346–1406 (2006).

17 Whether it is Hegel's sense, I will not conjecture. For Rawls on reconciliation, see *Justice as Fairness*, 3–4.

18 David Hume, *An Enquiry concerning the Principles of Morals*, ed. J. B. Schneewind (Indianapolis: Hackett Publishing 1983), 21.

19 The relevance of Hopkins's poem to my project was suggested to me by Benjamin Morgan and John Muse while I was a residential fellow at the Franke Institute for the Humanities.

20 Gerard Manley Hopkins, *Mortal Beauty, God's Grace: Major Poems and Spiritual Writings of Gerard Manley Hopkins*, ed. John F. Thornton and Susan B. Varenne (New York: Random House 2003), 25.

6. Against the Antipracticalists

1 Estlund, "Human Nature and the Limits (If Any) of Political Philosophy"; David Estlund, "What Good Is It? Unrealistic Political Theory and the Value of Intellectual Work," *Analyse and Kritik* 33 (2): 395–416 (2011); David Estlund, "Utopophobia," *Philosophy and Public Affairs* 42 (2): 113–134 (2014); Estlund, "Prime Justice"; and Estlund, *Utopophobia*.

2 Estlund, "Human Nature and the Limits (If Any) of Political Philosophy," 208–211.

3 I remember hearing the same lore in graduate school, and it rang true as a general description of questions asked after talks. The combative and dismissive tone of the two questions perhaps conveys something of the flavor of philosophical dialogue in the 1990s (and perhaps today). However, I ask the reader to set aside the tone as irrelevant to the points made here. Estlund, "Human Nature and the Limits (If Any) of Political Philosophy," 209–210.

4 Estlund, "Utopophobia," 114.

5 Estlund, *Utopophobia*, 117–141.

6 Estlund, *Utopophobia*, 111–114.

7 Estlund, *Utopophobia*, 112.

8 Estlund, *Utopophobia*, 17–18 and 76–80. He evinces an openness to call even this into question but at least grants it for the sake of his arguments.

9 Bill made his first appearance starring in Estlund, "Human Nature and the Limits (If Any) of People Philosophy." He is cast again in a smaller role in Estlund, *Utopophobia*, 95–98.

10 I heard David Estlund elaborate the case of Bill this way at a workshop at the University of Chicago.

11 Estlund, *Utopophobia*, 96–97.

12 Estlund, *Utopophobia*, 243–257 and 277–291.

13 Estlund, *Utopophobia*, 293–303.

14 Estlund, *Utopophobia*, 299–303.

15 Estlund, *Utopophobia*, 294.

16 Estlund, *Utopophobia*, 307–308.

17 You might wonder how anyone can be just if Bill is the Everyman. Perhaps some people are better than Bill, but not enough people to ever reach justice. Or, perhaps everyone is bad, but some measure of justice is still compatible with our Billish qualities, so we are discussing the contribution to this level of virtue.

18 Primo Levi discusses this as one legitimate form of shame that survivors experienced when they were liberated from the camps. For they had seen what human beings, like them, could willingly bring into the world. Primo Levi, *The Saved and the Drowned* (New York: Simon & Schuster 1988), 57–75.

19 Estlund, *Utopophobia*, 110.

20 Estlund, *Utopophobia*, 145–148.

21 Personally, I am sympathetic to the possibilist position of Benjamin Kiesewetter that insists on locating the discussion of deontic claims in the context of practical reasoning ("the deliberative context"). His papers are, I believe, brilliant defenses of the currently controversial position. However, I do not rest my case on any aspect of his view, arguing directly instead from the concept of justice and the theory of justice. See Frank Jackson and Robert Pargetter, "Oughts, Options, and Actualism," *Philosophical Review* 95 (2): 233–255 (1986); Benjamin Kiesewetter, "Instrumental Normativity: In Defense of the Transmission Principle," *Ethics* 125 (4): 921–946 (2105); and Benjamin Kiesewetter, "Contrary-to-Duty Scenarios, Deontic Dilemmas, and Transmission Principles," *Ethics* 129 (1): 98–115 (2018).

22 I follow Estlund in allowing myself to speak loosely in ways that suggest the truth of actualism. But as with Estlund, nothing turns on my doing so. My objection is to the practical upshot of the hopelessness of hopeless nonconcessive theories, whether we are to understand the deontic requirements in possibilist or actualist terms.

23 Estlund, *Utopophobia*, 197–220.

24 Estlund, *Utopophobia*, 201.

25 Estlund, *Utopophobia*, 207–220.

26 Estlund, *Utopophobia*, 221–240.

27 Kant, "Towards Perpetual Peace," 8:347.

28 Kant, *Metaphysics of Morals*, 6:223–6:228.

29 Ben Laurence, "An Anscombian Approach to Collective Action" in *Essays on Anscombe's Intention*, ed. Anton Ford, Jennifer Hornsby, and Frederick Stoutland (Cambridge: Harvard University Press 2010), 270–296.

30 But it is worth emphasizing a few qualifying points here about agency. The first is that structural injustice is often sustained by the activity of a bewildering array of agents: some do wrong, others support them in wrongdoing, still others are bystanders who are benefited and do nothing because of this, and so on. Injustice is the work of many hands, and so the attribution of responsibility will be complicated and often diffuse. For the most sophisticated discussion of this issue, see Iris Marion Young, *The Responsibility for Justice*.

31 Rawls, *The Law of Peoples*, 128. The Kant he paraphrases says, "If justice perishes, then it is no longer worthwhile for men to live upon the earth," 6:332.

32 Here I echo (I wouldn't put it exactly as he does) Kant, who writes, in critique of Moses Mendelssohn's cynicism, "It is quite irrelevant whether any empirical evidence suggests that these plans, which are founded only on hope, may be unsuccessful. For the idea that something which has hitherto been unsuccessful will therefore never be successful does not justify anyone in abandoning even a pragmatic or technical aim (for example, that of flights with aerostatic balloons). This applies even more to moral aims, which, so long as it is not demonstrably impossible to fulfil them, amount to duties." Kant, "Theory and Practice," 89.

33 The argument Estlund intends to refute is such a naked modus tollens. I think he succeeds in refuting it. Estlund, *Utopophobia*, 149–159.

7. Political Philosophy as Practical Reasoning

1 I say "in the first instance" because one can also have legitimate claims that arise from the fact that a situation is unjust.

2   How systematic one can be here is itself a substantial topic that nonideal theory must address. We can expect limitations, but even rough comparison and context-dependent weightings may be of use.

3   If we think about forming coalitions to overcome this change, there are many difficult questions about what compromises might be required to fashion a broader coalition and bring on board more powerful agents. The political ethics of such compromises is another normative area of nonideal theory.

4   Thanks to David Estlund for pressing this criticism of my view.

ACKNOWLEDGMENTS

This book would not have been possible without the tremendous support that I have received, especially from the Philosophy Department at the University of Chicago. First of all, I must thank Martha Nussbaum for her feedback on every step of the project, including invaluable comments on earlier papers and detailed comments on this manuscript, and also for her example as a practically engaged philosopher of the highest order. Dan Brudney gave me detailed comments on my manuscript, which he generously taught while it was in process. Jim Conant has supported the project at every step both logistically and intellectually. Gabriel Lear gave valuable feedback on material on the agent of change. I have benefited from many conversations with Chiara Cordelli and Jim Wilson over a series of invigorating lunchtime meetings at the Quadrangle Club. I also received extensive feedback on earlier versions of the manuscript from a working group of Anton Ford, Matthias Haase, and Matt Boyle. Pablo Gilabert and Burke Hendrix both gave me excellent feedback on the material on the agent of change when it was still in its earlier phases. Pablo Gilabert, whose work has shaped the argument of this book from start to finish, has given extensive, generous, and useful comments on the manuscript that touched every chapter.

I must give profuse thanks to the organizers of and participants in the conference "Agents of Change: A Book Manuscript Workshop" at the University of Chicago, including Matthew Boyle and Anton Ford, who funded the conference, and Amy Levine, who organized it. Thanks especially to my two commentators, Martha Nussbaum and David Estlund. David Estlund went far above and beyond the call of duty, supporting the project through its phases even while disagreeing with it vigorously. Having grappled with his generous feedback, I know the book manuscript is much better for it. I'm sure he still won't agree with my conclusions, but I have arrived at my views by thinking hard about his signal contributions for years. My debt to him is enormous.

I must also thank the participants in a variety of workshops and conferences where I presented relevant material. At the University of Chicago, these include the Practical Philosophy Workshop; the Political Theory Workshop; the Workshop on Moral, Political, and Legal Philosophy at the Law School; and the Thinking across Borders Conference at the Neubauer Collegium. I must also thank the Franke Institute for the Humanities, which gave me a faculty residential fellowship, where I developed and presented a precursor to some of this work. I must also thank the generous and creative philosophers at the Philosophy Department of Auburn University; the Center for Race, Philosophy, and Social Justice at Columbia University, including Bob Gooding-Williams; and the participants in the Virtue and Reasoning under Conditions of Social Oppression conference at Concordia University.

I must also thank two anonymous reviewers from Harvard University Press whose insightful comments led me to rethink huge swathes of the argument and organization of my text. Its current form owes much to their helpful interventions and creative suggestions. Their detailed and incisive remarks caused me to rethink the material at the heart of the book in chapters 2-4 in ways that greatly improved my argument.

Thanks also to my family—most of all to my wonderful wife, Julie Oppenheimer, who has supported me unwaveringly through all the ups and downs. Even in the midst of high-stakes organizing drives, she made sure I had the time I needed to bring this manuscript into being. As a union organizer, she is also the primary agent of change in our family. By the lights of my own view, she completes in deed what I conceive only in thesis. She is a political thinker in her own right, and I learn every day from her own rich theoretical engagement with practice.

Portions of Chapter 1 were first published as "Constructivism, Strict Compliance, and Realistic Utopianism," *Philosophy and Phenomenological Research* 97: 433–453 (2) (2018), © 2017 Philosophy and Phenomenological Research, LLC. Chapter 4 includes text first published as "The Question of the Agent of Change," *Journal of Political Philosophy* 28: 355–377 (4) (2020), © 2019 John Wiley & Sons Ltd.

INDEX